**LIN TSO** is a leading expert in listed options. He is the author of six previous books on stocks, options, and investing. Mr. Tso was educated both in China and in the United States, including graduate work at the Johns Hopkins University. A veteran investment analyst, he has been active in the areas of mergers and acquisitions.

# COMPLETE GUIDE TO LISTED OPTIONS CALLS & PUTS

Here is a comprehensive guide to listed options for stock traders and investors who want to investigate the why's and how's of making money in an up and down market.

The listed options market has grown phenomenally in the past decade because of the versatile investment medium that enables the trader and investor to profit despite the market direction. Listed options also appeal to conservative and speculative investors.

Inside you will find complete and practical coverage of the many-faceted possibilities of the listed option market. The various forms and combinations of "writing" and "buying" techniques are stressed, along with the multiplying applications of the "spreading" strategy.

The intricacies of these and other hedging techniques are concisely defined so that you, as an investor or trader, can explore the uses, risks, and rewards of trading in listed calls and puts.

PRENTICE-HALL, INC.
Englewood Cliffs, New Jersey 07632

A SPECTRUM BOOK

LIN TSO

# COMPLETE INVESTORS GUIDE TO LISTED OPTIONS: CALLS & PUTS

*Library of Congress Cataloging in Publication Data*

Tso, Lin, security analyst.
  Complete investor's guide to listed options.

  (A Spectrum Book)
  Includes index.

  1. Stocks.  2. Put and call transactions.
1. Title.
HG6042.T76     332.64′52     80-22175
ISBN 0-13-161216-6
ISBN 0-13-161208-5 (pbk.)

A SPECTRUM BOOK

Printed in the United States of America

10  9  8  7  6  5  4  3  2  1

Prentice-Hall International, Inc., *London*
Prentice-Hall of Australia Pty. Limited, *Sydney*
Prentice-Hall of Canada, Ltd., *Toronto*
Prentice-Hall of India Private Limited, *New Delhi*
Prentice-Hall of Japan, Inc., *Tokyo*
Prentice-Hall of Southeast Asia Pte. Ltd., *Singapore*
Whitehall Books Limited, Wellington, *New Zealand*

*Once again, as always,*
*to my dearest Sou Cheng*
*for her love, devotion, and unbounded help*

## PART I
### ELEMENTS OF CALL OPTIONS, 3

### 1
### OPTION BASICS, 5
OVERVIEW, 5

WHY PEOPLE BUY CALL OPTIONS, 6

WHY PEOPLE SELL CALL OPTIONS, 7

### 2
### LISTED OPTION MARKET, 8
OVERVIEW, 8

ARBITRAGE, 10

### 3
### CHARACTERISTICS OF CALL OPTIONS, 12
OVERVIEW, 12

OPTION PREMIUM, 13

### 4
### ANALYSIS OF CALL OPTIONS, 16
OVERVIEW, 16

IN-THE-MONEY OPTION TECHNIQUES, 19

# contents

## PART II
### CALLING BUYING, 21

### 5
### CALL OPTION BUYING STRATEGIES, 23

OVERVIEW, 23
OPTION-BUYING APPLICATIONS, 23

## PART III
### CALL SELLING, 27

### 6
### WRITING CALL OPTIONS, 29

OVERVIEW, 29

### 7
### COVERED OPTION WRITING STRATEGIES, 32

OVERVIEW, 32

### 8
### ELEMENTS OF OPTION WRITING PORTFOLIOS, 35

OVERVIEW, 35
IF-CALLED-AWAY OPTION WRITING PORTFOLIOS, 39

### 9
### VARIABLE HEDGING STRATEGIES, 42

OVERVIEW, 42
UNCOVERED OPTION WRITING, 42
PARTIALLY UNCOVERED OPTION WRITING, 44

## PART IV
### CALL SPREADING, 47

### 10
### CALL SPREADING BASICS, 49

OVERVIEW, 49
BASIC CONCEPTS, 50

### 11
### CALL TIME SPREADS, 53

OVERVIEW, 53
RATIO SPREADING, 57

### 12
### CALL PRICE SPREADS, 58

OVERVIEW, 58
BULL VERTICAL SPREAD TECHNIQUES, 58
BEAR VERTICAL SPREAD TECHNIQUES, 60
SANDWICH SPREADS, 63
DIAGONAL SPREADS, 65

### 13
### CALL MARGINS, 67

OVERVIEW, 67
SPREAD MARGINS, 70

# PART V
## FUNDAMENTALS AND TECHNIQUES, 75

## 14
### PUT BASICS, 77

OVERVIEW, 77
BASIC COMPONENTS, 77
MIRROR-IMAGE CONCEPT: PUTS VERSUS CALLS, 77
TWO SIDES TO THE GAME, 79
PUT PREMIUMS, 79

## 15
### SIMPLE PUT STRATEGIES, 81

OVERVIEW, 81
FROM THE PUT BUYER'S VIEWPOINT, 81
FROM THE PUT SELLER'S VIEWPOINT, 83
SUMMARY OF SIMPLE STRATEGIES, 84

# PART VI
## PUT BUYING, 85

## 16
### PUT BUYING: WHY AND HOW, 87

OVERVIEW, 87

## 17
### LONG PUT, 90

OVERVIEW, 90
SPECULATION, 90
SHORT-SALE ALTERNATIVE, 91
PROTECTION, 93
WHAT PUTS TO BUY, AND WHEN, 94
TO SELL OR TO EXERCISE? 95
PUT BUYING AS A TRADING VEHICLE, 96
ALTERNATIVE RISK-MINIMIZING VEHICLES, 96

## 18
### LONG PUT, LONG STOCK, 98

OVERVIEW, 98
COMPLETE HEDGE, 99
LONG PUT, LONG STOCK VERSUS LONG PUT, LONG CALL, 100

# PART VII
## PUT SELLING, 103

## 19
### PUT SELLING BASICS, 105

OVERVIEW, 105
THE PUT SELLER'S OBLIGATIONS, 106
COVERED VERSUS UNCOVERED PUT WRITING, 106
HOW TO CHOOSE WHICH PUT TO WRITE, 108
PUT WRITING MARGINS, 109

# 20

## SHORT PUT, 110

OVERVIEW, 110

STEP-BY-STEP WRITING
PROCEDURE, 111

PUT SELLING TO EARN PREMIUM
INCOME, 112

PUT SELLING TO ACQUIRE STOCK
BELOW MARKET PRICE, 113

MULTIPLE-EXERCISE-PRICE
PUT WRITING, 115

HOW TO MEASURE VOLATILITY,
115

MEANS OF DEFENSE, 116

# 21

## SHORT PUT, SHORT STOCK, 118

OVERVIEW, 118

HEDGED PUT WRITING, 118

HOW TO SELECT THE STRIKE
PRICE, 119

# 22

## SHORT PUT, LONG STOCK, 121

OVERVIEW, 121

# PART VIII
## PUT SPREADING, 123

# 23

## PUT SPREADING:
## WHY AND HOW, 125

OVERVIEW, 125

BASIC CONCEPTS, 125

SPREAD CONSTRUCTION, 127

PUT SPREAD MARGINS, 128

# 24

## PUT TIME SPREADS, 130

OVERVIEW, 130

BASICS OF PUT TIME
SPREADING, 130

PRINCIPAL APPROACHES TO PUT
TIME SPREADS, 132

# 25

## PUT PRICE SPREADS, 135

OVERVIEW, 135

BULLISH APPROACH: SELL
HIGHER, BUY LOWER STRIKE, 136

HOW TO CALCULATE THE POTEN-
TIAL SPREAD PROFIT/RISK, 137

BEARISH APPROACH: BUY HIGHER
STRIKE, SELL LOWER STRIKE, 138

HOW TO ROLL A BEAR PUT PRICE
SPREAD, 139

# PART IX
## OTHER MULTIPLE OPTIONS
## AND MARGINS, 141

# 26

## STRADDLES, 143

OVERVIEW, 143

STRADDLE BASICS, 143

LONG STRADDLE, 144

SHORT STRADDLE, 146

BULLISH VERSUS BEARISH
APPROACH, 147

SHORT STRADDLE, LONG
STOCK, 148

HOW TO CALCULATE STRADDLE
MARGINS, 150

# 27
COMBINATIONS, 152

OVERVIEW, 152
COMBINATION BUYING, 153
BASIC APPROACHES, 155
COMBINATION SELLING, 158
COMBINATION VERSUS
STRADDLE, 161

# 28
PUT MARGINS, 162

OVERVIEW, 162
LONG PUT, 163
LONG PUT, LONG STOCK, 163
SHORT PUT, 163
SHORT PUT, SHORT STOCK, 164
PUT SPREAD MARGINS, 165
STRADDLE MARGINS, 166
COMBINATION MARGINS, 166

# TAXES AND STRATEGY SELECTION

# PART X
TAX
CONSIDERATIONS, 171

# 29
TAX PLANNING FOR
OPTIONS, 173

# 30
TAX STRATEGY
FOR HOLDERS, 175

THE BASIC CONSIDERATION:
DISPOSAL, 175
TAX STRATEGY FOR CALL
HOLDERS, 176
TAX STRATEGY FOR PUT
HOLDERS, 177

# 31
TAX STRATEGY FOR WRITERS,
180

TAX STRATEGY FOR CALL
WRITERS, 181
TAX STRATEGY FOR PUT
WRITERS, 182

# PART XI
STRATEGY AND PORTFOLIO
CONSTRUCTION, 185

# 32
OPTION STRATEGY SELECTION
GUIDE, 187

IN TERMS OF INVESTMENT
OBJECTIVES, 187
IN TERMS OF STRATEGY
CATEGORIZATION, 188
IN TERMS OF BULL- VERSUS
BEAR-MARKET
INSTRUMENTS, 189

# 33
NEW OPTION
TRADING TOOLS, 191

CALL OPTION PRICE INDEX, 191
OPTION STRATEGIES RELATIVE
TO PREMIUM LEVELS, 192
LOW-PREMIUM-LEVEL
STRATEGIES, 192
LOW- OR HIGH-PREMIUM-LEVEL
STRATEGIES, 192

## 34
### OPTION PORTFOLIO STRATEGIES, 193

PROTOTYPE PORTFOLIO, 193
ANATOMY OF PROTOTYPE PORTFOLIO, 195

## PART XII
### WORKSHOP AND QUESTIONNAIRE, 199

## 35
### OPTION WORKSHOP, 201

POSSIBLE CONSEQUENCES, 201
APPLYING WORKSHEET FORMULA, 202
POSSIBLE CONSEQUENCES, 202

## 36
### CALL OPTION QUESTIONNAIRE, 204

LISTED OPTIONS AND LISTED OPTIONS MARKETS, 204
OPTION VALUES, 205
VARIOUS OPTION STRATEGIES, 205
OPTION BUYING AND ITS TECHNIQUES, 205
OPTION WRITING AND ITS TECHNIQUES, 206
RATIO WRITING AND ITS TECHNIQUES, 206

OPTION SPREADING AND ITS TECHNIQUES, 206
OPTION STRADDLING AND ITS TECHNIQUES, 206
PUT OPTION AND ITS TECHNIQUES, 207
OPTION MARGINS, 207
TAXES, 207
OPTION PORTFOLIOS, 207

## 37
### PUT OPTIONS QUESTIONNAIRE, 209

PUT BASICS, 209
SIMPLE STRATEGIES, 209
PUT BUYING, 209
LONG PUT, 209
LONG PUT, LONG STOCK, 209
PUT SELLING, 209
SHORT PUT, 211
SHORT PUT, SHORT STOCK, 211
SHORT PUT, LONG STOCK, 211
PUT SPREADING, 211
PUT TIME SPREADS, 211
PUT PRICE SPREADS, 212
STRADDLES, 212
COMBINATIONS, 212
PUT MARGINS, 213

GLOSSARY, 214

INDEX, 221

## HOW TO MAKE MONEY IN OPTIONS IN EITHER UP OR DOWN MARKETS

For most stock traders or investors, speculating on stock price changes has traditionally meant speculating on stock price *increases*. But as stock market gyrations of recent years have clearly shown, price changes are by no means always increases. Stock prices can—and normally do—*drop,* as sharply as they can rise. *The Complete Investors' Guide to Listed Options—Calls and Puts,* however, shows you the how's and why's of making money in *up* or *down* markets.

### A Tool for Speculative or Conservative Investors

Since its opening in the 1970's, the listed options market has grown by leaps and bounds and may come to dwarf even the New York Stock Exchange. This popularity is understandable, not only because listed options provide a way to make money regardless of market direction but also because this highly versatile investment medium appeals to speculative and conservative investors alike. Options are inherently neither speculative nor conservative. They can be used in speculative or conservative ways, however.

### The Scenario for Speculators

For speculative investors, listed options provide a means of achieving a never-before-attainable degree of leverage. Sometimes options can go up several hundred percent in a matter of weeks. Naturally, leverage works both ways. It can magnify a loss on the downside as much as it can magnify a gain on the upside. Moreover, options can expire worthless, meaning a total loss of the option purchase price. (Investors need not ride options all the way down, however, since a highly liquid secondary option market usually makes it possible to get out with only a limited loss.)

Traditionally, traders and speculators rely primarily on *selling short* as a means of making

# preface

money in stocks they believe are likely to go down. In a short sale, a person sells borrowed stock in the hope of buying it back later—a process known as *covering*—at a lower price, thus realizing a profit on the difference between the sale and purchase prices. Short selling has certain disadvantages, though. The idea of selling something they don't own is hard for many investors to grasp. Moreover, short selling exposes traders and speculators to unlimited risks. If the stock goes up instead of down, short sellers have to cover, or buy back borrowed stock, at higher prices. Short sellers also expose themselves to the possibility of margin calls.

Thus, up until now most investors haven't had a practical investment vehicle with which to speculate on the down side of stock price movements. Puts can provide such a vehicle. (A *put* is an option that gives the buyer the right to *sell* 100 shares of stock at a fixed price during a fixed period of time, whereas the more familiar *call* is an option that gives the buyer the right to *buy* similar securities.)

An investor who has grown accustomed to the "up together, down together" relationship between stock and call option prices must learn to shift gears when thinking of put options. As stock prices decline, prices of call options go down, but those of put options *increase* in value. Essentially, puts offer a cheap, highly-leveraged, and limited-risk way of speculating on the down side of stock price movements. That concept may require some adjustment on the part of the average investor, who typically thinks in terms of bigger and better as the only road to profit. But once the idea *is* understood, investors gain a better balanced market perspective, in which the search for profit opportunities is no longer necessarily linked to rising stock prices. Put options make it as feasible to invest for profit in down markets as in up markets.

Put options are not, of course, free from risk. They're not for those investors who can't afford to lose the price paid for the option. But for investors who can afford the risk and who understand how puts work and how they can be used, the ability to participate in declining markets as well as rising markets can mean an important expansion in money-making opportunities.

## The Scenario for Conservative Investors

For the more conservative investor, listed calls provide a low-risk means of obtaining higher yields without significantly increasing portfolio exposure. Investors can generate additional premium income by writing options on the core stocks of their portfolios, those they mean to hold anyway. (Listed options are probably the only investment medium that entail a gain instead of a loss at the start!)

The rate of return on an options portfolio can considerably exceed that on a straight debt, equity, or mixed portfolio. According to one estimate, every $1 million committed to the regular writing of call options on a diversified list of stocks should produce $250,000 (to which the dividends are added and the commissions and portfolio losses subtracted).

Whether you invest conservatively, speculatively, or somewhere in between, it is worthwhile exploring the uses, the opportunities, the strategies, and the risks of the versatile listed option.

## A Method Book

This book is essentially a method book, designed to give comprehensive and practical coverage to the listed options market. Particular stress is placed on the varying forms and combinations of *writing* and *buying* techniques of listed options, and on the multiplying applications of *spreading* and other multiple-option strategies.

Worksheet methods are used to illustrate writing, buying, spreading, and other hedging techniques. To simplify calculations in case studies, dividends, commissions, and other transaction costs generally are disregarded. (Readers are advised to consult their own brokers for such important transaction costs.)

## Complete Integration And Updating

This book is designed to provide investors with fundamental information concerning the possible uses, risks and rewards of trading in listed calls and puts. It is an integration and updating of two earlier books, *How to Make Money in Listed Options* and *How to Make Money Trading Listed Puts*.

Chapters on taxation encompass the extensive changes made by the Tax Reform Act of 1976 and the Revenue Act of 1978. Tax law change affecting calls and puts and Internal Revenue Service interpretations make it imperative for investors in the options market to weigh the implications of income-tax exposure when designing their option strategies. Careful planning can result not only in increased after-tax profits but in the avoidance of tax pitfalls.

While the tax chapters in this book may serve as outlines of tax considerations to investors in their strategy planning, *investors must consult with their own legal advisers and accountants.*

## One-Volume Reference Library

It is my earnest hope that this book will provide a one-volume reference library on listed options for traders, brokers, students of options, and investors seeking either above-average returns and/or leveraged profits with predetermined risks.

Since the present book draws material from two previous books, I remain indebted to a number of individuals who offered valuable suggestions, including Edwin Burton, Leon Pomerance, James J. Horan, Richard Jo Brignoli, Jerry Goldsmith, Martin Presler, Kenneth L. Marsh, Warren H. Bree, and Martha J. Ogborn.

Lin Tso
New York City

# LISTED CALLS

# ELEMENTS OF OPTIONS

# PART I

## OVERVIEW

### What

An *option* is a business contract that allows its holder to buy or sell stock in 100-share units at a certain price (known as the *exercise price* or *strike price*) within a certain period of time, regardless of how high or low the price of the stock (known as the *underlying security*) moves during that time.

### Why

*Buying* call options offers the possibility of acting with a degree of risk predetermined to realize a potentially large profit from a relatively small investment.

*Selling* (writing) call options offers an opportunity to increase the income derived from investments. Also, option writing enables investors to reduce substantially the cost of their securities.

### How

For the rights granted by the option, the option buyer pays and the option seller (writer) receives a certain amount of money. The option seller keeps the option money whether or not the option is exercised.

### The Option Concept Defined

What is an option? *Webster's New World Dictionary* gives the following definitions:

1. A choosing; choice
2. The right or liberty of choosing
3. Something that is or can be chosen
4. The right to buy or sell something at a fixed price

### Similarity to Insurance

Options have been common in Europe for more than three centuries. For instance, when a grower of tulip bulbs was worried about the safe arrival of a shipment he had contracted to deliver, he would buy an "option" from another grower on an equivalent amount of the merchandise at the prevailing price, as insurance.*

* Interestingly, the price paid for a *stock* option is called the "premium," the same term used in the insurance business for the price of an insurance policy.

# option basics

The option would cost him a relatively small amount of money to insure against a possibly costly breach of contract.

### A Rather Common Instrument

Options are still used extensively, both by individuals and by businesses. An option is a more common instrument than you may realize. When you buy an automobile, for instance, you have a chance to buy many accessories, such as power brakes or power steering, that are termed "optional"; that is, "elective," or at your choice. Or, when you buy a house under construction, a number of items, such as fireplaces, appliances, and the basement, have become optional.

### A Way to Limit Loss

To understand this aspect of options, imagine a real estate developer who wants to acquire land on which to build a large apartment house or an office building. The project involves buying out a number of small lots indispensable to his required large plot of ground. Instead of risking a very costly failure, the developer could buy an option, for a relatively small consideration, on each of the small lots. If he were unable to obtain options on all property segments, he could abandon the project, his loss limited to the cost of the acquired options.

### Elements of Property Options

Such options on property normally are composed of three important items: (1) a description of the property to be acquired; (2) the price at which the property may be acquired; and (3) the time period during which the buyer may exercise the right to acquire.

If the option-holder selects not to exercise the purchase rights during the option period, the option expires. The option writer (the property owner) keeps the option money regardless of whether the option is exercised.

### Similar Elements of Stock Options

A stock option contract also has three basic ingredients: (1) a description of the item the option buyer may purchase from the seller (writer) of the option; (2) the price at which the item may be purchased or sold; and (3) the time period during which the buyer must exercise the right to purchase.

For the rights granted by the option, the option buyer pays and the option writer (seller) receives a certain amount of money. The option writer keeps this money whether or not the option is exercised.

### Characteristics of Listed Options

In the case of listed* options, each option is for 100 shares of a specific, widely held, actively traded security. In option parlance, this security is known as the "underlying security."

The price at which the option buyer may purchase the stock from the option writer is the "strike price" or the "exercise price."

The expiration date is the last day on which the option buyer is entitled to exercise the option to purchase the security.

For a given stock, with its options listed on one of the national exchanges, there may be trading, at the same time, in both calls and puts with varying exercise prices and expiration dates.

### Option Market Liquidity

Since options have long been available on the over-the-counter market and have not made much headway, what has made the listed options market so successful? One simple answer: liquidity. This liquidity comes from the creation of a centralized, ready market, which was, in turn, made possible by the standardization of expiration dates and strike prices for listed options contracts. Exactly what it means to options investors to be able to liquidate their positions at any time in the listed market is discussed in Chapter 2.

# WHY PEOPLE BUY CALL OPTIONS

Buying call options provides to many investors the attractive combination of a potentially large

* "Listed" options are standardized options contracts traded specifically in options exchanges such as the Chicago Board Options Exchange.

profit from a relatively small investment, with a known and predetermined risk.

*Example:* Investor A bought 100 shares of XYZ at $45 per share, at a total cost of $4,500.

Investor B bought a call option on 100 shares of XYZ at $45 per share, for $300 as the cost of the call option.

Here are the obvious advantages for Investor B over Investor A:

1. Higher leverage: If XYZ rises from $45 to $65 per share, Investor A will have a profit of $2,000, amounting to a 44.4-percent return on his investment of $4,500. On the other hand, Investor B will have a profit of $1,700 ($2,000 − $300, the cost of the option), amounting to a 567-percent return on his much smaller investment of $300.
2. Limited and predetermined risk: If XYZ declines from $45 to $25 per share, Investor A will lose $2,000, or 44.4 percent on his $4,500 investment. Investor B's loss will be limited to $300. In fact, Investor B knows in advance that the most he can lose is the price he has paid for the option, $300. While relatively modest in absolute amount, the loss of $300 would constitute a 100-percent loss of Investor B's option capital. On the other hand, theoretically, Investor A could lose the entire $4,500 if XYZ went down to zero. Investor A, however, has an ultimate advantage over Investor B: while Investor B has no recourse after the expiration of his option, Investor A could always hold on to his stock for possible eventual recovery.

# WHY PEOPLE SELL CALL OPTIONS

Writing (selling) call options offers investors an opportunity to increase the income derived from their investments, sometimes significantly. Also, writing enables investors to reduce substantially the costs of their securities.

*Example:* If you presently own 100 shares of Xerox at $70 per share, you might consider writing one October 70 option for $750.

The advantages in doing this are twofold. First, you receive an immediate cash flow of $750 to work with.

Second, the $750 in option premium has the effect of reducing your investment in 100 shares of Xerox from $7,000 to $6,250, amounting to a 10.7-percent cost reduction.

## Cost Reduction and Downside Protection

This same $750, or 10.7-percent cost reduction, also provides you with that amount of protection on the downside; that is, if Xerox declines 7½ points, or 10.7 percent, from the price level at which you bought the stock, you still break even.

However, if Xerox should remain unchanged at expiration, the option would expire worthless, and the $750 option premium would, in effect, constitute an increase in the overall return on capital.

## Drawbacks and Limitations

Investors should weigh the drawbacks and limitations inherent in options carefully against the potential rewards.

Call sellers (writers), for instance, give up almost all of the benefits of a possible advance in the price of the underlying stock in return for the option premium received.

Call buyers lose the premium they paid for the right (option) to buy the underlying stock at a specified price within a specific period of time if the option expires unexercised.

Most option investors believe that more money has been made on the writing (selling) side than on the buying side, meaning, actually, that more money has been lost on the buying side than on the writing (selling) side.

# OVERVIEW

## What

Radically different, especially structurally, from the over-the-counter option market, the listed market is a continuous auction market in standardized option contracts, in which holders and writers may liquidate their positions as easily and as simply as they do other securities listed on major exchanges.

## Why

The listed option market enables an option investor to liquidate a position when and if desired. This makes possible a whole array of defensive and aggressive techniques that was never available in the over-the-counter option market.

## How

The national option exchanges provide for the resale of options through their secondary-market-making ability.

## Exchange-Traded Option Market

While trading in options is nothing new, what is new is the emergence of an active, organized market as a result of trading in listed call options on five listed options exchanges—the first two being the Chicago Board Options Exchange (CBOE) and the American Stock Exchange (AMEX).

The securities industry marked the beginning of a new era on April 26, 1973, when the CBOE began its trading in call options on a limited number of New York Stock Exchange stocks. The list of such stocks has steadily expanded.

## Emerging Major Investment Vehicle

Not since the height of the growth-stock craze of the late 1960s has Wall Street displayed such enthusiasm as it has over options trading.

According to former AMEX chairman Paul Kolton, "Only a small portion of the potential universe for options trading has been tapped at this point." The most commonly

# listed option market

heard estimate is that only 5 percent of active brokerage-house clients have so far engaged in options trading. Conceivably, though, listed options could emerge as a major investment vehicle, comparable to mutual funds in the 1950s, and 1960s.

### Secondary-Market-Making Ability

Perhaps the single most important feature of listed options is the option writer's ability to liquidate a position when and if desired. This makes possible a whole array of defensive and aggressive techniques unavailable with OTC options.

The national options exchanges provide for the resale of options through their secondary-market-making ability. Instead of being merely an inert derivative of the market in the underlying stock, listed options have developed into a kinetic instrument with market value of their own.

### Commodity Futures Concept and Strategies

To begin with, the listed options exchanges borrowed the futures concept of delivery months from the commodity market. The listed options exchanges have also successfully applied most of the key commodity strategies to the options market. Essentially, the CBOE is a commodity exchange using options on stocks rather than on commodity futures.

### Quality List

While options are available at only a fraction of the price of their underlying securities, they provide a low-cost participation in quality stocks due to the stringent listing requirements on listed options exchanges.

The listing requirements of the CBOE are even more stringent than those of the nation's major stock exchanges. These strict requirements help supply the options writer with a quality list from which to select.

### Eligibility Standards

To have its options eligible for listing on the CBOE, for example, the underlying security must meet certain requirements, including (1) a minimum of 10 million outstanding shares, of which 80 percent are held by the general public; (2) a minimum of 10,000 stockholders; and (3) a minimum price of $10 per share at the time of approval for listing.

In addition, the issuing corporations of the underlying securities (1) must have earned a minimum $500,000 per year in operating profits after taxes for the five years preceding the listing; (2) must not have been in default on their obligations during the past ten years; and (3) must have earned all dividends paid on all classes of securities for the five years preceding the listing. Similar standards apply for all exchanges.

### Options Clearing Corporation

The listed options exchanges are served by a central Options Clearing Corporation that performs a unique role in options trading. Immediately after sales and purchase orders are matched and executed, the direct connection between the purchaser and the seller ends. The Options Clearing Corporation assumes the obligation and becomes the purchaser to the seller and seller to the purchaser. It guarantees all options transactions that clear through it, assuring the purchaser that the stock will be delivered and the seller that he will be paid.

### "Certificateless" Securities

Options are called "certificateless" securities because customarily no certificates are issued to show ownership of exchange-traded options. The customer's position is evidenced by the confirmations and periodic statements that the customer receives from the broker.

Despite the rapid volume growth, markets have been orderly and technical foul-ups few. High-volume trading in certificateless securities has been achieved, and option transactions clear in one day, compared with five days for stock clearing.

### Basic Option Strategies

Probably the most versatile of available investment vehicles, listed options have applications limited only by imagination. Some of them are quite conservative, others more speculative. Listed options sometimes act as insurance policies to lock in profits, sometimes as high-leveraged means of maximizing profitability, sometimes as hedges to contain losses from other risk transactions.

To explain options at the most fundamental level, if you believe the price of a stock will increase, you buy a call option. On the other hand, if you believe the price of that stock you own will stand still or decline but you still want to hold the stock, you sell a call option.

An ever-growing number of options are bought as hedges against existing positions. Call option purchase can guarantee a purchase price against a short position. Conversely, call option writing (selling) can often guarantee a sale price against a long position.

Because there are many reasons to sell or to buy call options, buying or selling pressures can create relative price variances between options with various striking price and expiration dates.

## Possible Combinations

Because of the possible combinations of striking prices and expiration dates, there can be many different options traded on one underlying stock.

In combination with positions in other securities, options can produce portfolio configurations with risk/reward possibilities that are not obtainable in other investment media.

For instance, it is possible to guard against price changes by means of protective hedging, which uses a combination of buying and selling calls. It is also possible to establish aggressive spread and hedge positions, with limited risk, that are designed to take advantage either of market swings or movements in the market or price changes in a particular security.

Indicative of the growth potential of option-oriented portfolios is the rapid growth of option funds. Actually, hedged funds have been created to invest only in the options market. Listed options funds enjoy strong merchandising appeal because of their arbitrage characteristics. Let's examine this important technique more closely.

# ARBITRAGE

## Exploiting Price Differential

Essentially, arbitrage is accomplished by an offsetting transaction in two securities or in a related security of the same company. Specifically, arbitrage involves almost simultaneous purchase and sale of the same security (or substantially identical securities) in different markets in order to profit from a price differential.

By means of convertible securities, arbitrage seeks to cash in on profits resulting from price differential regardless of the direction of the general market or of underlying stocks.

## Relative versus Absolute Price Relations

Determination of likely relative price relationships between convertible securities is easier than forecasting the absolute price of the underlying securities. Generally, conventional investing methods are aimed at forecasting the absolute price some time in the future. As opposed to conventional investing, arbitrage does not depend upon such variables as disappointing earnings, compression of price/earnings (P/E) multiples, and so on.

## Objective Mathematical Approach

The analysis of convertible securities lends itself to an objective mathematical approach far more successful than conventional investment techniques. In the last analysis, arbitrage is a mathematical investment method that can, by varying and combining a number of basic techniques, be made to design a hedged portfolio that will profit within a range of rising, stable, and falling prices.

Arbitrage has long been a significant and steady source of income to many New York Stock Exchange member firms and other professional investors. It has been particularly profitable during periods of market weakness where other investment areas have been moribund. Generally, Wall Street professionals have performed arbitrage activities primarily for their own accounts because of the difficulty of finding enough situations to satisfy external demand.

### Broadened Arbitrage Opportunities

The growth of listed options has considerably broadened arbitrage opportunities.

Like other arbitrage methods, option arbitrage involves identifying options that are either underpriced or overpriced relative to the price of the underlying security. The overvalued option is sold short against the purchase of the undervalued option.

### Summary

While the listed options market is radically different, especially structurally, from the over-the-counter options market, strategies involving the use of options for both the buyer and the writer remain essentially the same.

Despite differences in contract terms in different option markets, all share three inherent characteristics: capital-protection possibilities, income-producing possibilities, and trading possibilities.

Underlying such profit-making possibilities are arbitrage and hedging methods used to attain capital-protection and income-generating possibilities, as well as to maximize trading possibilities to profit from market movements in any direction.

## OVERVIEW

### What

With a liquid secondary market, a listed call option is essentially a short-life warrant. It is a wasting asset, its value diminishing with time and completely vanishing on expiration date.

### Why

With two options of equal life, a higher price will generally be paid for an option providing greater upside leverage coupled with greater downside risk protection than for one with less upside leverage and less downside protection.

### How

Since an option sells at a fraction of the price of the underlying security, small price changes in the price of the underlying security can result in large percentage changes in the price of the option.

A listed call option has three essential ingredients: namely, the specific security the option buyer may purchase from the seller or writer of the option; the price at which the security may be purchased (or sold); and the time period during which the buyer must exercise or lose the right to purchase.

### Time Period

The time period during which the option buyer must exercise or lose the right to purchase amounts to the life of an option.

The price that the option buyer pays for that right to buy or not to buy the underlying security generally is in recognition of the time value placed upon the option's upside profit potential and limited downside risk.

### Time Value

An option is a wasting asset, its value diminishing with time and completely vanishing on expiration date.

Everything else being equal, the longer the life remaining in an option, the larger the premium. Conversely, the shorter the life remaining in an option, the smaller the premium. For

# characteristics of
# call options

example, everything else being equal, a three-month option is invariably cheaper than a six-month option.

The life of a conventional (over-the-counter) option may be whatever buyer and seller mutually agree. By and large, however, such options are granted for periods ranging between thirty days and one year.

On the other hand, listed options have only three clearly defined time periods: namely three months, six months, and nine months.

### Short-Life Warrant

With a liquid secondary market, a listed call option functions essentially the same as a short-life warrant. (A warrant is a company-issued right to buy stock.) The main differences between such an option and a warrant are that:

1. A listed call option is of relatively short duration, as its longest possible maturity is only nine months.
2. Listed calls are issued by option writers while warrants are issued by companies.

### Perpetual Regeneration

A listed call option has a major advantage over a warrant in that the former enjoys a perpetual regeneration of new warrants at new strikes and new expiration dates.

It has been the practice of the national options exchanges to issue a new series of option contracts for the same underlying security when a substantial price change occurs in that security.

Unlike the market situation with stocks, where the number of shares that can be traded is fixed, no predetermined number of options exists. How many options there are depends solely on the number sellers are willing to write and buyers are willing to buy.

### Strike Prices

Listed call options can be traded with the same expiration date, but different strike prices.

Strike prices are, as a rule, fixed at five-point intervals for securities trading below 50, ten-point intervals for securities trading between 50 and 100; and twenty-point intervals for securities trading over 100.

With over-the-counter options, the strike price is automatically reduced on the ex-dividend date, by the exact value of any dividends, rights, or stock distributed to shareholders.

On the other hand, the strike price of listed options is not reduced by cash dividends but does reflect all other distributions. Cash dividends on a long stock position accrue to the option writer.

### Compelling Mathematics

Since an option sells at a percentage of the price of the underlying security, small price changes in the price of the underlying security can result in large percentage changes in the price of the option.

From the standpoint of both writer and buyer, the mathematics of listed options are compelling. The option writer obtains additional income from his portfolio, while at the same time reducing his risk. The premium received from option writing can be considered as a partial hedge against a possible decline in the prices of the stock. The buyer maximizes the number of shares to be controlled with minimum cost.

# OPTION PREMIUM

The key to option trading is the amount of money, called the "premium," that a buyer pays to a seller (or writer) for the right to buy 100 shares of a given stock within a certain time limit. The writer of the option keeps the premium whether or not the option is exercised.

The premium is payable at purchase of the option and is not applicable to the purchase price of the stock at exercise of the option. The premium, however, does become part of the cost basis of the stock if the option is exercised.

### General Yardsticks

While there is no precise formula for calculating the amount of premium, there are some general yardsticks:

The amount of the premium varies with the market price and volatility of the underlying stock as well as with its time duration and striking price.

Other factors influencing the size of the premium include market trends, the cost of money, and the level of general interest or lack of interest in options.

### Supply and Demand Factors

Essentially, the premium is a reflection of supply and demand.

In times of generally rising stock prices, there is less interest in writing call options but more interest in buying them. Thus, the level of option premiums tends to rise.

Conversely, in times of generally weak or declining stock prices, there is greater interest in writing call options but less interest in buying them. Premiums thus tend to decline.

### Volatility

A major premium-influencing factor is the volatility of the underlying security.

As a general rule, an option for a traditionally volatile stock is likely to command a higher premium than the option for a stock that normally trades in narrow price limits. A stock that fluctuates widely presents more risk to the option writer; therefore, the option buyer has a greater chance to exercise the option profitably.

### Premium Cost of Short- and Long-Term Options

Percentagewise, the largest premium is often paid for the shortest period of time.

The increment of premium for the period between the nearest expiration date and the next longest usually is significantly less than the premium for the first three months.

As a rule of thumb, 90-day call options range from 8 to 12 percent of the market price of the stock. Six-month options run from 10 to 16 percent, or higher in the case of very volatile stocks.

An option on a stock selling for $20 per share usually costs, percentagewise, more than an option on a stock selling for $60.

### Premium Components

With a liquid secondary options market, the price of the option can be considered as having three components: intrinsic or tangible worth, discounted potential appreciation, and premium. "Premium," in this sense, means that portion of the option price the buyer pays in excess of intrinsic worth.

During a call option's life, the option will usually sell at a premium—meaning more than the option's tangible worth. The size of the premium essentially reflects the option's upside leverage and limited downside risk.

Generally, a larger premium will be paid for an option providing greater upside leverage coupled with greater downside risk protection than for one of equal life with less upside leverage and less downside protection.

Normally, an option will command a price in excess of its actual tangible worth. The amount option buyers are willing to pay over an option's tangible worth is called "premium" in the narrow sense of the term. Option buyers are willing to pay such a premium in the expectation that the underlying security will rise and the option will develop more value.

### Mathematical Relationship at Expiration

At expiration, the option price will reflect itself directly in terms of its mathematical relationship to the underlying security. In other words, the only remaining value of an option at expiration will be its tangible value. This is the amount (if any) that the exercise price of the option is below the current market value of the underlying security.

### Three Basic Price Relationships

When traded on the national exchanges, listed options maintain three basic price relationships with the underlying security, namely: options "at market," options "in the money," and options "out of the money."

### At-Market Options

At-market options are options whose striking prices are equal to the market value of the underlying stock.

When one sells an option at market against a long position, one is usually seeking above-average return. Generally, the writer of options at market believes that his annual return will, on average, be greater than he could realize by being just long on common stocks.

### In-the-Money Options

In-the-money options are options whose strike prices are below the current market price of the underlying stock.

Thus, options with strike prices below the market price are said to have tangible worth or intrinsic value. This in-the-money aspect is in addition to value for time remaining.

One would sell these options if one were generally short-term bearish on the market. Another important factor motivating such option writing is the desire to increase overall return by selling options against stocks held in one's portfolio.

### Out-of-the-Money Options

Out-of-the-money options are options with strike prices above the market value of the underlying stock. Such options are said to have no tangible worth. This does not mean, however, that the call will not command a value. Usually, only at or very near an option's expiration date does it not maintain a premium.

When a call has no tangible worth, the entire price the option sells for constitutes its premium.

Since there is an optimistic bias in out-of-the-money options, it would make sense to buy stocks and sell out-of-the-money options if you believe the stocks you are buying are not going to change very much in price. However, when you buy such a stock, be sure that you would like to own it anyhow and are willing either to surrender the stock or close out the call if the price of the security goes up.

For an investor who owns the stock, an out-of-the-money option can be used to maximize potential return and, at the same time, derive some income from the long position.

# OVERVIEW

## What

Buying a call option is an alternative to investing in the underlying security. On the other hand, selling (writing) a call option serves the dual purpose of at least partially protecting capital and earning an income from that capital.

## Why

For a fraction of the price of the underlying stock, the call option buyer can speculate on the stock's near-term movements. On the other hand, selling (writing) options probably is the only investing approach that starts with cash receipt (getting paid in the form of premium dollars in advance in return for issuing an option contract).

## How

The degree of upside leverage (the principal attraction for option buyers) is dependent upon the actual movement of the underlying security. Dividing the projected percentage move of the call option by the projected percentage move of the underlying security amounts to the potential leverage an option provides.

Of all kinds of options, the call option is by far the most popular form, accounting for the great majority of all option transactions.

Essentially a call option purchaser anticipates an increase in the value of the underlying security by investing a fraction of the cost of the stock as a means of obtaining greater leverage on his investment.

Probably the single most important attraction of purchasing call options is leverage. In essence, leverage presents the possibility of very large percentage gains on the predetermined premium risk within very short time periods.

## Speculative Opportunities

Since options may be purchased for only a fraction of the underlying stock's market value, they provide attractive vehicles for speculation.

Opportunities include day-to-day trading by aggressive investors. Often, a price move of several points in the underlying security can produce 40-percent or more gain in the option

# analysis of call options

in a single day. A significant number of options have more than doubled in one session.

### Predetermined Risk

Leverage runs either way, however. A large number of options have declined more than 50 percent in one trading session.

Offsetting the risk, however, is the purchaser's knowledge that the most he can lose is the premium, no matter how far the underlying stock may decline. Call option buyers are only risking the cost of the call, which is considerably less than the price of the stock, but they stand to profit from any appreciation in the price of the stock.

### Alternate Courses

Buying an option is an alternate course to investing in the underlying security. In many instances, it is less risky and less expensive to control shares of XYZ with an option than it is to go long on the stock.

The key to determining these alternate vehicles lies in weighing the risk-reward parameters and the leverage factor of the option.

### Leverage Factor

1. For a cash purchase: As a rule of thumb, for the same amount of money involved in an outright acquisition of 100 shares of stock, you can control far more shares through the use of calls.
2. For a margin purchase: Buyers of a call option achieve great leverage by establishing a position in a selected stock several times larger than a margin position (based on the current 50-percent margin).

### Magnification Factor

The magnifying effect of potential option profitability is indicated by the following comparisons:

Two investors are impressed with the future prospects of the same stock. Each has about $5,000 in investable cash. Mr. A decides to buy 200 shares of the stock at $50 and margin his purchase. Under current margin requirements he puts up 50 percent of the market value, or $5,000. Mr. B buys ten calls (1,000 shares) at the strike price of $50, for a premium of $500 per call, or $5,000.

Now, suppose the stock moves to $75 within the next six months. Mr. A, who bought 200 shares on margin, would have a profit of $5,000 ($15,000 less the $5,000 debit in his margin account and less $5,000 initial investment). On the other hand, Mr. B could exercise his ten calls at $50 and immediately sell the 1,000 shares at $75, thereby realizing a profit of $20,-000 ($25,000 less the $5,000 he paid for the ten calls).

### Reward Parameters

For the same amount of cash outlay, Mr. B would gain $20,000 from his ten calls, or 400 percent on his money.

Mr. A, however, would gain $5,000, or only 100 percent on this investment. The relative leverage between Mr. B and Mr. A is four to one.

### Near-Term Movements

Thus, the buyer's side of an option contract is where the leverage lies and, consequently, where the big profits are. For a fraction of the price of the underlying stock, the option buyer can speculate on the stock's near-term movements.

### Risk of Total Loss

Leverage can operate in reverse, of course. At worst, a total loss of premium money in a relatively short period of time can result when the underlying shares fail to reach the strike price before the option runs out. If options are not exercised before expiration, they lose all value.

In the preceding example, Mr. B could lose his entire $5,000 if the stock were to become worthless. On the other hand, Mr. A could hold on to his stock for possible recovery. Total erosion of stock value is highly unlikely (though theoretically possible) because, as a result of the strict listing requirements by the national options exchanges, the underlying stocks are generally blue-chip quality.

### Resale Market

The option buyer need not, however, ride all the way down, because of the existence of a continuous listed options market. He can limit his loss just as he can in the stock market.

A rule of thumb calls for an option buyer to consider getting out while he still has 75 percent of his premium money intact.

The ability to resell listed options at any time on the national exchanges serves to limit option losses and to realize profits with less stock price movement than in the OTC market.

In the OTC market, it is extremely difficult to sell a call option with the market price below the strike price. The holder of an OTC option can rarely, if ever, obtain any reasonable value for the time remaining in his option contract.

## Cushion Factor

A cushion factor tends to support the price of a listed option as it descends.

The same cushion factor has been noted in the behavior of commodity futures markets. In a number of key commodity markets, the premium widens when commodity prices decline, then narrows again when commodity prices recover. The closer commodity prices get to their floor, the more pronounced the effect of the floor becomes. The premium is a reflection of the value commodity futures traders place on the limited risk.

Just as with commodity futures, listed options have a predetermined downside risk. Consequently, if a listed option still has a meaningful period of exercisable life remaining, it tends to develop into an increasingly attractive candidate for purchase as its price descends simply because its potential loss is becoming progressively smaller even though its possible gains are highly speculative.

## Relative Percentage Moves

The degree of upside leverage an option provides depends on the actual movement of the underlying security.

In order to determine the rate at which a call option will appreciate relative to the percentage advance of its underlying security, one must project a specific stock move. Dividing the resulting percentage move of the call option by the projected percentage move of the underlying security gives the potential leverage an option offers.

One formula calls for option purchases only when the purchaser envisions a price move in the underlying security of approximately three times the premium at risk.

## Option-to-Double Formula

To determine the percentage move required for the call price to double to maturity, divide the sum of twice the option's cost plus the exercise price by the price of the underlying stock thus:

$$\text{Required percentage move for call to double at maturity} = \frac{2(op) + sp}{mp}$$

where $op$ = option premium
$mp$ = market price
$sp$ = exercise price

## Option-to-Break-Even Formula

For an option buyer to break even at maturity, it is necessary for the call's intrinsic value at expiration to equal the option's cost.

To determine the percentage of the underlying stock advance required for a call option buyer to break even, divide the price of the call plus its exercise price by the price of the underlying stock thus:

$$\text{Option breakeven} = \frac{op + sp}{mp}$$

where $op$ = option premium
$mp$ = market price
$sp$ = exercise price

## Option-to-Become-WorthlessFormulas

The following two formulas are used to measure the extent of stock decline before an option becomes worthless at expiration:

1. Formula A, for call options with positive intrinsic value: To determine the percentage by which the underlying stock must decline to make the call worthless at expiration, divide the option's intrinsic value by the price of the underlying stock.

$$\text{Formula A} = \frac{piv}{mp}$$

where $piv$ = positive intrinsic value
$mp$ = market price

2. Formula B, for call options with negative intrinsic value: To determine the percentage, the underlying security must decline to make the call worthless at expiration, divide the negative intrinsic value by the price of the underlying stock.

$$\text{Formula B} = \frac{niv}{mp}$$

where $niv$ = negative intrinsic value
$mp$ = market price

## Intrinsic Value

The intrinsic value of a call option is the difference between the market value of the underlying security and the strike price of the option.

A call option is said to be in the money when its strike price is below the market value of the underlying security. A call option is said to be out of the money when its strike price is above the market price of the underlying security.

## Relative Leverage and Risk

The existence of both in-the-money options and out-of-the-money options has considerably broadened investment opportunities. The greatest leverage is usually obtained with the out-of-the-money option and the least with the in-the-money option.

However, purchasers of out-of-the-money options stand a greater chance of losing all the funds invested than buyers of in-the-money options.

In assessing the relative risk of in-the-money and out-of-the-money options, the total amount of dollar exposure per option must be weighed.

# IN-THE-MONEY OPTION TECHNIQUES

A significant number of "in the money" option buying techniques are available to sophisticated investors, illustrated here with actual option-buying situations from past markets.

## Technique 1: High-Leveraged Call Options

*Example:* On April 21, 1975, the July 60 option on Union Carbide (NYSE–63⅛–UK) was in the money 3⅛ points; its price at 60 indicated an actual cost of 2⅞. Buying this option constituted a fairly inexpensive way to control a $60-plus stock in a dynamic uptrend. An advance of 2⅞ points, or only 4.5 percent, from the current market level would enable the July 60 option to move point for point with the common. Current P/E ratio of 7 was less than half its ten-year average P/E of 13.5.

Two weeks later, on May 5, 1975, UK had moved 3¼ points, or 5 percent, from 63⅛ to 66⅜. Its July 60 option jumped 50 percent, from 6 to 9, indicating the dynamics of high-leveraged calls.

Investors who had bought the original call could then either have taken a quick 50-percent profit (before commissions) or ventured for further possible gains.

## Technique 2: Low-Cost Dynamic Call Options

*Example:* A low-cost, dynamic, in-the-money call option was available on May 5, 1975, on the October 25 call option on International Harvester (NYSE–28½–HR). Since the option was in the money 3½ points, its price at 5⅛ indicated an actual cost of 1⅝, which was an attractive six-month-plus call on a recession-resistant growth stock. HR, a leading manufacturer of agricultural equipment, was in an uptrend despite the recession. Technically, it had achieved a breakthrough at 27, with an upward objective of 32 to 34. Estimated 1975 earnings of $6 per share indicated a P/E of 4.8, versus its twelve-year average P/E of 11. A 6.0-percent yield is indicated by dividends of $1.70.

## Technique 3: Parity Call Options

In these situations, a one-point increase or decrease in the underlying stock price usually results in movement of only a fraction of a point in the option's premium. However, once an option reaches parity (the premium plus the exercise price equals the price of the stock), the premium is likely to move point for point with the stock.

*Example:* The July 15 option on International Telephone & Telegraph (NYSE–20½–ITT), on April 21, 1975, was available at 5¾ against the common stock price of 20½.

After two weeks, on May 5, 1975, the common had advanced 1⅜ points, or 6.7 percent, from 20½ to 21⅞, while the July option had moved 1⅛ points, or 20 percent, from 5¾ to 6⅞. The option advance was in line with the generally point-for-point movement with the common.

When you are considering the purchase of the underlying security of these parity options, you may find it more attractive to buy the option instead. The difference in capital could be placed in high-yield instruments.

## Short Options at Parity

Consideration should be given to closing out option writing positions that were established at much lower levels if the short option is selling near parity.

## Technique 4: Conservative Hedging Call Options

Conservative hedge writers should consider writing in-the-money options for both maximum downside protection and high returns.

*Example:* One illustration of this conservative hedging technique was the July 40 option on Alcoa (NYSE–46–AA) on May 20, 1975.

With the July option 6 points in the money, an actual premium of 1⅞ was available on the nine weeks remaining in the option.

This conservatively capitalized company, producing about half the United States' aluminum cans, primarily used for soft drinks, is recession-resistant and sometimes even countercyclical.

Based on lower 1975 earnings of $4.25 (versus $5.14 in 1974), current P/E was 10.8.

## Technique 5: No-Premium Call Options

*Example:* Illustrative of the technique of buying call options at no premium was the possibility of purchasing, on January 21, 1975, the April 15 option of IT&T, then quoted at 16¾.

With the April 15 option selling at 1¹⁵⁄₁₆, the option purchaser would pay a ³⁄₁₆ premium based on the stock price of 16¾.

(Lack of premium for buying a call option is probably due to an excess of option writiers over option buyers.)

Since the strike price of 15 was below the stock price of 16¾ the April 15 option was said to be in the money. In-the-money options normally are more expensive to buy due to their intrinsic value.

Also illustrative of no-premium call options was possible purchase of the July 20 option, on June 12, 1975, on IT&T, which was quoted at 22⅞ on that date.

With the July 20 option available at 2⅞, it indicated zero cost on the option as the stock was 2⅞ points in the money.

## Technique 6: Discount Call Options

Probably one of the best risk-reduction and profit-maximizing option techniques is to buy discount instead of premium. (The availability of options "at discount" is usually due to an excess of option writers over option buyers.) Some deep-in-the-money options are available at discount.

*Example:* Illustrative of the discount option buying technique was the possibility of purchasing, on June 12, 1975, the July 30 option at 13¼ of General Motors (NYSE–43⅜–GM), which was trading at a ⅛-point discount:

| | | |
|---|---|---|
| GM common | | 43⅜ |
| GM April 30 option: | | |
| Exercise price | 30 | |
| Premium | 13¼ | |
| | | 43¼ |
| Discount | | ⅛ |

## Deep-in-the-Money

Option premiums generally approximate intrinsic value more closely as the option becomes deeper in the money, and they rise above intrinsic value as the underlying security declines toward the strike price.

# CALL BUYING

# PART II

## OVERVIEW

### What

Buying call options provides a significant number of applications, ranging from the conservative to the speculative.

### Why

Purchasers of call options have three principal objectives: (1) leveraged participation with limited capital; (2) short-term trading; and (3) insurance.

### How

Among the most important applications are: (1) participation vehicle as an alternative to buying the underlying stock; (2) limited-risk method; (3) establishing a position in advance of funds; (4) locking up profits; (5) trading-against method; (6) hedging against short sale; (7) controlling more stock with the same money; and (8) buying stock at below-market price.

### Essential Objectives

People purchase listed call options for one or more of three reasons: (1) leveraged partici-

pation with limited capital; (2) short-term trading; and (3) insurance. Option buyers have developed sophisticated applications of these general objectives.

## OPTION-BUYING APPLICATIONS

### Speculative Alternative to Stock Purchase

Option buying can be an alternative to the purchase of stock. In addition to the leverage factor, the purchase of a call option limits the investor's downside exposure to the cost of the call.

*Example:* On April 21, 1975, it was possible to buy either or both the July 15 option and the October 15 option of Tesoro Petroleum (NYSE–16–TSO).

TSO was one of the few oil producers looking for higher per-share earnings in 1975 than in 1974. Also bullish was the expected rise to 700 million tons of coal reserves under lease or option by midyear. TSO had a strong base forming at 13½ to 15. Its

# call option
# buying strategies

1974 high was close to 29. Current P/E ratio was a low 3.

Both the July 15 option at 2¾ and the October 15 option at 3⅝ were attractive. For an extra $87, the October 15 option for an additional three months was preferred. A less aggressive strategy was to buy the stock and then wait until it reached the 20 level before writing options to gain higher option premium.

A month later, on May 20, 1975, TSO had advanced 3⅝, or 22.6 percent, from 16 to 19⅝. The July 15 option had jumped 82 percent, from 2¾ to 5, and the October 15 option 70 percent, from 3 to 5¾.

Investors who had taken these option positions could have taken an 82 or 70 percent (precommissions) profit on the respective July 15 or October 15 options. Or, they could have ventured for further possible gains since TSO continued to be statistically cheap.

*Example:*  Another illustraiton of call speculation was the possible purchase on May 5, 1975, of the October 30 call option of Kresge (NYSE–28⅞–KG).

At a cost of 3⅞, KG's October 30 call option had considerable speculative appeal. Fundamentally, its year-ahead prospects remained strong despite expected lower earnings. Technically, the recent upside breakout on increased volume favored further advance. With support at 24–26, the price objectives for KG were indicated at 31 to 33 for the near term.

## Limited-Risk Method

This approach, which can be described as buying options and investing the difference, provides an opportunity to benefit from a stock price rise while protecting the investor against an adverse price movement.

The limited-risk technique involves purchasing call options on the same number of shares of stock that would otherwise have been bought outright and investing the balance in some short-term fixed-income securities.

*Example:*  On June 12, 1975, you decided to take a 100-share position in Syntex (NYSE–39¾–SYN.)

Instead of buying 100 shares of Syntex for $3,975, you decided to take a far more limited risk by purchasing an October 40 call for 5⅛ that, for a three-month-plus period, have enabled you to participate in the possible rise of the stock.

Meanwhile, since you had used only part of the fund that otherwise would be required to buy 100 shares of Syntex, you invested the balance, amounting to $3,462, in short-term fixed-income securities.

## Establishing a Position in Advance of Funds

Investors buy call options to nail down the price of a stock they intend to buy six or nine months later. One primary use of this "buy now, pay later" method is to establish a position in a stock in advance of an expected inflow of money.

*Example:*  Assume that Homestake Mining (NYSE–52¾–HM) appeared attractive to you on June 12, 1975, for possible recovery in the price of gold, but you did not expect to have the funds to buy HM until late October.

In order not to miss a possible resurgence of gold prices, you bought an October 50 call of 7⅝, indicating a premium of 4⅞ points, since the October 50 call was 2¾ points in the money. In effect, the October 50 call guaranteed you, through its exercise, a definitive price until it expired. If, as expected, HM had risen to 60, you could have exercised your option and acquired 100 shares of HM at $50 per share.

## Trading-Against Method

The holder of a listed call option may trade (short the stock) against the option. This practice has become one of the most important reasons for buying options, for it can be quite profitable to the holder, especially in a "trading market" (one that fluctuates wildly).

A listed option contract is operable until it expires or is exercised. A trade or trades against an option do not nullify the option contract. As long as the original call option remains intact, the holder of the call can trade repeatedly against the option until its expiration. As many as ten trades could conceivably occur during a six-month period. Following are the important reasons for trading against.

1. Trading under a protective umbrella: Such trades are made under the protective umbrella of the option and with the holder's risk predetermined. Each time a trade is made, that trade is fully protected against unlimited loss should the trader's judgment be wrong.

The number of opportunities to make trades against an option is limited only by the fluctuation of the stock and the trader's ability to judge the stock's movements.

2. Trading in No-Trend Markets: When there is no definitive trend in stock prices, options can be used as a limited (instead of a full-fledged) commitment. Such options allow a certain measure of participation before the market gives a clearer indication of its direction.

Thus, regardless of what happens to the price of the underlying stock, the holder's maximum risk in any long call option position is the total price of the option premium.

*Example:* Instead of buying XYZ at 50, you buy a three-month call with a strike price of 50 at a premium cost of $300.

If XYZ rises to 60, your call will gain in value and can be exercised at a profit.

If XYZ declines to 40, your loss will be limited to the premium cost of $300 instead of the $1,000 you would have lost had you bought the stock at 50.

If, when your call expires, the stock is still depressed, you could purchase another call if you feel it should recover a good portion of its decline.

3. Trading for short-term movements: Through continuous trading of a security against an option, the investor is in a position to benefit from short-term reactions to a basic trend of the security, especially when an initial profit has been insured.

*Example:* Assume that you paid $300 for a three-month call on XYZ with a strike price of 50. If XYZ rises to 60, you could sell it short and lock in a $1,000 gain.

Should the stock continue to advance, you could exercise your call to cover the short sale. If XYZ, instead, fell back to 55, you could cover your short sale by buying the stock, while continuing to be in a position to profit through the use of your call. If the stock advanced once more to 60, you could repeat the operation.

## Hedge against Short Sale

You may hedge the risk you have assumed in a short sale by buying a call option.

You can protect your short sales with a call because the option increases in value as the stock goes up. Your risk is limited to the costs involved in buying the option.

The alternative is to risk having to cover a short sale at a higher price, perhaps incurring a substantial loss.

Should the market go against you, the call can be exercised to cover the short position. If the stock declines, the call can be allowed to expire, leaving a profitable short position.

*Example:* You feel XYZ is overvalued at $60 and decide to sell short. In order to protect yourself, you buy a call at the same price. If the stock declines, say to $50, you buy 100 shares at that level to cover your short position, and take a 10-point profit less the cost of your call, which you allow to expire.

If the stock rises, you will be able to exercise your call in order to cover your short position.

It will very rarely be possible to sell short at the exact strike price of the listed option. The differential between the short-sale price and the strike price may be positive or negative and must be considered in addition to the call premium when evaluating the cost of the hedge.

In the above, we assume that the price of a listed call option and that of its underlying stock will move up and down in unison. In fact, since the two are traded in different markets and on different exchanges, they indicate movements not exactly in unison between the listed option and the underlying stock.

## Controlling More Stock with the Same Money

Because the price of an option usually accounts for a small percentage of the value of the underlying security, one can control a large amount of stock with a relatively small amount of money.

A rule of thumb is that a call option buyer controls about five to ten times the stock he could normally control with the same available capital. The same amount of money required to margin 100 shares of stock probably could be used to buy five calls.

## Releasing Cash while Maintaining Market Position

Through a listed call option one may release one's funds by selling the stock while still maintaining control over the same number of shares during the life of the option.

### Buying at Below-Market Price

Under certain conditions a stock can be acquired through its options at less than the cost of the underlying security, especially if the stock has a low dividend yield.

### Acquiring an Option at No Cost

Suppose you buy stock and a call at the same time. If the stock advances to a point where the profit will pay the cost of the call, you can sell the stock and have the call for nothing.

### Averaging Down

Assume that a stock you bought has declines in price. You may buy a listed call option on the same stock as a means of averaging down.

If the stock recovers during the life of the call, either partially or completely, you could end up either with a gain or with your loss reduced.

# CALL SELLING

## PART III

## OVERVIEW

### What

A call option seller (writer) contracts to deliver, upon demand, a specified number of shares at a fixed price, on or before a specified date, to the option buyer. In return, the buyer pays the seller (writer) a premium (option money) at the time of the option sale.

### Why

The seller (writer) of call options has two basic objectives: (1) to generate additional income from his stock; and (2) to acquire price protection by at least partially offsetting loss in a falling market.

### How

It is on the seller's (writer's) side that the smaller but more consistent dollar is to be made. Accumulation of smaller gains can substantially enhance overall investment returns.

The writer or seller of call options has two basic objectives: (1) to generate additional income from his stock, and (2) to acquire price protection by at least partially offsetting loss in a falling market.

By its unique features, listed call option writing serves the dual purposes of protecting capital and earning a high income from that capital. More often than not, these two goals are irreconcilable with other investing techniques.

Option writers are paid premium dollars in advance in return for issuing an option contract. Option writing probably is the only investing approach that starts with the receiving of cash. The receipt, however, eventually may not prove to be a gain. It may just be a downside cushion, or it may simply lure the investor into buying stock he wouldn't ordinarily buy.

Many experienced option writers believe that call buyers are generally wrong in their expectations for moves in the underlying security. They also believe that call buyers who pay relatively high premiums for very short time periods (usually periods of three to six months) are wrong more often than not.

This belief is, of course, by no means unchallenged. According to some statistics, most

# writing
# call options

# 6

options were exercised with gains for the buyers. Many options are believed to have been exercised well in advance of their expiration date.

## The Active Role of the Listed Call Writer

In the OTC market, a call writer can do nothing but wait for the buyer to call away his stock. More often than not the call buyer may have no wish to do so, since often it would be less expensive for the buyer to convert than to call the stock.

With a liquid listed options market, the writer can assume an active role. For example, in a sharp rise of the underlying stock, the option loses premium and approaches its intrinsic worth. The writer may repurchase the option and either sell the next higher strike at a large premium or the call further out at a large premium.

## Three Basic Courses

As a writer or seller of a call option, you contract to deliver, upon demand, a specified number of shares at a fixed price, on or before a specified date, to the option buyer. In return, the buyer pays you a premium at the time of the option sale.

During the life of the call option, one of the following three basic courses may develop:

1. The stock moves above the strike price and is called away.
2. The stock does not move either way and the call expires.
3. The stock moves below the strike price and the call expires.

*Example:* Should XYZ rise above the strike price of $50, the buyer would exercise his option and you would be obligated to deliver the stock to him at $50. The loss of the gain you would sustain as a result of the stock's rising above the strike price would be reduced by the premium you have already received.

Should XYZ fail to move either way, or trade below during the life span of the option, you would pocket the premium and retain the stock.

## Built-In Advantages

The built-in advantages enjoyed by covered option writers versus long common stock

holders or call buyers are obvious, especially in periods of market uncertainty.

In an up market, the covered writer earns the premium and possibly a favorable strike price differential. In a flat market, the writer earns the premium. In a down market, the writer may profit if the decline is less than the premium received. The writer loses only when the decline is more than the premium received.

These advantages are even more compelling when the market is vulnerable to serious correction after a strong and sharp upward movement.

In large part, most of the advantages for option writers are based on the nature of the options instrument itself. It is on the writer's side that the smaller but more consistent dollar is to be made. Accumulation of smaller gains can substantially enhance overall investment returns.

## Capital-Protection Features

In addition to augmenting overall portfolio returns, judiciously used listed options can achieve two other important capital-protection objectives, even for conservative portfolios. These are (1) reducing net cash outlay in stock purchases through writing call options simultaneously on stocks being bought; and (2) hedging the investment position.

As the national options exchanges expand coverage of the most widely held and traded stocks, portfolio managers gain more opportunities for option writing.

Besides generating more income, portfolio option writers can, at the same time, limit downside risk by selling options on the core portfolio stocks (those they would hold through any market decline).

## The Other Side of the Coin: Profit Limitation

While option writers gain downside protection, they may well forgo some of the upside potential. Should the underlying stock rise substantially, profit potential is limited to the additional dollars received for selling the option. By writing an option on the underlying security, the security owner gives up an opportunity for any gain resulting from an increase in the price of the underlying stock above the exercise price. In the options market, money made by purchasers represents gains given up on the underlying stocks by the option writers.

It is very important to remember that most options written have been exercised.

### Hedged Percentage

Generally, the option writer has to think like a banker, especially in understanding the time value of money. He should look at the market from a mathematical or percentage point of view.

The investment objective of the professional option writer is to achieve a higher-than-normal rate of return on his investment with reduced risk. He favors a hedged percentage by usually forgoing the potential for a large gain.

This hedged percentage can be quite considerable on a cumulative basis, however. A return of 15 to 18 percent a year is possible for even the most conservative writers.

### Arithmetic and Reality

Options can result in impressive annual gains for aggressive option writers. For instance, an option sold for a 10-percent premium and exercised in a month would amount to an annualized rate of 120 percent, quite astonishing but frequently overlooked arithmetic.

The above annualized rate of return refers only to the income received by the option writer from the premium, and ignores any price movement of the long underlying stock position.

The annualized rate is obtained by dividing the option premium by the current price of the underlying security and adjusting for the length of time remaining in the option.

However, the exercise of a listed call after one month of its life is very rare. Even in cases that theoretically might justify such an exercise,

the call holder can do better by liquidating his call than by exercising it. Only in cases where the stock has risen so sharply that the option sells for a discount from true worth is there likely to be an early exercise.

### "Total Return" Concept

Option-oriented portfolios focus on the "total return" on invested capital: dividends, premiums, and capital gains earned from option writing activities. Unlike options traded over the counter, the writer of listed options retains cash dividends earned on the underlying stock during the time prior to exercise.

The rate of total return on an options portfolio could measurably exceed that on a straight debt, equity, or mixed portfolio.

### Cumulative Average Yield

Most high-quality stock portfolios have a cumulative average yield well below that obtainable from high-quality bond portfolios. Now options provide a valid method to increase the yield of high-quality stock portfolios without substantially increasing the risk.

Percentage-minded investors or portfolio managers can do very well by repeatedly selling call options against a portfolio. If judiciously used, option writing can turn a high-quality portfolio into an income portfolio without buying or selling a single stock.

To an increasing number of sophisticated money managers, writing call options is becoming a useful tool to enhance the total portfolio return.

### Long-Range Performance

According to industry studies, writing options on stocks held in a portfolio can produce better long-term investment results than just buying and holding stocks.

## OVERVIEW

### What

Writing a covered call option means that the writer (seller) owns the underlying security against which he has written (sold) an option.

### Why

Generally, the writer (seller) (1) feels comfortable holding or buying the underlying stock at its present price level; and (2) is willing to sell the underlying stock at the strike price plus the premium received.

### How

Covered call option writing has two principal applications:

1. It provides a way to sell stocks already owned at a price level above the prevailing market price.
2. It provides an intermediate-term hedge when call option writers (sellers) believe that certain stocks are due for an intermediate-term consolidation after a sharp rise.

There are two broad classes of written options, covered and uncovered. A covered option is one for which the writer owns the underlying stock.

An option written against cash is known as an uncovered option or a naked option. An uncovered writer must deposit and maintain sufficient funds with his broker to assure delivery of the stock if the call is exercised. Uncovered option writers expose themselves to great risks. When an investor sells an uncovered call option, the potential for loss is theoretically unlimited.

As long as a naked option is not exercised, it is possible for its writer to realize profits. This has been the case during periods of declining and generally stable stock prices.

### Scope of Covered Option Writing

In addition to writing covered options against underlying common stocks, covered options can also be written against warrants, convertible bonds, convertible preferreds, or listed options of the same security. One may even borrow stock to deliver short. The specific action an option writer chooses to take will de-

# covered option writing strategies

7

pend upon his overall strategy as well as his current market judgment.

In the majority of call writings, however, a covered option writer either owns the underlying security or buys it at the time he writes the option. Generally, the writer (1) feels comfortable in holding or buying the stock at its present level; and (2) is willing to sell the stock at the strike price plus the premium received.

### Larger Hedged Component

Since the equity investment is a much larger component of a written position than the option, security selection is the key to a successful writing position.

Fundamentally, option writers are well advised to write call options only for stocks that are within their historical price range and P/E relationships. Regular investment criteria should be applied to the process of stock selection.

### Determination of Option Value

Some options advisory services have developed proprietary computer programs that regularly evaluate all call option writing opportunities in terms of potential return on investment, downside protection, and so on.

While most experts agree on the wisdom of writing an overvalued option and purchasing an undervalued option, the problem of how to determine "overvalued" or "undervalued" options is a real one. An increasing number of options-evaluation services resort to computer programs to "determine" the "normal value" of an option. When a significant deviation from the "normal value" occurs in the price of an option, it is said to call for purchase or sale of that option accordingly.

### Normal-Value Calculations

The following factors are generally considered the basic components that go into determination of the "normal value": the price and volatility of the stock, the yield of the stock, the strike price of the option, and the time remaining before expiration.

1. Stock price: Since an option sells for a fraction of the price of its underlying security, option value partly reflects the value of the underlying security. Everything else being equal, a higher priced stock normally commands a higher priced option than does a lower priced stock.
2. Stock volatility: Option buyers normally are willing to pay more for options on stocks of higher volatility, with correspondingly higher possibilities for profitable exercise or disposal of options.
3. Stock yield: The impact of stock yield on option value is obvious, because stock yield is part of the total yield on the weighing scale of option writers. Higher stock yield may compensate for lower option premium return. By the same token, the level of money cost also is reflected in option price. Higher money cost to maintain the option writer's stock position causes him to compensate for it with a higher premium.
4. Option strike price: The direct relationship between the strike price and option value is apparent.
5. Time factor: Since options are wasting assets, the value vanished at expiration, time is an important factor in the determination of their value. Everything else being equal, longer duration options normally command a higher price than shorter duration options. The diminishing rate in the value of an option generally accelerates toward the end of the time period. In-the-money options, however, maintain their value almost to the last day of expiration.

Combined with fundamental research on underlying securities, normal-value calculations help determine the most advantageous strike price and expiration date of the options to be written or bought.

### The Use of Normal-Value Calculations

While normal-value calculations are also very useful to option buyers in search for value, such calculations are more frequently used by option writers than by option buyers.

Option writers depend more on such calculations to locate call-writing situations that are believed to be overvalued. In addition, the normal-value concept helps option writers to know how to close out their positions—usually just when the option reaches normal value.

## *Broad Option Writing Strategies*

Based on the total return concept discussed above, option writing can be designed to cope with varying market conditions.

In a stable and moderately advancing market, option writers seek a rate of return that is higher than that obtainable by nonwriters.

In a declining market, option writing portfolio risks are cushioned by premiums received.

Generally, it is desirable for writers to issue calls for more distant contract months, primarily because these yield more premium dollars, which also serve to provide more protection against downside risk.

The following are several of the most important call option writing strategies:

1. Intermediate-term hedge: When option writers believe certain stocks are due for an intemediate-term consolidation after a sharp rise, they may take in premium money while waiting for further gains.
2. Selling at above-market price: Option writing is used as a means of selling stocks already owned at a price level above the current market. Even if the price of the stock declines, the option writer is better off—by the amount of the premium—than if he had not written an option.
3. "Buy-back": If the underlying security declines to a level that forfeits most of the option premium received, consideration should be given to disposing of the stock. If the writer decides to sell the stock, he should buy back the outstanding call obligation to eliminate the remaining time exposure.
4. Buy-stop order: As an added defense to the buy-back strategy, option writers should try to limit the risk that might result from a sharp price recovery by entering a buy-stop order to purchase a second 100-share position in XYZ at the original strike price. At the expiration of both calls, option writers might sell still a third call option to take in additional premium.
5. Step-down protection: As a variation of the above strategy, option writers might retain the stock, despite the price drop, in the following way: buy back the outstanding call obligation to eliminate the remaining time exposure, thus paving the way for selling more-distant calls that invariably carry larger premiums.
This strategy is based upon the assumption that the second more-distant call is written at the same striking price as the first. Should a call with a lower striking price become available, the writer could issue such a call with new premium to shelter him from a further stock price drop.

# OVERVIEW

### What

Option writing selection essentially is a trade-off between downside protection and expected return.

### Why

Normally, expected return declines as downside protection increases. Conversely, such return rises as downside protection decreases.

### How

For return, premium plus dividends should be large enough to earn an annual return of approximately 20 percent or more.

Downside protection in the form of premium should be no less than 10 percent of the writer's (seller's) commitment.

### Measures of Option Premium

Since the call writer's potential profits are limited to option premiums, methods of measuring premium are of paramount importance.

The size of the premium can be assessed from the viewpoint of return as well as from that of risk protection.

### Return and Protection

From the viewpoint of return, premium plus dividends should be large enough to earn an annual return of approximately 20 percent or more. From the viewpoint of risk protection, downside protection in the form of premium should be no less than 10 percent of the writer's commitment.

Option writing for return and protection is based on the following criteria:

1. Return on cash flow* ($rcf$): The immediate return on actual dollar commitment, indicating leverage based on cash flow.

$$rcf = \frac{\text{call option premium } (op)}{\text{market price of stock } (mp)}$$

* For simplification, $rcf$ is calculated on the basis of cash stock purchase instead of a purchase on margin. For a margin account, its leverage is increased by a multiplier of two, as follows:

$$rcf = 2\left(\frac{op}{mp}\right)$$

# elements of option writing portfolios

8

2. Maximum yield on investment (*my*): This quantity represents the theoretically maximum realizable return under optimal conditions.

$$my = \frac{op + (sp - mp) + d}{mp}$$

Where
$op$ = call premium
$sp$ = strike price
$mp$ = market price
$d$ = expected dividend (until option expiration)

3. Annualized return (*ar*): This quantity represents a conservative estimate of annual return based on the maximum length of holding period.

$$ar = \frac{360}{\text{number of days to expiration}} \times \left(\begin{matrix}\text{the lessor of} \\ rcf \text{ or } my\end{matrix}\right)$$

4. Downside breakeven (*db*): This constitutes the downside price for breakeven:

$$db = mp - op - d$$

5. Downside breakeven percentage (*dbp*): This represents the percentage of stock decline for breakeven

$$\frac{mp - db}{mp}$$

### *Tradeoff Nature*

Option writing selection essentially is a tradeoff between downside protection and expected return. Normally, such return declines as downside protection increases.

### *Maximum Return*

In one-to-one option writing, the maximum return to the writer (before dividends) is the difference between the strike price plus the option price on the one hand and the stock price on the other. This assumes that the market price is lower than the strike price. The maximum return occurs at expiration, when the stock sells at or above the option's exercise price and is not exercised.

The principal source of the option writer's gain will come from option premium. He will benefit, however, also from any increase in the stock price up to the exercise price.

### *Premium with or without Tangible Worth*

For a call option with tangible worth or intrinsic value, the premium represents the excess differential between the current stock price and the option's exercise price. For a call option without intrinsic value, the entire option price represents its premium.

### *Low P/E, High Yield Writing Portfolios*

The core of conservative option writers', writing portfolios should be stocks with low P/Es and high yields. Table 8.1 illustrates one such portfolio, based on February 24, 1975, closing prices:

**TABLE 8.1 EXAMPLE OF LOW P/E, HIGH-YIELD PORTFOLIO CORE FOR CONSERVATIVE OPTION WRITING APPROACH**

| | 1974–75 High-low | 2/24/75 Stock Price | P/E | Dividend | Yield | 2/24/75 Option price |
|---|---|---|---|---|---|---|
| **Pennzoil** | 30½–12¾ | 20¼ | 6 | $1.20 | 5.9% | 2½ (July 20) |
| **Gen. Tel.** | 26⅝–16⅛ | 21¾ | 10 | $1.80 | 8.3% | 3 (July 20) |
| **Texaco** | 32⅞–20 | 26¼ | 4 | $2.00 | 7.6% | 2¾ (July 25) |
| **Gulf** | 25¼–16 | 20⅝ | 4 | $1.70 | 8.3% | 3 (July 20) |
| **Goodyear** | 18⅜–11¾ | 15¾ | 7 | $1.10 | 7.0% | 2⅜ (July 15) |
| **Kennecott** | 49½–25⅝ | 33¼ | 6 | $2.60 | 7.8% | 2¾ (July 35) |
| **U.S. Steel** | 50–35⅜ | 49¼ | 4 | $2.80 | 5.7% | 4⅛ (July 50) |

## Possible Workout against
## Key Measurements

### TABLE 8.2 SUMMARY OF A POSSIBLE WORKOUT AGAINST KEY MEASUREMENTS

| | Return on Cash Flow (rcf) | Maximum Yield on Investment (my) | Annualized Return (ar) | Downside Breakeven (db) | Percentage of Decline for Breakeven (dbp) |
|---|---|---|---|---|---|
| Pennzoil | 12.3% | 12.3% | 29.5% | $17.25 | 14.8% |
| Gen. Tel. | 13.8% | 9.2% | 22.1% | $18.00 | 17.2% |
| Texaco | 10.5% | 9.0% | 21.6% | $22.67 | 13.6% |
| Gulf | 10.3% | 11.3% | 24.7% | $16.92 | 18.0% |
| Goodyear | 15.0% | 13.2% | 31.7% | $12.92 | 18.0% |
| Kennecott | 8.3% | 16.8% | 19.9% | $29.42 | 11.5% |
| U.S. Steel | 8.4% | 12.3% | 20.2% | $43.96 | 10.8% |

### Pennzoil
Stock price = 20¼ (2/24/75)          P/E = 6

Dividends = $1.20          Yield = 5.9%

#### Option Strategy
Buy stock at 20¼ (2/24/75)

Sell July 20 call option at 2½ (2/24/75)

#### Option Worksheet

(1) Return on cash flow = 12.3%
(2) Maximum yield on investment = 12.3%
(3) Annualized return = 29.5%
(4) Downside breakeven = $17.25
(5) Downside breakeven percentage = 14.8%

### General Telephone & Electronics
Stock price = 21¾ (2/24/75)          P/E = 10

Dividends = $1.80          Yield = 8.3%

#### Option Strategy
Buy stock at 21¾ (2/24/75)

Sell July 20 option at 3 (2/24/75)

#### Option Worksheet

(1) Return on cash flow = 13.8%
(2) Maximum yield on investment = 9.2%
(3) Annualized return = 22.1%

(4) Downside breakeven = $18.00
(5) Downside breakeven percentage = 17.2%

### Texaco
Stock price = 26¼ (2/24/75)          P/E = 4

Dividends = $2          Yield = 7.6%

#### Option Strategy
Buy stock at 26¼ (2/24/75)

Sell July 25 call option at 2¾ (2/24/75)

#### Option Worksheet

(1) Return on cash flow = 10.3%
(2) Maximum yield on investment = 9.0%
(3) Annualized return = 21.6%
(4) Downside breakeven = $22.67
(5) Downside breakeven percentage = 13.6%

### Gulf Oil
Stock price = 20⅝ (2/24/75)          P/E = 4

Dividends = $1.70          Yield = 8.3%

#### Option Strategy
Buy stock at 20⅝ (2/24/75)

Sell July 20 option at 3 (2/24/75)

#### Option Worksheet

(1) Return on cash flow = 10.3%
(2) Maximum yield on investment = 11.3%

(3) Annualized return = 24.7%
(4) Downside breakeven = $16.92
(5) Downside breakeven percentage = 18.0%

(3) Annualized return = 19.9%
(4) Downside breakeven = $29.42
(5) Downside breakeven percentage = 11.5%

## Goodyear Tire & Rubber
Stock price = 15¾ (2/24/75)      P/E = 7

Dividends = $1.10      Yield = 7.0%

### Option Strategy
Buy stock at 15¾ (2/24/75)

Sell July 15 option at 2⅜ (2/24/75)

### Option Worksheet

(1) Return on cash flow = 15.0%
(2) Maximum yield on investment = 13.2%
(3) Annualized return = 31.7%
(4) Downside breakeven = $12.92
(5) Downside breakeven percentage = 18.0%

## Kennecott
Stock price = 33¼ (2/24/75)      P/E = 6

Dividends = $2.60      Yield = 7.8%

### Option Strategy
Buy stock at 33¼ (2/24/75)

Sell July 35 option at 2¾ (2/24/75)

### Option Worksheet

(1) Return on cash flow = 8.3%
(2) Maximum yield on investment = 16.8%

## U.S. Steel
Stock price = 49¼ (2/24/75)      P/E = 4

Dividends = $2.80      Yield = 5.7%

### Option Strategy
Buy stock at 49¼ (2/24/75)

Sell July 50 option at 4⅛ (2/24/75)

### Option Worksheet

(1) Return on cash flow = 8.4%
(2) Maximum yield on investment = 12.3%
(3) Annualized return = 20.2%
(4) Downside breakeven = $43.96
(5) Downside breakeven percentage = 10.8%

### Portfolio Strategy
Buy 1,000 shares of the above seven stocks

Sell 10 calls on each above stock

### Portfolio Investment and Projected Returns

The $43,106 annualized return on $187,-130 investment (projected in Table 8.3 and based on 100-percent cash purchase) amounts to a portfolio return of 23.0 percent.

The percentage return would be much greater if a 50-percent margin instead of 100-percent cash is used.

### TABLE 8.3 SUMMARY OF PORTFOLIO INVESTMENT AND PROJECTED ANNUALIZED RETURNS

| | 1,000-share Purchase | Cost of Cash Purchase (10 × Cost of 1,000 Shares) | Annualized Return | |
|---|---|---|---|---|
| | | | Percentage | Dollars |
| Pennzoil | $2,025 | $ 20,250 | 29.5% | $ 5,974 |
| Texaco | $2,625 | $ 26,250 | 21.6% | $ 5,670 |
| Gen. Tel. | $2,175 | $ 21,750 | 22.1% | $ 4,807 |
| Gulf | $2,063 | $ 20,630 | 24.7% | $ 5,096 |
| Goodyear | $1,575 | $ 15,750 | 31.7% | $ 4,993 |
| Kennecott | $3,325 | $ 33,250 | 19.9% | $ 6,617 |
| U.S. Steel | $4,925 | $ 49,250 | 20.2% | $ 9,949 |
| | | $187,130 | | $43,106 |

### Portfolio Balance

Most of the strike prices used in the foregoing examples are close to the present market prices of their underlying securities.

Generally, conservative equity portfolios write longer term options at strike prices lower than the current market price of the underlying security.

On the other hand, the more aggressive equity portfolios incline toward shorter term options with strike prices that are above the current market price of the security.

A proper balance between longer term, strike-below-market writes and shorter term, strike-above-market writes should be structured, varying with individual portfolios, depending upon their relative emphasis on return and capital protection.

### Options-Oriented Portfolios

A properly structured options-oriented portfolio is designed to produce returns of 20 to 25 percent, indicating gains of from $20,000 to $25,000 on an option capital of $100,000. (A floor of $100,000 option capital is advised for writing call options on a diversified list of stocks.) This 20- to 25-percent gain will provide a downside cushion of like amounts in a down market. In other words, the option writer could still break even despite a 20- to 25-percent decline in his portfolio.

To achieve appreciation objectives of 20 to 25 percent, options-oriented portfolios should, of course, exclude writing any call options of premium sizes that, if exercised on expiration date, would produce less than a 20-percent annualized return. Nor would such portfolios consider writing options with premiums that provide less than 10-percent downside protection.

# IF-CALLED-AWAY OPTION WRITING PORTFOLIOS

### Major Reservoir

One major reservoir of call writing situations that helps achieve the dual objectives of return and protection for options-oriented portfolios is the writing of call options with an eye toward their "called-away" possibilities.

An option is said to be called away when its buyer exercises his right to purchase the underlying stock for a given price within a given period of time and, thus, calls the stock away from the option writer who must deliver the stock so called.

### Short-Term If-Called-Away Writes

The following situations illustrate if-called-away call options for possible realization of gains over the short term:

*Example:* On May 5, 1975, writing either the July 40 option (premium 2⅜) or the October 40 option (premium 4⅛) against Kennecott common (NYSE–38–KN) offered the potential for attractive returns should the underlying stock have been called away.

The KN July 40 option would have brought in 2⅜ points in option premium, plus two points from appreciation of the stock if it had been called away at 40, for a total 4⅜ points. This return equals 13.1 percent on an 11-week option, or 61.9 percent annualized, exclusive of dividends.

The KN October 40 option would have produced 4¼ points. Together with the same two-point appreciation, this would total 6⅛: 18.1 percent over the short term, or 85.6 percent annualized.

A 6.8-percent yield was available on KN's dividends of $2.60. Its P/E ratio of 10.4 was indicated on estimated 1975 earnings of $3.65. Technically, KN was emerging strongly from a several-months' sidewise move, as indicated by attainment of recovery highs on expanded volume.

*Example:* Another if-called-away call writing possibility existed on May 5, 1975, when the sale of the July 45 call option at 4¾ against 100 shares of Deere (NYSE–45½–DE) would have protected the stock down to 40¾.

If DE had been called away at 45, the gains for the option writer would have amounted to 4¼, plus dividends, less commissions.

Fundamentally DE was favorably situated as the technological leader in agricultural equipment, a vitally important American industry that should continue to prosper despite recession as a growing world population depends on U.S. farmers for sustenance. Estimated 1975 earnings of $6.20 indicated a

P/E ratio of 7.3 versus its 12-year average P/E of 10.5. Its yield was 4 percent on indicated dividends of $1.80.

Technically, DE remained bullish after a sharp move from the September low of 28. While a long-term objective beyond 60 was projected from the underlying base formation, interim profits appeared possible for a number of writing operations.

*Example:* Also illustrative of short-term hedges was possible writing on May 5, 1975, of a July 30 call option on American Cyanamid (NYSE–28¾–ACY) to produce 2¼ points in option premium that would have protected the stock down to 26½.

For the 11 weeks available on this short-term option the return was 8.5 percent (40.2 percent annualized) exclusive of dividends. Should the stock have been called away at expiration, the writer would have realized an additional appreciation of 1¼ points, plus 2¼ points from option premium. The total was thus 3½ points, or 13.2 percent on 11 weeks (62.4 percent annualized).

Fundamentally, a streamlined ACY was expected to hold its ground in a recession year. Technically, ACY had an overall favorable pattern.

## Intermediate-Term If-Called-Away Writes

The following situations are used to illustrate if-called-away call options over the intermediate term.

*Example:* On June 3, 1975, an intermediate-term writing situation existed in the sale of an October 15 call option at 3¼ against 100 shares of Merrill Lynch (NYSE–16¼–MER), thereby reducing the cash outlay to 13 on a fully paid cash basis.

If MER remained unchanged at expiration, the covered writer would have realized $385, including $325 from option premium and $60 from dividends, or a $29.6-percent return in 19 weeks.

Technically, MER has paused in the 14 to 18 zone within an overall favorable formation.

*Example:* Another illustration of this type of call writing was Federal National Mortgage which, on April 21, 1975, was available for 17.

Its October 20 option produced 1¾ points in option premium, plus 3 points from appreciation on stock if called away at 20. The total realized would have been 4¾ points, a return of 70 percent in six months (140 percent annualized) on a cash invest-

ment of $675 for a margin account (50-percent margin on stock, less $175 in option premium).

*Example:* Another if-called-away writing possibility was available on June 3, 1975, involving the purchase of 100 shares of Ford (NYSE–36⅝–F) and the sale of an October 40 option at 4.

If the F October 40 call were to be exercised, the return to the writer would have amounted to $8.58, including 4 points from the option premium, $1.20 from dividends, and 3⅜ from appreciation, indicating a return of 26.3 percent.

Technically, Ford continued in a long-term base area.

## Buy-Wait-Write

Writers of call options with an eye toward their called-away possibilities can either buy shares and concurrently write calls against them or buy shares first and then wait for some appreciation before writing calls against them.

*Example:* Illustrative of such a course was the possible purchase on April 21, 1975, of Delta (NYSE–36–DAL).

An option premium of 4½ was available to a DAL October 40 option writer. This premium, plus 3¾ points from appreciation on the stock if called away, would realize 8¼ points, indicating a return of 42.9 percent in six months (85.7 percent annualized) on the cash investment of $1,350 for a margin transaction (50 percent margin on stock, less $450 in option premium).

*Example:* The strategy involving the buying of stock first and waiting for higher option premium was evident to those who bought Tesoro Petroleum (NYSE–TSO) first at 16 on April 12, 1975, and then waited until it reached the 20 level before writing options to gain higher option premium.

By May 20, 1975, TSO reached 19⅝. The option writer was now in a position to sell the July 15 option at 5, thereby protecting the stock down to 14⅝, or 25 percent.

The selling of options against a portfolio is no more speculative than is the owning of stocks themselves.

Options are sold by individuals, funds, trusts, or anyone who has a continuous portfolio of common stocks.

Previously, while long-term growth segments of portfolios were used to take care of future actuarial funding obligations and as a hedge against inflation, separate segments of portfolios were geared toward income in order to meet current obligations.

As options on more of the most widely held common stocks begin to be traded on the national options exchanges, fund fiduciaries will expand their option writing operations to take advantage of the high total yields obtainable.

## OVERVIEW

### What

Also known as ratio writing, variable hedging involves writing (selling) one covered option and one or more uncovered options.

### Why

Selling (writing) more than one option is a protective strategy. The price of the underlying stock can decline further before a hedge position shows a loss because the writer has received more premium money.

### How

When a ratio (variable) writer determines the number of calls to be written (sold) against a 100-share position, the ratio is a function of his risk preference. In the determination of the ratio to be written, the upside risk from uncovered calls should be weighed against the additional downside protection.

Since variable hedging primarily deals with partially uncovered option writing, it serves as a bridge between covered and uncovered option writing. A full understanding of uncovered option writing should precede our discussions of variable hedging or ratio option writing strategies.

## UNCOVERED OPTION WRITING

An uncovered or "naked" option is written without the writer owning the underlying stock.

Essentially, naked option writing is based on the belief that call option buyers are usually wrong within their time frame.

Principally market bears, naked option writers speculate on a downward course of the stock during the life of their contracts.

So long as the option is not exercised, it is possible for writers of uncovered options to realize profits. This has been the case during periods of declining or generally stable stock prices.

### Writing against Cash

An uncovered option is written against cash. It represents substantial risk, should there

# variable hedging strategies

be a sharp rise in the price of the underlying stock.

Example: An option writer might decide that XYZ is not a stock he wishes to own. But, since he considers the premium to be attractive, he decides to sell the call without owning the stock.

He must post the required minimum 30-percent margin, reduced by the amount of premium. In a sense he is now in a short position.

If XYZ declines, the entire option premium will be profit.

But if XYZ rises, he may at some future date be forced to choose among buying the stock in the open market to cover the call, assuming an actual short position at the strike price with the stock selling at a higher price level, or buying back the option.

## Risk

Uncovered option writing is extremely risky, and a naked writer may incur losses limited only by the amount of the increase in the price of the underlying security.

Only very sophisticated investors of substantial means should engage in uncovered writing. The exchanges require substantial cash from sellers of naked options to assure themselves that the option writers (or sellers) will be able to meet their obligations.

In addition to maintaining a specified amount of margin on deposit in his account, an uncovered option writer may at any time be called upon to purchase the underlying security at its then-prevailing market price in order to be able to deliver it at the strike (exercise) price.

Moreover, the uncovered (naked) writer has no control over *when* he might be required to buy and deliver the underlying security. Indeed, he may be given an exercise notice at any time when the underlying security price exceeds the exercise price.

Given this extremely high degree of risk, uncovered option writers seek much larger percentage gains than those sought by covered option writers. The maximum profits for uncovered writers, however, are limited by the premium paid for the option by the buyers, less commissions. On the other hand, the risk to uncovered writers is unlimited until they close

their positions. To reduce their risk exposure, naked option writers tend to write short-term call options.

## Similarity to Short Sales

In assessing risk, uncovered option writing is not unlike a short sale of the underlying stock. Each transaction generally has the same effective exposure, except that the uncovered option writer's risk is cushioned somewhat by the amount of the premium.

## Possible Recourses

What can happen when an option writer selling a naked call is wrong about the stock and finds himself in a bind when the stock on which he has sold a naked call option rises in price?

Following are the possible courses of action to defend a position when the market begins to move away from a naked seller.

## Defense 1: Buy In

Like the covered writer, an uncovered writer may usually cancel his obligation at any time prior to being assigned an exercise notice by executing a "closing purchase" transaction, thus terminating his obligation to deliver the stock.

In other words, the naked option writer can "buy in" an option he has previously written as long as the option hasn't been exercised. His gain or loss depends on the difference between the premium originally received and the price later paid.

## Defense 2: Taking Cover

An uncovered option writer may also buy the underlying security during the life of the option, thereby becoming a covered writer. Taking cover amounts to a substantial investment in a stock about which the writer was wrong.

## Defense 3: Offsetting Call Option

The uncovered option writer may buy an offsetting call option on the same security to cover his naked option sale. For example, if he sold a McDonald option naked at 50 and got worried when the underlying shares reached 60, he would simply buy a call on McDonald at 60.

### Defense 4: Buy-Stop

A fourth course of defense is to enter a "buy-stop" order at a price that is generally calculated on the basis of the striking price plus option premium. The purpose of the buy-stop order is to limit an unknown loss.

# PARTIALLY UNCOVERED OPTION WRITING

### Hedged Strategies

Instead of completely naked writing, the writer may choose to hedge high position partially. He may wish to combine the writing of covered and uncovered options on the same underlying stock.

Known as "variable hedging" or "ratio writing," this strategy involves writing one option that is covered and one or more options that are uncovered.

The additional downside protection provided by the additional premium income, however, must be weighed against the risk of incurring a loss on the uncovered option or options.

### Writing Multiple Options

Since the premium is a small percentage of the price of the underlying stock, a significant decline in the price of the stock can quickly wipe out the protection offered by the premium.

An alternative course is to write more than one call to achieve greater price protection. The sale of two options will allow the price of the underlying stock to decline further before a hedge position shows a loss, because the writer has twice the premium to offset a decline in the price of the underlying stock. Also, the writer benefits from lower commissions per option.

When the underlying security sells at a price far below the strike price, aggressive writers tend to increase the number of calls per 100

shares of stock. They may own 100 shares and issue two or more calls.

### Variety of Hedges

An investor who is moderately bearish might wish to sell three calls against a 200-share long position.

A more aggressive writer, convinced of a more substantial downside move, might sell two or even three calls against a 100-share long position.

These combinations provide a variety of hedges and are attractive to a writer seeking greater protection when he anticipates a declining market in the underlying stock.

### How to Determine Ratio

When a ratio writer determines the number of calls to be written against a 100-share position, the ratio is a function of his risk preference.

In the determination of the ratio to be written, the upside risk from uncovered options should be weighed against the additional downside protection.

### Position-One, Sell-Two Strategy

The most frequently employed ratio writing is to "position one, sell two," or to buy 100 shares of stock and issue two call options.

The theory behind position one, sell two is that most stocks generally fluctuate within a range of no more than 25 percent above and 25 percent below the strike price in a six-month period.

The profit-protection zone generally sought by ratio writers applying the position-one, sell-two strategy extends 25 percent up and 25 percent down from the strike price. The closer to the strike price the underlying security remains, the greater the profit to the writer becomes.

### Selection Criteria

Thus, in selecting stocks for position-one, sell-two writing, hedge writers generally favor those that are likely to stay within the parameters of their protection zone and, preferably, close to the strike price.

## Profit Band

The protection zone covered by these two parameters constitutes the "profit band." Ratio writers will remain profitable so long as the stock stays between the upside and downside parameters.

These upside and downside parameters also constitute the upside and downside break-even points.

## Downside Parameter

Downside parameter is obtained by reducing the purchase price by the total premium received from writing two or more call options.

## Upside Parameter

Upside parameter is computed by more complicated formulas, as follows:

1. When stock cost is below the strike price:

$$\text{Upside parameter} = \frac{\text{Premium received} + \text{Difference between stock cost and strike price}}{\text{Number of uncovered options}} + \text{Strike price}$$

2. When stock cost is above the strike price:

$$\text{Upside parameter} = \frac{\text{Premium received} - \text{Difference between strike price and stock cost}}{\text{Number of uncovered options}} + \text{Strike price}$$

## How to Establish a Profit Band

The following are several illustrations of how ratio writers establish a profit band.

*Example:* On June 3, 1975, a ratio writer may have wished to sell two October 45 calls at 5½ per call on a 100-share long position on Syntex (NYSE–43⅝–SYN).

The 11 points from option premium protect the stock down to 32⅝ as the downside parameter. The upside parameter is 57⅜.

A profit band of from 32⅝ to 57⅜, amounting to 24¾ points, is thus established, within which the partial hedger will realize a profit.

Technically, SYN had marked time between 38 and 45 after its recent run-up.

*Example:* On April 21, 1975, Syntex appeared attractive for ratio writing as follows: writing two Syntex October 40 calls at 8⅝ each against 100 shares at 43⅛.

The sale of two calls realized 17¼ points, which protected the 100-share position down to 25⅞, or 40 percent below the current market. The breakeven point was only 2¾ points above Syntex's lowest price during the 1973–75 period.

No upside loss would have occurred until the 54 area was reached. Thus, a wide profit zone of 28¼ points was created between 54⅛ and 25⅞.

The foregoing strategy provides a broad profit possibility without requiring the investor to guess correctly which direction the stock or the market will take.

*Example:* An aggressive ratio writer on June 3, 1975, might have considered selling two July 80 calls at 4¾ points per call of Xerox (NYSE–76¼–XRX) against 100 shares of stock purchased.

The premiums from the two calls, totaling 9½ points, protected the stock down to the downside parameter of 66¾. The upside parameter was 93¼.

The above parameters established a 26½-point profit range, from 66¾ to 93¼. A short-term reaction was indicated for XRX.

*Example:* Another ratio writing appeared sensible on Avon Products (NYSE–48⅝–AVP) on June 5, 1975, when the ratio writer could have sold two October 50 calls at 6⅛ per call. The option premiums, totaling 12¼ points, would have protected the stock down to 36 points. The upside profit limit was 63⅝.

The position of the ratio writer would have remained profitable as long as AVP swung within the 27¼-point zone (between 63⅝ and 36⅜).

*Example:* Another illustration of this ratio writing method was the possible purchase on June 5,

1975, of 100 shares of Disney (NYSE–51¼–DIS) and the sale of two January 60 calls at 6⅝ per call.

The 13¼ points from option premiums would have protected the stock down to 38 as the downside parameter. The upside parameter was 82.

The position of the ratio writer would have remained profitable as long as DIS fluctuated in the broad range of 38 to 82.

DIS's primary uptrend started to ease as it came under increasing selling pressures.

## Modified Strategy

As a modification of the above strategy, the option writer may decide initially to write only one option for each 100 shares of stock owned, then subsequently to write a second option with a lower exercise price if the price of the underlying stock decreases.

## Three-against-One Strategy

The three-against-one strategy can provide additional defense against a possible deep downward move.

*Example:* Illustrative of this ratio strategy was the possible sale on April 21, 1975, of three October 50 calls on Homestake Mining (NYSE–43⅞–HM) against 100 shares. At 5 each, the three calls would have realized $1,500, protecting the stock position down to 28⅞, or 34 percent below the market.

No upside loss would have occurred until 60⁹⁄₁₆. Thus, a profit zone of 31¹¹⁄₁₆ points was created.

This three-to-one strategy on HM was appropriate primarily for a venturesome hedger who was not particularly bullish on gold stocks.

# CALL SPREADING

# PART IV

## OVERVIEW

### What

Essentially, a spread is the dollar difference between the buy and sell premiums.

### Why

Its objective is to capture the difference in premiums between the "long" option and the "short" option.

### How

A conventional spread is "long" on the option with a striking price higher than the market price but "short" on the option with a striking price lower than the market price.

### "Old" versus "New" Meanings of Spread

Let's trace the historical background and meaning of "spread." Prior to the advent of listed options, a spread in the options world was a special type of "straddle" with the put and call exercisable at different strike prices. What is a straddle? A straddle consists of one put and one call with a common strike price and a common expiration date. The spread of pre-listed-option days never enjoyed much popularity.

A spread is *now* defined as a partial hedge consisting of a long position* in one option contract and a short position in another contract of the same type (call or put) on the same underlying stock.

A call spread consists of long and short positions in calls. A put spread consists of long and short positions in puts. Only call spreads, are discussed in this chapter, but many points apply equally to put spreads.

### Two Options in One

Similar to straddles, spreads are actually two separate option contracts in one. Although composed of two distinctly individual options, a spread option order cannot be executed unless both sides of the order are executed because the two orders in one are entered as a unit order.

---

* A "long" option position is the position of the holder or buyer of an option contract. A "short" option position is the position of the writer or seller of an option contract.

# call spreading basics

# 10

# BASIC CONCEPTS

The concept of spreads was borrowed from the commodity futures markets and adapted to listed options. Essentially, spreads are an application of the technique of arbitrage to options, utilizing the basic concepts of price differentials and time dissipation of premium.

### Spread Premiums

A spread is the dollar difference between the buy and sell premiums. Its object is to capture the difference in premiums between the long option and the short option. A spreader is concerned with the extent of spread between the premium paid and the premium received in establishing the spread position. The prices at which the spread order is executed are no concern to him.

### Spreads in Debit

If the cost of the long option is more than that of the short option, the spread is expressed as a debit.

*Example:*  If you had made a spread on Eastman Kodak (NYSE–99⅛–EK) by buying an EK October 90 option at 13¾ and selling EK October 100 at 8½ (based on June 17, 1975, closing prices), you would have been 5¼ points in debit:

| | |
|---|---|
| Buy EK October 90 at | 13¾ |
| Sell EK October 100 at | 8½ |
| Debit | 5¼ |

The debit resulted from the fact that you were long the more expensive option and short the less expensive option.

### Spreads in Credit

Conversely, if the cost of the long option is less than the short option, the spread is expressed as a credit.

*Example:*  If you had made a spread on Avon Products (NYSE–31¼–AVP) by buying AVP April 30 at 3⅞ and selling AVP April 20 at 11¼ (based on January 27, 1975, closing prices), you would have been 7⅜ points in credit:

| | |
|---|---|
| Sell AVP April 20 at | 11¼ |
| Buy AVP April 30 at | 3⅞ |
| Credit | 7⅜ |

This credit resulted from the fact that you were short the more expensive option and long the less expensive option.

### Even Spread

If the cost of the long option equals the cost of the short option, the spread is said to be even.

### Spread Margins

Before the advent of listed options, option margin rules were based on the notion that shorting calls was extremely risky. To effectuate a spread on IBM, for example, would be a proposition requiring very high margin.

Under changed margin requirements regarding the hedging of listed options, the long option is, under certain conditions, considered adequate margin for the short position.

### Call-Backed Call versus Stock-Backed Call

As a result of the changed margin requirements for spreads, the leverage for call-backed-call optioning and that for stock-backed-call writing has considerably widened, as illustrated by the following example.

*Example:*  This example is based on a comparison of writing an October 40 call at 6½ backed by 100 shares of Honeywell (NYSE–39¾–HON) versus the same call backed by an October 30 call bought at 12⅜.

In the stock-backed call, cash layout on a 50-percent margin and after premium deduction of 6½ was $1,337.50:

| | |
|---|---|
| Buy 100 HON at | $3,975.00 |
| 50% margin | 1,987.50 |
| | $1,987.50 |
| Less premium | 650.00 |
| Cash layout | $1,337.50 |

On the other hand, in the call-backed call, the cash outlay after premium deduction is 5⅞:

| | |
|---|---|
| Buy HON October 30 at | $1,237.50 |
| Sell HON October 40 at | 650.00 |
| Cash layout | $ 587.50 |

The call-backed-call leverage in the foregoing example is well over two to one compared with the stock-backed-call leverage.

### *Margin Requiements: Bull versus Bear Spreads*

Different margin requirements cover bull spreads and bear spreads:

1. A bullish spread is long the more expensive option and short the less expensive option.
2. A bearish spread is long the less expensive option and short the more expensive option.

### *Bull Spread Margins*

The short position in a bull spread is considered covered in respect to margin requirements provided that the long position, which must be paid for, (1) has the *same* or *lower strike* price than the short position, and (2) has the *same* or *later expiration* date than the short position.

As illustrations we use Disney options of different expiration months and different strike prices, based on July 11, 1975, closing prices. Note that Disney (DIS) closed at 53⅜ on July 11, 1975:

| Option | July | October | January |
|---|---|---|---|
| Disney 60 | 3/16 | 3⅜ | 5¼ |
| Disney 50 | 4⅛ | 7⅝ | 9¾ |
| Disney 45 | 8⅝ | 11 | 12¾ |

1. Different strike prices

***Example:*** Same expiration month: When the "long" position has the same expiration month as the short position:

| | |
|---|---|
| Buy DIS January 50 at | 9¾ |
| Sell DIS January 60 at | 5¼ |
| Margin requirement | 4½ |

***Example:*** *Later expiration month:* When the long position has a later expiration month than the short position:

| | |
|---|---|
| Buy DIS January 60 at | 5¼ |
| Sell DIS October 60 at | 3⅜ |
| Margin requirement | 1⅞ |

2. Different expiration months

***Example:*** *Same strike price:* When the long position has the same strike price as the short position (the immediately preceding example also applies here):

| | |
|---|---|
| Buy DIS January 60 at | 5¼ |
| Sell DIS October 60 at | 3⅜ |
| Margin requirement | 1⅞ |

***Example:*** *Lower strike price:* When the long position has a lower strike than the short position:

| | |
|---|---|
| Buy DIS October 45 at | 11 |
| Sell DIS July 50 at | 4⅛ |
| Margin requirement | 6⅞ |

### *Bear Spread Margins*

If one buys the higher strike price and sells the lower strike price (a bearish spread), the margin requirement will be the differential between strike prices plus the long option premium, minus the short option premium.

***Example:*** Illustrative of the above requirement was the following example based on January 27, 1975, closing prices of Upjohn. If you had bought UPJ July 50 at 2⅛ and sold UPJ July 45 at 3⅛, the requirement would have been $500 (strike price differential), plus 2⅛ (long option premium), less 3⅛ (short option premium):

| | |
|---|---|
| Strike price differential | $500.00 |
| Long option premium | +212.50 |
| | $712.50 |
| Short option premium | −312.50 |
| | $400.00 |

**Example:** Also illustrative of bear spread margin requirements was the following example based on January 27, 1975, closing prices. If you had bought UPJ October 50 at 3⅜ and sold UPJ October 40 at 5¾, the margin requirement was $1,000 (strike price differential), plus 3⅜ (long option premium), less 5¾ (short option premium):

| | |
|---|---|
| Strike price differential | $1,000.00 |
| Long option premium | +337.50 |
| | $1,337.50 |
| Short option premium | −575.00 |
| | $ 762.50 |

**Example:** A third illustration of the margin requirement of another bear spread (buying higher strike price and selling lower strike price with the same expiration month) follows, based on January 27, 1975, closing prices. If you had bought an April 30 option of Avon Products (NYSE–31¼–AVP) at 3⅞ and sold AVP April 20 at 11¼, the margin requirement would have been $1,000 (strike price differential), plus 3⅞ (long option premium), less 11¼ (short option premium):

| | |
|---|---|
| Strike price differential | $1,000.00 |
| Long option premium | +387.50 |
| | $1,387.50 |
| Short option premium | −1,125.00 |
| | $ 262.50 |

## Anatomy of a Bear Spread

The preceding bear spread example on Avon Products shows what can happen to the spreader in terms of profit or loss if Avon (1) goes down to 20 or less; (2) stays within the spread range (between 20 and 30); or (3) rises to 30 or higher.

1. If Avon goes down to 20 or less: Profit is $737.50 (11¼ less 3⅞), since both options are worthless, plus the $262.50 margin deposit is retained.
2. If Avon stays within range of 20 and 30: The spread could narrow. Profit would be difference of the new spread (7⅜).
3. If Avon rises to 30 or higher: The maximum loss is $262.50, which is the difference between the two strike prices (20 to 30) less the credit differential of $737.50.

At a premium cost of $262.50, the above spreader on Avon would risk a maximum $262.50 to make $737.50 in the three months between January 27, 1975, and the end of April 1975.

## Low-Risk Option Vehicle

The risk of a spread, whether bearish or bullish, is limited to the amount of the spreader's premium money plus his entry and exit costs.

Together with covered writing, spreads are considered relatively low-risk option vehicles. The cost of spreading (call-backed call) is relatively modest versus that for covered writing (stock-backed call), a comparison of which was made earlier in this chapter.

A bearish spread provides the investor with a vehicle of limited potential loss instead of selling (shorting) an option naked.

## OVERVIEW

### *What*

Also known as horizontal or calendar spread, a time spread is the purchase of a listed call option and the sale of a listed call option having the same exercise price but different expiration months.

### *Why*

An investor need only put up the difference between the prices of the two call options, because the long option is deemed adequate to cover the short option.

### *How*

The potentially most promising spreads are those of relatively volatile stocks with a relatively small premium differential between the two options.

A whole array of spread techniques is available for sophisticated investors, depending on their investment and hedging objectives as well as on their view of market trends and of particular underlying stocks.

Despite the differences in makeup, various spreads have something basic in common: all of them consist of simultaneously buying and selling options on the same stock, with different strike prices and/or different expiration months.

Thus, despite their varying construction, all forms of spreading contain simultaneous long and short positions.

The two principal forms of spread techniques are the horizontal spread and the vertical spread. Variations of the principal types are diagonal spread and sandwich spread.

### *Horizontal Spread*

Also called a "calendar" or "time" spread, a horizontal spread is the purchase of a listed option and the sale of a listed option having the same exercise price but different expiration months. A horizontal spread is considered a relatively conservative option approach.

### *Vertical Spread*

Also called a "money" or "price" spread, a vertical spread is the purchase of a listed option and the sale of a listed option having the same expiration month but different strike prices.

# call time spreads

### Diagonal Spread

A diagonal spread is the purchase of a listed option and the sale of a listed option combining different strike prices and different expiration months.

### Sandwich Spread

Also known as a "butterfly," a sandwich spread consists of the sale of two intermediate listed options and the purchase of two listed options with strike prices being of equal distance from the short calls in the ratio of 1:2:1.

If the long calls are not of equal distance, there will be additional risk exposure.

### Bull Horizontal and Bear Horizontal

Horizontal spreads encompass two kinds: bull horizontal spreads and bear horizontal spreads.

Bull horizontals are designed to exploit changes in relative premiums, from a bullish situation, with spreads on different expiration months but with the same strike price. In bull horizontals, you long the option with the more distant expiration month and short the option with the nearby month expiration. The option for the more distant month invariably costs more in option premium than the option for the closer month.

Bear horizontals are designed to generate a cash flow return, from a bearish situation, on spreads of different expiration months but of the same strike price. In bear horizontals, you long the nearby-month expiration and short expiration for the more distant month.

The point difference in time spreads will usually be greatest if the underlying stock is selling at or near the exercise price shortly before the expiration of the near-term option.

### Spread Opportunities with Higher Potential

The potentially most rewarding spread opportunities generally exist in situations where the purchased contract has a more distant expiration month than the one sold.

### Small-Capital-Expenditure Vehicle

Under margin requirements on spreads, the long option is deemed adequate to cover the short option. As a result, an investor need only put up the difference between the prices of two options. The new margin requirements have made spreads a small-capital-expenditure vehicle and one of the more attractive option possibilities for investors.

### How to Select Stocks for Spreads

The potentially most promising spreads are those of relatively volatile stock with a small spread premium differential between two options. In the following sections, several important pointers for time spreading are discussed.

### Relative Volatility

While some degree of volatility is desirable for time spreading, avoid positioning time spreads where the underlying security could advance or decline from the strike price by more than 50 percent for a stock under 50, 30 percent for a stock between 50 and 100, and 25 percent for a stock over 100.

### Small Spread Premium

A narrow spread premium differential is requisite to time spreading. Spread premium differential is that between premium paid for the long position and the premium received for the short position.

Also, avoid positioning a time spread if the option premium on the long position is less than 10 percent of the price of the underlying security.

### Strike Price

Generally, you should avoid a time spread when the strike price is at a point substantially below the price of the underlying security.

In the selection of a strike price for time spreading after a major market decline, it is generally more desirable to select one that is above the present market price of the underlying security.

## Spreading Profit versus Near-Term Expiration

A spreader will probably have made the bulk of his profit when the market price of the underlying security is close to the strike price with approximately one month remaining in the life of the near-term option. Avoid waiting until the very end of the near-term option to take spreading profit.

## Low-Cost Long Call

At the expiration of the near-term option, you will be left with a long call at a very low cost if the underlying security is trading at or near the strike price.

## Multiple Options

It enhances the possibility of spread profits if you start by reducing per-option commission costs through doing spreads in quantities. Since commission costs are heavy in setting up spreads, it is advisable to do them in multiples of five or ten. One possible approach: do no fewer than ten calls for spreads under $1; no fewer than five calls for spreads between $1 and $3; no fewer than three calls for spreads over $3.

## Spread Risks

Spread risks can be summarized as follows:

1. Spread orders are relatively difficult to execute.
2. Early exercise can destroy a spread. If the short side of a spread is exercised, a whole new set of circumstances arises.
3. Lifting a leg* of the spread can significantly increase risk. Anyone lifting a leg on a spread should recognize the greatly increased exposure to market fluctuations.
4. Tax consequences can make a successful spread unprofitable.

---

* "Lifting a leg" of a spread simply means undoing one side of a combination option consisting of the purchase of one option and the sale of another option on the same stock.

## Historical Premium-Differential Relationships

An illustration of how to exploit the present option premium differential versus its historical premium differential follows:

**Example:** A horizontal spread could have been structured on IBM (NYSE–203½–IBM) June 17, 1975, by sale of a nearer-term option to reduce the cost of a more-distant-term option:

| | |
|---|---|
| Buy IBM January 200 at | 28 |
| Sell IBM October 200 at | 21¼ |
| Debit | 6¾ |

Historically, the premium differential between an intermediate-term IBM option and a far-term IBM option with three months separating them was wider than the premium debit of 6¾ indicated in this spread.

The spreader's possible profit was predicated upon a possible widening of the premium spread of 6¾.

## Low-Cost Spreads on Fluctuating Stocks

While narrow premium spreads are generally available on stable stocks, they don't come too often on volatile stocks that normally fluctuate over a wide zone.

**Example:** A low-cost spread on a widely moving stock was found available on May 5, 1975, on Homestake (NYSE–44¾–HM) involving the purchase of an HM October 50 call at 4½ and the sale of an HM July 50 at 3, with a 1½ point debit.

Since the long position had a later expiration month than the short position, the short position was considered covered. Requirement was $150 (4½ less 3). The maximum loss was limited to $150 (the premium differential) plus commissions.

HM had been fluctuating in a wide band for over nine months, with a recent trading range of 40 to 49.

## Spread Widening with Near-Term Expiration

The following two spreads are illustrative of spreads widening as near-expiration premiums drop.

**Example:** One was the possible purchase on February 24, 1975, of a July 80 option at 8¾ on

Xerox (NYSE–78⅝–XRX) and the sale of XRX April 80 at 5⅜, with a 3⅜ debit:

| | |
|---|---|
| Buy July 80 | 8¾ |
| Sell April 80 | 5⅜ |
| Debit | 3⅜ |

As XRX April 80s drew close to expiration, their premium would have dropped, probably widening the spread to 5 or perhaps 6 points.

***Example:*** The other situation involved the possible purchase on February 14, 1975, of a July 70 option at 13¼, also on Xerox, and the sale of XRX April 70 at 10⅞, with a 2⅜-point debit:

| | |
|---|---|
| Buy XRX July 70 | 13¼ |
| Sell XRX April 70 | 10⅞ |
| Debit | 2⅜ |

As XRX April 70 drew toward expiration, its premium would drop, widening the spread probably to 4 or 5 points.

### Exploiting the Expiration-Time Tool

Generally, the horizontal spread can serve as an instrument for exploiting the near-term-expiration option as its expiration time draws near.

The most propitious time for exploiting expiration time is when the upside visibility of the underlying security beyond the strike price is unclear and the near-term, "out of the money" option is still carrying a large premium.

***Example:*** Illustrative of expiration-time exploitation was the possible purchase on March 28, 1975, of a July 50 option (far term) at 4⅜ on Philip Morris (NYSE–48¾–MO) and the sale of MO April 50 (near term) at 1$^{13}/_{16}$:

| | |
|---|---|
| Buy MO July 50 at | 4⅜ |
| Sell MO April 50 at | 1$^{13}/_{16}$ |
| Debit | 2$^{9}/_{16}$ |

### Double-Edged Strategy

Such a horizontal spread can serve double-edged purposes. Should the underlying security rise above the strike price, the near-term option might be selling at only slightly more than the earlier price, because, as a rule, "in the money," near-term options lose whatever premium over intrinsic value they may be carrying.

At this point, the spreader could buy back the near-term option at a price probably not appreciably higher than the price originally sold for.

### More Expensive Option at Reduced Risk

The upshot of the foregoing strategy is that the spreader can carry a more expensive option at reduced cost and thus with reduced risk.

Should the underlying security fail to go beyond the strike price, the near-term option would become worthless. In that case, the spreader would use the option premium received from the near-term option to reduce the cost of his distant-month option.

### How to Reduce Spread Cost to Zero

***Example:*** To illustrate the foregoing strategy was a possible spread on Proctor and Gamble (NYSE–PG), which closed at 96 for the week ending March 28, 1975.

If you had sold one PG April 90 option at 6½ and simultaneously bought one PG July 90 option at 9¾, you would have had a debit of 3¼ points:

| | |
|---|---|
| Buy PG July 90 at | 9¾ |
| Sell PG April 90 at | 6½ |
| Debit | 3¼ |

If, at the end of April, PG had been selling at 90 or slightly below, the April 90 call you had sold short would have been worthless but the July 90 call might have been selling around 6 or 6½ for a potentially good profit.

Or, alternately, you could then have sold a higher-strike option (PG July 100) around 3¼, which would have reduced your cost on the July 90 call to zero.

### Below-Intrinsic-Value Options

Spreaders should be aware of spreading risks involving "deep in the money" options selling at below their intrinsic value.

***Example:*** Illustrative was what would have been a bad spread on March 12, 1975, involving the purchase of a July 30 option at 8¾ on Alcoa (NYSE–37½–AA) and the sale of an AA April 30 option at 7¼:

| | |
|---|---|
| Buy AA July 30 at | 8¾ |
| Sell AA April 30 at | 7¼ |
| Debit | 1½ |

Since AA April 30 at 7¼ was ¼ point below the intrinsic value (7¼ plus the strike price at 30, totaling 37¼, or ¼ below the market price of 37½), a spread involving such deep-in-the-money options as the short position should be avoided.

### Possible Early Exercise

Spreading involving such deep-in-the-money options runs the further risk of possible early exercise of the options. In that event, the spreader incurs commission expenses in purchasing and selling the required number of shares of the underlying security.

### Only Useful to Arbitrageurs

Such below-intrinsic-value options are useful only to professional arbitrageurs who could execute a simultaneous transaction by purchasing the underlying security at 37½ and exercising the call at 7¼, thereby earning a comparatively risk-free ⅛ or ¼ point.

# RATIO SPREADING

Just as ratio writing comes in varying forms, so ratio spreading covers a whole range of possibilities, including using different strike prices, different expiration months, or a combination of different strike prices *and* different expiration months.

### Different Strike Prices

To illustrate one of the most frequently used forms of ratio spreading, we use the purchase of one option and the sale of two or more options of the same stock having different strike prices but the same expiration month.

*Example:* Assuming that XYZ July 60 is trading at 5 and XYZ July 70 at 2, with common being quoted at 58:

| | |
|---|---|
| Buy 1 XYZ July 60 at | $500 |
| Sell 3 XYZ July 70 (at $200) | $600 |
| Credit | $100 |

In the event that the option premiums trade at their intrinsic value at expiration, the risk and profit potential would be as follows:

| | | |
|---|---|---|
| Downside risk | = | 0 |
| Upside risk | = | 75½ |
| Maximum profit point | = | 70 |

Since XYZ at 58 has about 30 percent before rising above 75½ at expiration, the spread is profitable.

If XYZ trades at 70 at any time near the end of the option period, the 60 call is worth about 10 while the 70 call approximates zero in value. The profit to the spreader is approximately $1,100 ($1,000 + $600 − $500).

### Two-against-One Ratio Spreading

Instead of the foregoing three-against-one ratio spreading, we also can construct a two-against-one ratio spreading.

*Example:* When Xerox was trading at 76¾, its April 70 option and April 80 option were worth 11 and 5⅛, respectively.

A possible ratio spread of one long call (April 70 at 11) against two short calls (April 80 at 5⅛ each) could be structured as follows:

| | |
|---|---|
| Buy 1 XRX April 70 at | 11 |
| Sell 2 XRX April 80 (at 5⅛ each) | 10¼ |
| Debit | ¾ |

### Reverse Horizontal Hedge

Ratio spreading that involves the purchase of two near-term options and the sale of one far-term option of the same strike price is also called a reverse horizontal hedge.

Structurally, a reverse horizontal hedge is essentially as follows:

Buy two XYZ July 30
Sell one XYZ Oct. 30

One of the primary purposes of this spread construction is to develop a free call with a hedge.

# OVERVIEW

### What

Also known as a "vertical" or "money" spread, a price spread is the purchase of a listed option and the sale of a listed option that have the same expiration month but different striking prices.

### Why

Bull vertical spreads are designed to exploit changes in the price of the underlying security.

Bear vertical spreads are designed to exploit changes in relative premiums.

### How

Bull vertical spreads involve buying low-strike options and selling high-strike options, for the same period. Profit is made on the upside.

The reverse of bull vertical spreads, bear vertical spreads involve buying higher-strike options and selling (shorting) lower-strike option. Profit is made on the downside.

### Bull Vertical versus Bear Vertical

Like other forms of spreading techniques, vertical spreads consist of bull verticals and bear verticals.

Bull verticals, also known as bull perpendicular spreads, are designed to exploit changes in the price of the underlying security. This objective is generally achieved by buying the lower-strike-price option and selling (shorting) the higher-strike-price option.

Bear verticals are designed to exploit changes in relative premiums. The objective is generally achieved by buying the higher-strike-price option and selling (shorting) the lower-strike-price option.

# BULL VERTICAL SPREAD TECHNIQUES

### Profit Made on Upside

The key to successful bull spreading is finding situations with narrow premium spreads. Profit is made on the upside.

# call price spreads

12

## Low-Cost Bull Perpendicular Spreads

**Example:** An interesting bull perpendicular spread on June 13, 1975, on Deere (NYSE–41–DE), involved the purchase of 10 DE October 40 calls and the sale of 10 DE October 45 calls, with a premium spread for 2¼ (plus ⅛ discretion*):

Buy 10 DE October 40
Sell 10 DE October 45

DE had to move to 45 for the spread to reach maximum profit potential.

At 45, October 45s are worth zero and October 40s are worth 5, for a profit of $2,625. Breakeven point for this trade is DE at 42½ at expiration.

**Example:** On June 17, 1975, another bull perpendicular spread on Deere, then available at 39½, could have been constructed as follows:

| | |
|---|---|
| Buy DE October 40 at | 4 |
| Sell DE October 45 at | 2 |
| Debit | 2 |

The maximum profit potential for this bull spread would have been obtained if DE had moved up to 45.

Technically, DE was undergoing correction of its recent upswings.

**Example:** Another bull perpendicular spread appeared attractive on June 17, 1975, on Eastman Kodak (NYSE–99⅛–EK):

| | |
|---|---|
| Buy EK October 90 at | 13¾ |
| Sell EK October 100 at | 8½ |
| Debit | 5¼ |

A net cash flow of only $525 would have controlled a $99 stock for 18 weeks.

If EK had remained at 99⅛ at expiration, the return would have been 73.8 percent in that time span.

## Discount Spreads

Probably one of the best risk-reduction option techniques is to buy discount instead of

premium. As a group, spreads provide a fertile field for discount purchases. The following examples illustrate such discounts.

**Example:** On June 3, 1975, on General Electric (NYSE–47⅜–GE) you could have bought the July 45 call for 4⅛ and sold the July 50 call for 1¹⁵⁄₁₆, with a premium difference of 2³⁄₁₆.

Since the July 45 call had an intrinsic value of 2, you actually would have obtained a discount of ³⁄₁₆ instead of paying a premium for the spread.

**Example:** Also illustrative of discount spreads was a possible spread on June 3, 1975, on Johnson & Johnson (NYSE–96–JNJ) when you could have bought the July 90 call for 9⅛ and sold the July 100 call for 3¾, with a premium difference of 5⅜ points.

Since the July 90 option had an intrinsic worth of 6 points, the spreader actually would have obtained ⅝ point in discount instead of paying a premium on the spread.

## Spreads as a Trading Vehicle

Since spreads fluctuate with the price of the underlying security, they also constitute a trading vehicle for sophisticated investors.

**Example:** On March 28, 1975, a bull spread was feasible on Minnesota Mining (NYSE–MMM) when you could have bought MMM October 35 for 5½ and sold MMM October 55 for 4 for a spread of 1½:

| | |
|---|---|
| Buy MMM October 35 at | 5½ |
| Sell MMM October 55 at | 4 |
| Debit | 1½ |

MMM is known for its relatively wide-fluctuating movements.

## Other Vertical Illustrations

**Example:** On June 3, 1975, another pair of bull verticals were feasible: one on Upjohn (NYSE–47⅜–UPJ) and the other on Black & Decker (NYSE–35⅞–BDK).

The UPJ vertical would have involved the purchase of UPJ July 45 for 4⅞ and the sale of UPJ July 50 for 2½, with a premium difference of 2⅜, with a ⅛ discretion:

---

* Discretion means the room for freedom of action given the broker in executing a given order.

| | |
|---|---|
| Buy UPJ July 45 at | 4⅞ |
| Sell UPJ July 50 at | 2½ |
| Debit | 2⅜ |

If the stock had risen to 50, the spreader would have realized 2⅝ points, or 110.5 percent, on the invested premium cost in seven weeks.

UPJ's technical pattern was favorable despite its edging toward the next obstacle of 48 to 53 supply.

The BDK spread was one where you could have bought BDK October 35 for 5⅜ and simultaneously sold BDK October 40 for 3½, with a premium difference of 1⅞:

| | |
|---|---|
| Buy BDK October 35 for | 5⅜ |
| Sell BDK October 40 for | 3½ |
| Debit | 1⅞ |

### *Buy Low Strike, Sell High Strike*

The importance of doing low-cost bull vertical spreads cannot be over-emphasized. Bull vertical spreads involve buying low strike options and selling high strike options.

***Example:*** On April 21, 1975, the July 35 and July 40 options on Chase Manhattan (NYSE–33¼–CMB) provided an opportunity for a strike differential spread. CMB had experienced an earnings recovery in recent quarters. While banks' extremely wide yield-cost spreads were unlikely to last, spreads were expected to be wider in the next few years than they had been in the recent past.

CMB's then P/E of 5 was one of the lowest among major money-center banks, as compared with its own ten-year average P/E ratio of 11.5.

A bullish spread on CMB's July 35 and July 40 options would have involved the purchase of the low strike at 2⅛ and the sale of the high strike at ⅞, with a 1¼-point debit:

| | |
|---|---|
| Buy CMB July 35 at | 2⅛ |
| Sell CMB July 40 at | ⅞ |
| Debit | 1¼ |

With CMB at 35 or lower at expiration, the maximum loss would have been limited to the $125 in premium differential, plus commissions.

The maximum profit would have occurred when CMB sold at 40 or higher, in which case the gain would have been $375, or a 300-percent return on the invested $125, the cash required under the margin rules.

### *Other Interesting Spreads*

Other interesting spread examples were the following situations available on April 23, 1975:

1. General Telephone & Electronics (GTE)

| | |
|---|---|
| Buy GTE July 20 at | 1.5625 |
| Sell GTE July 25 at | .4375 |
| Debit | 1.1250 |

Maximum gain = 3.875
Maximum loss = 1.125

2. Minnesota Mining (MMM)

| | |
|---|---|
| Buy MMM July 55 at | 5.375 |
| Sell MMM July 65 at | 2.000 |
| Debit | 3.375 |

Maximum gain = 6.625
Maximum loss = 3.375

## BEAR VERTICAL SPREAD TECHNIQUES

### *Buy High Strike, Sell Low Strike*

The reverse of bull vertical spreads, bear vertical spreads involve buying options at higher strike prices and selling (shorting) options at lower strike prices.

The purpose of a bear vertical is to receive the profit from a large decline in the price of the underlying security, as the best profit results if both options expire worthless. Profit is made on the downside.

### *Margin Requirement*

The margin requirement for bear spreads is different from that for bull spreads because a bear spread is long the cheaper option and short the more expensive one. The required margin is equal to the difference between strike prices minus premium differential.

## Calculating Margin

**Example:** Illustrative of the method of calculating margin requirements on bear verticals was a possible bear vertical spread on Upjohn (NYSE–37½–UPJ) on February 14, 1975, that would have involved the purchase of a UPJ July 40 call at 4½ and the sale of UPJ July 30 at 9¾, with a premium differential of 5¼ on the credit side:

| | |
|---|---|
| Buy UPJ July 40 at | 4½ |
| Sell UPJ July 30 at | 9¾ |
| Credit | 5¼ |

The strike price differential between UPJ July 40 and UPJ July 30 was 10 points.

Since the spreader took in 5¼ points (long the cheaper option and short the more expensive one), the margin requirement of this spread was based on the following calculation:

| | |
|---|---|
| Strike price differential | 10 |
| Premium differential | − 5¼ |
| Margin requirement | 4¾ |

In other words, the option premium differential of $525 was applied toward reducing the margin requirement to $475, which would also be the limit to the spreader's loss.

**Example:** Also illustrative of margin calculations for bear verticals was the possible spread on Burroughs (NYSE–BGH) on March 7, 1975, when it was possible to sell BGH July 80 at 19¾ and buy BGH July 90 at 12⅝, with a premium differential of 7⅛ on the credit side:

| | |
|---|---|
| Sell BGH July 80 at | 19¾ |
| Buy BGH July 90 at | 12⅝ |
| Credit | 7⅛ |

The strike price differential between July 90 and July 80 was 10 points.

Calculations of the margin requirement for this BGH bear vertical are:

| | |
|---|---|
| Strike price differential | 10 |
| Premium differential | − 7⅛ |
| Margin requirement | 2⅞ |

## Strike-Prices Relative to Premiums

Generally, in bear verticals, the lower-strike-price option sold by the spreader is usually somewhat in the money while the higher-strike-price option bought is usually somewhat out of the money.

In the illustration on Upjohn, for example, the UPJ July 30 option (lower strike) sold was in the money relative to UPJ common at 37½. On the other hand, the UPJ July 40 (higher strike) bought was out of the money relative to the price of the underlying security.

## Bear Vertical Illustrations

The following possible bear verticals appeared attractive on April 18, 1975. They constitute additional examples of such spreads for illustrative purposes:

1. Bear vertical on IBM
   a. Premium differential

| | |
|---|---|
| Sell IBM July 180 at | 38½ |
| Buy IBM July 200 at | 22 |
| | 16½ |

   b. Strike price differential

| | |
|---|---|
| IBM July | 200 |
| IBM July | 180 |
| | 20 |

   c. Margin requirement

| | |
|---|---|
| Strike price differential | 20 |
| Premium differential | 16½ |
| | 3½ |

   d. Maximum gain = 16½
      Maximum loss = 3½

2. Bear vertical on Texas Instruments (TXN)
   a. Premium differential

| | |
|---|---|
| Sell TXN October 80 at | 34 |
| Buy TXN October 90 at | 24¾ |
| | 9¼ |

b. Strike price differential

| | |
|---|---|
| TXN October | 90 |
| TXN October | 80 |
| | 10 |

c. Margin requirement

| | |
|---|---|
| Strike price differential | 10 |
| Premium differential | 9¼ |
| | ¾ |

d. Maximum gain = 9¼
Maximum loss = ¾

3. Bear vertical on McDonald (MCD)
   a. Premium differential

| | |
|---|---|
| Sell MCD July 40 at | 10 |
| Buy MCD July 45 at | 6¾ |
| | 3¼ |

b. Strike price differential

| | |
|---|---|
| MCD July | 45 |
| MCD July | 40 |
| | 5 |

c. Margin requirement

| | |
|---|---|
| Strike price differential | 5 |
| Premium differential | 3¼ |
| | 1¾ |

d. Maximum gain = 3¼
Maximum loss = 1¾

4. Bear vertical on General Electric (GE)
   a. Premium differential

| | |
|---|---|
| Sell GE July 35 at | 13 |
| Buy GE July 40 at | 7⅜ |
| | 5⅝ |

b. Strike price differential

| | |
|---|---|
| GE July | 40 |
| GE July | 35 |
| | 5 |

c. Margin requirement

| | |
|---|---|
| Strike price differential | 5 |
| Premium differential | 5⅝ |
| | ⅝ |

d. Maximum gain = 5⅝
Maximum loss = zero

## *Key Measurements*

Option strategy is determined by the following key considerations:

1. Premium differential (*pd*) represents the maximum potential, being the difference between the more expensive low-strike option price and the less expensive high-strike option price.
2. Maximum loss (*ml*) represents option capital (*oc*), which is equal to the differential between the two strike prices less premium differential (*pd*).
3. Profit-loss differential (*pld*) represents the differential between premium differential (*pd*) and maximum loss (*ml*).
4. Profit leverage (*pl*) represents the magnitude of gain, measured by profit-loss differential (*pld*) as a percentage of option capital (same as *ml*).
5. Downside breakeven (*db*).
6. Downside breakeven percentage (*dbp*).

## *Possible Workout against Key Measurements*

Refer to Table 12.1 on the next page.

### *McDonald (MCD)*

Stock price = 41⅛ (2/24/75)
MCD July 30 = 12⅛
Option prices = MCD July 40 = 6⅜

### *Option Strategy*

| | |
|---|---|
| Sell MCD July 30 | 12⅞ |
| Buy MCD July 40 | 6⅜ |
| Profit differential (*pd*) | 6½ |

| Stock | Prem. Differential (*pd*) | Maximum Loss (*ml*) | Profit Loss Differential (*pld*) | Profit Leverage (*pl*) |
|---|---|---|---|---|
| McDonald | $650 | $350 | $300 | 86% |
| Polaroid | $337 | $163 | $174 | 107% |
| Disney | $587 | $413 | $174 | 42% |

Margin requirement (option capital) = $1,000 − $650 = $350

### Option Worksheet

(1) Premium differential (*pd*) = $650
(2) Option capital (*oc*) = $350
(3) Maximum loss (*ml*) = $350
(4) Profit-loss differential (*pld*) = $300
(5) Profit leverage (*pl*) = 86%

## Polaroid (PRD)

Stock price = 20¾ (2/24/75)

Option prices = PRD April 15 = 6¼
PRD April 20 = 2⅞

### Option Strategy

| Sell PRD April 15 | 6¼ |
|---|---|
| Buy PRD April 20 | 2⅞ |
| Profit differential (*pd*) | 3⅜ |

Margin requirement = $500 − $337 = $163

### Option Worksheet

(1) Premium differential (*pd*) = $337
(2) Option capital (*oc*) = $163
(3) Maximum loss (*ml*) = $163
(4) Profit-loss differential (*pld*) = $174
(5) Profit leverage (*pl*) = 107%

## Disney (DIS)

Stock prices = 39¾ (2/24/75)

Option prices = DIS July 30 = 11¾
DIS July 40 = 5⅞

### Option Strategy

| Sell DIS July 30 | 11¾ |
|---|---|
| Buy DIS July 40 | 5⅞ |
| Profit differential (*pd*) | 5⅞ |

Margin requirement = $1,000 − $587 = $413

### Option Worksheet

(1) Premium differential (*pd*) = $587
(2) Option capital (*oc*) = $413
(3) Maximum loss (*ml*) = $413
(4) Profit-loss differential (*pld*) = $174
(5) Profit leverage (*pl*) = 42%

# SANDWICH SPREADS

With its risk known in advance, a sandwich is designed for accounts that seek protected-gain opportunities, if the stock goes up higher than expected or declines more than anticipated.

### Multiple Option Structure

Structurally, a sandwich spread consists of sale of two intermediate calls in the middle and purchase of two calls with strike prices equidistant from the short calls in a ratio of 1:2:1. If the long calls are not of equal distance, there is additional exposure to risk.

### Financial Leverage

Ideally, the sale of two intermediate strike calls will finance the purchase of the long calls. In other words, the cash received from the middle strike calls equals, or nearly so, the cash spent to purchase the long calls. A small cash difference, however, does not eliminate opportunity.

The profit potential can be calculated in advance. While moderate, the percentage gain per dollar of cash investment is potentially enormous.

### *Key Considerations*

1. Option capital (*oc*) represents the differential between the negative (debit) spread and the positive (credit) spread.
2. Common strike differential (*csd*).
3. Potential profit (*pp*) represents the difference between *csd* and *oc*.

For evaluating sandwich spreads quickly, take the common strike differential less the net initial cash difference. The balance is the potential profit.

At expiration, the maximum cash gain is at the middle strike price for the underlying stock.

### *Possible Workout against Key Measurements*

*Upjohn (UPJ)*

Stock price = 34⅞ (2/24/75)
UPJ April 40 = 1¾
Option prices = UPJ April 35 = 3¾
UPJ April 30 = 7

### *Option Strategy*

Buy 1 UPJ April 40 at 1¾
Sell 2 UPJ April 35 at 3¾
Buy 1 UPJ April 30 at 7

| | | |
|---|---|---|
| (1) | Buy 1 UPJ April 30 at | 7 |
| | Sell 1 UPJ April 35 at | 3¾ |
| | Debit spread | 3¼ |
| (2) | Sell 1 UPJ April 35 at | 3¾ |
| | Buy 1 UPJ April 40 at | 1¾ |
| | Credit spread | 2 |

### *Option Worksheet*

(1) Debit spread = 3¼
(2) Credit spread = 2
(3) Option capital (*oc*) = 1¼
(4) Common strike differential (*csd*) = 5
(5) Profit potential (*pp*) = *csd* − *oc* = $375
(6) Profit leverage (*pl*) = $\frac{pp}{oc}$ = 300%

*Xerox (XRX)*

Stock price = 78⅝ (2/24/75)
XRX April 90 = 2⅜
Option prices = XRX April 80 = 5⅜
XRX April 70 = 10¾

### *Option Strategy*

Buy 1 XRX April 90 at 2⅜
Sell 2 XRX April 80 at 5⅜
Buy 1 XRX April 70 at 10¾

| | | |
|---|---|---|
| (1) | Buy 1 XRX April 70 at | 10¾ |
| | Sell 1 XRX April 80 at | 5⅜ |
| | Debit spread | 5⅜ |
| (2) | Sell 1 XRX April 80 at | 5⅜ |
| | Buy 1 XRX April 90 at | 2⅜ |
| | Credit spread | 3 |

### *Option Worksheet*

(1) Debit spread = 5⅜
(2) Credit spread = 2⅜
(3) Option capital (*oc*) = 5⅜ − 2⅜ = 3
(4) Common strike differential (*csd*) = 10
(5) Profit potential (*pp*) = *csd* − *oc* = $700
(6) Profit leverage (*pl*) = $\frac{pp}{oc}$ = 233%

**TABLE 12.2 SUMMARY OF POSSIBLE WORKOUT AGAINST KEY MEASUREMENTS ON A PACKAGE OF THREE STOCKS**

| | Debit Spread (*ds*) | Credit Spread (*cs*) | Option Capital (*oc*) | Common Strike Differential (*csd*) | Potential Profit (*pp*) | Profit Leverage (*pl*) |
|---|---|---|---|---|---|---|
| UPI | $325 | $200 | $125 | $500 | $375 | 300% |
| XRX | $537 | $237 | $300 | $1,000 | $700 | 233% |
| EK | $463 | $219 | $244 | $1,000 | $756 | 310% |

## Eastman Kodak (EK)

Stock price = 86⅛ (2/24/75)

EK April 100 = 1¹¹⁄₁₆

Option prices = $\begin{array}{l} \text{EK April } 90 = 3\frac{7}{8} \\ \text{EK April } 80 = 8\frac{1}{2} \end{array}$

### Option Strategy

| | |
|---|---|
| Buy 1 EK April 80 at | 8½ |
| Sell 1 EK April 90 at | 3⅞ |
| Debit spread | 4⅝ |
| | |
| Sell 1 EK April 90 at | 3⅞ |
| Buy 1 EK April 100 at | 1¹¹⁄₁₆ |
| *Credit spread* | 2³⁄₁₆ |

### Option Worksheet

(1) Debit spread = 4⅝

(2) Credit spread = 2³⁄₁₆

(3) Option capital (*oc*) = 2⁷⁄₁₆

(4) Common strike differential (*csd*) = 10

(5) Profit potential (*pp*) = *csd* − *oc* = $756

(6) Profit leverage $(pl) = \dfrac{pp}{oc} = 310\%$

### Portfolio Strategy

The initial phase of a spread portfolio for a pilot option money management program is suggested on a small scale:

15 spreads each on McDonald, Polaroid, and Disney as outlined above.

15 sandwiches each for Upjohn, Xerox, and Eastman Kodak as outlined above.

## Portfolio Investment and Projected Returns

The profit potential projected above, though not large in amount, is extraordinarily high in terms of the gain per dollar of cash investment, particularly with sandwich spreads.

The potential profit leverage amounts to 155 percent based on a profit of $37,189 on an option capital of $23,925.

# DIAGONAL SPREADS

### Combining Different Strikes and Different Expirations

Basically, a diagonal spread is a combination spread involving long and short positions of *both* different strike prices *and* different maturity months.

Whereas horizontal spreads and vertical spreads consist of simultaneously buying and selling options on the same stock with different strike prices *or* different expiration months, diagonal spreads involve such buying and selling with different strike prices *and* different expiration months.

### Another Multiple Option Structure

Both diagonal spreads and sandwich spreads are forms of multiple option structures. Whereas the sandwich spread consists of

---

**TABLE 12.3 SUMMARY OF PORTFOLIO INVESTMENT AND ITS POSSIBLE RETURNS**

| Portfolio Options | No. of options | Unit price | Option Capital (15 × unit price) | Potential Profit | Profit Leverage |
|---|---|---|---|---|---|
| McDonald | 15 | $350 | $ 5,250 | $ 4,515 | 86% |
| Polaroid | 15 | $163 | $ 2,445 | $ 2,616 | 107% |
| Disney | 15 | $413 | $ 6,195 | $ 2,602 | 42% |
| Upjohn | 15 | $125 | $ 1,875 | $ 5,625 | 300% |
| Xerox | 15 | $300 | $ 4,500 | $10,485 | 233% |
| Eastman Kodak | 15 | $244 | $ 3,660 | $11,346 | 310% |
| | | | $23,925 | $37,189 | |

the sale of two intermediate options and the purchase of two options with strike prices at equal distance from the short options in the ratio of 1:2:1, diagonal spreads combine simultaneous long and short positions combining different strike prices and different expiration months.

# OVERVIEW

## *What*

Margin is amount of borrowing or credit that a broker is permitted to extend to his customers in call option transactions.

## *Why*

For investors, margin is designed to achieve leverage. Borrowed money serves to magnify the investor's gains if the investment is based on sound and correct judgment. Leverage can, of course, work against the investor, leading to the perils of margin calls.

For the broker, strict margin requirements serve to protect him for his lending through cash or collateral deposited by the borrowing investor.

## *How*

Initially, the Federal Reserve Board has established the initial margin requirement for purchased long or sale short of equity securities.

For maintenance, the New York Stock Exchange provides the minimum equity level required of an account after meeting the initial margin requirements.

Brokers recompute an investor's margin requirement daily. If an account requires more money, it must be supplied immediately.

## *Margin's Two Edges*

"Margin" is the term used in the marketplace to indicate borrowing from a broker in order to achieve leverage. In return, the broker needs protection for his lending, which is provided through a cash or collateral deposit by the borrowing investor.

Leveraged investment with borrowed money serves to magnify gains when the investment realizes a gain. Conversely, leverage works against an investor to magnify his losses if his investment decisions prove to be wrong. Investors should be fully aware of the perils of "margin calls," or the necessity to supply more as well as of the possibilities of involuntary liquidation of their accounts if margin calls are not met.

# call margins

# 13

## Three Sets of Margin Requirements

For any given margin security, an investor is required to comply with the highest of the three sets of margin requirements established, respectively, by the Federal Reserve Board via Regulation T, the New York Stock Exchange, and the brokerage house (a New York Stock Exchange member firm).

## Margin and Credit Relationships

Since the Options Clearing Corporation (OCC) acts as the central clearing house for listed options transactions, it requires each clearing member firm either to deposit the underlying stock or to maintain margin with the OCC in any one or any combination of the three specified types of margin:

1. Cash
2. U.S. Treasury Bills
3. A letter of credit issued by a commercial bank rated acceptable by OCC

In return, clearing member firms are responsible for adequate deposit (physical stock certificates or margin money) which a nonclearing member firm, in turn, is required to obtain from its own customer.

## Regulation T

Regulation T of the Federal Reserve Board governs, among other things, the amount of credit (if any) that initially may be extended by a broker to his customer.

For purposes of Regulation T, listed options have no loan value. Full payment for the purchase of such options must be made within the required time limit, although they may be purchased either in a special cash account or in a margin account.

Brokerage firms are also required to comply with the margin requirements of the exchanges of which they are members. AMEX margin requirements for listed options are similar to those of the New York Stock Exchange.

Moreover, brokerage firms may impose house rules that are never less, but rather more, strict than those of Regulation T and the exchanges.

## Margin-Account-Only Transactions

Certain transactions *must* take place in margin accounts.

Generally, covered writing transactions may be effected in a margin account or in a special cash account, but only if the underlying security is held in the account.

Uncovered writing transactions and spread transactions in listed options must take place in a margin account.

A call option may be exercised in a special cash account if full cash payment is made promptly.

Where a call held in a margin account is exercised, the initial margin requirement of Regulation T applies to the purchase price of the stock.

However, if a call is exercised in a margin account and the underlying stock is sold on the same day, no additional margin is required under Regulation T if the proceeds from the sale exceed the exercise price of the call.

## Initial Margin Requirement

Since January 1974 the Federal Reserve Board has established the initial margin requirement at 50 pecent for purchase long or sale short of equity securities.

Both the NYSE and the AMEX require an initial margin minimum of $2,000 that applies to all new securities transactions and commitments. Thereafter, the maintenance margin provisions apply.

The $2,000 initial margin (also called "minimum account equity") rule has exceptions:

1. If a proposed purchase will cost less than $2,000, the customer need not deposit more than the actual purchase price for the transaction.
2. An equity of $2,000 is required after certain so-called speculative transactions, including short sales or uncovered option transactions.

## Maintenance Margin

Under NYSE maintenance margin provisions, an investor is generally required to maintain a minimum 25-percent equity in the account. Defined as the customer's ownership interest in the account, equity is calculated by subtracting his debit balance from the present market value of the securities in the account. Margin calls are made if securities value declines to this minimum maintenance level.

The NYSE and the AMEX have established similar minimum maintenance margin requirements for specific classes of transaction, as follows:

1. Margins for covered option transactions: No margin is required for sale of call options against a long position. The long position can be either long stock in the account, properly margined, or the broker's possession of an escrow receipt or an option-guarantee letter issued by a bank or trust company approved by OCC.
2. Margins for uncovered options transactions: For sale of call options without long stock, the requirement is 30 percent of the current market value of the underlying security
   a. *plus* 100 percent of any excess of the current market value of the underlying security over the aggregate exercise price of the call (in the money)
   b. or *minus* 100 percent of any excess of the aggregate exercise price of the call over the current market value of the underlying security (out of the money), with a minimum requirement of $250 per option contract.

In other words, if the stock is selling higher than the strike price (in the money), the margin requirement is, as stated in *item 2a* above, 30 percent of the market price of the stock *plus* the differential between the market price and the strike price. If, on the other hand, the stock is selling below the strike price (out of the money), the margin requirement is, as stated in *item 2b*, 30 percent of the market price of the stock, *minus* the differential between market price and strike price.

*Example:* *Short Uncovered Option with Market Price Same as Strike Price:* Assuming that an investor wrote one uncovered Weyerhaeuser (WY) October 40 for 3½ when WY common stock was at 40 (based on June 24, 1975, closing prices), the maintenance margin would have been:

| | |
|---|---|
| 30% of WY ($4,000 × .30) | $1,200 |
| In the money | + 0 |
| Out of the money | − 0 |
| Maintenance margin requirement | $1,200 |

The option premium of $350 received from sale of the uncovered WY October 40 option could have been used to satisfy part of the maintenance margin requirement. If, however, the equity in the account was less than $2,000 at the time of the transaction, the initial margin requirement of $2,000 had to be satisfied.

*Example:* *Short Uncovered Option with Market Price Above Strike Price:* If, thereafter, WY went up to $50, the maintenance margin requirement would have been:

| | |
|---|---|
| 30% of WY ($5,000 × .30) | $1,500 |
| In the money ($5,000 − $4,000) | +$1,000 |
| Maintenance margin requirement | $2,500 |

*Example:* *Short Uncovered Option with Market Price Below Strike Price:* If WY, thereafter, went down to $35, the maintenance margin requirement would have been:

| | |
|---|---|
| 30% of WY ($3,500 × .30) | $1,050 |
| Out of the money ($4,000 − $3,500) | − 500 |
| Maintenance margin requirement | $ 550 |

## Sale of Put Options

No margin is required on sale of a put option against short stock.

On the sale of a put option without short stock, the minimum maintenance requirement is 25 percent of the market price of the underlying stock (1) *plus* the differential between the market price and the strike price, if the market price is lower than the strike price; or (2) *minus* the differential between the market price and the strike price, if the market price is higher than the strike price.

# SPREAD MARGINS

Following is a summary of margin requirements on spreads where a long call may margin a short call.

## Margins on Bull Horizontal Spreads

Bull horizontal spreads are those where the long option expires no earlier than the "short" option.

The maintenance margin requirement on such spreads is the *lesser* of (1) the margin required against the short option if treated as uncovered, with a $250 minimum per option contract, or (2) the excess, if any, of the aggregate exercise price of the "long" option over the aggregate exercise price of the "short" option.

***Example:*** *Long Far Expiration, Short Near Expiration at Same Strike Price:* Assume an investor wrote one Honeywell (HON) October 40 for 5¼ and, at the same time, bought one HON Jaunary 40 for 7 when HON common was at $40 (based on June 25, 1975, closing prices).

This bull horizontal spread would have qualified for spread margin treatment because the long position would have expired no earlier than the short position. The maintenance margin requirement would have been the lesser of:

| | |
|---|---:|
| 30% of HON ($4,000 × .30) | $1,200 |
| In the money | + 0 |
| Out of the money | − 0 |
| | $1,200 |

*or*

| | |
|---|---:|
| Strike-price differential ($4,000 − $4,000) | = 0 |
| Maintenance margin requirement | = 0 |

No maintenance margin is required on the "short" position because the "long" position more than covers the "short" position:

| | |
|---|---:|
| Long position (January 40) at | 7 |
| Short position (October 40) at | 5¼ |
| | 1¾ |

In addition to the $525 from writing HON October 40, which was applicable toward the $700 purchase price of the long position, an additional $175 would have been required to satisfy the requirement that a long option must be paid for in full. In addition, the initial margin requirement also had to be met if the equity in the account was less than $2,000 at the time of the transaction.

## Margins on Bear Horizontal Spreads

Bear horizontal spreads are those where the long option expires earlier than the short option. In other words, you long the near expiration and short the far expiration on the same stock, with the two options having the same strike price.

Spread margins are not applicable to bear horizontal spreads. Such margins apply only to those spreads where the number of long options equals or exceeds the number of short options.

Uncovered short options must be margined as uncovered call options.

***Example:*** *Long Near Expiration, Short Far Expiration at Same Strike Price:* Assuming that an investor wrote a Boeing (BA) October 30 for 4⅜ and, at the same time, bought a BA July 30 for 3½ when BA common was at 31⅛ (based on June 25, 1975, closing prices), this bear horizontal spread would not have qualified for spread margins because the long position expired prior to the short position.

In this case, the short position had to be margined as an uncovered short and the long position had to be paid in full.

## Margins on Vertical Spreads

Vertical spreads involve buying and selling (shorting) options on the same stock having the same expiration month but different strike prices.

Spread margins are applicable to verticals where long options have the *same* expiration month as short options.

***Example:*** *In-the-Money Vertical Spread:* Assuming that an investor wrote a General Motors (GM) October 35 for 11⅜ and, at the same time, bought a GM October 40 for 7½ when GM common was at 46 (based on June 25, 1975, closing prices), the maintenance margin requirement would have been the lesser of

| | |
|---|---|
| 30% of GM ($4,600 × .30) | $1,380 |
| In the money ($4,600 − $3,500) | +$1,100 |
| | $2,480 |

*or*

Strike-price differential ($4,000 − $3,500) = $500
Maintenance margin requirement = $500

As always, the minimum account equity of $2,000 must be met if the equity in the account is below that amount at the time of the transaction.

The difference between the premium received from the short position and the premium paid for the long position ($1,138 − $750 = $388), would have been applicable to the initial margin requirement.

***Example:*** *Out-of-the-Money Vertical Spread:* If GM common later declined to $30, the maintenance margin requirement would have been the lesser of

| | |
|---|---|
| 30% of GM ($3,000 × .30) | $900 |
| Out of the money ($3,500 − $3,000) | −500 |
| | $400 |

*or*

Strike-price differential (4,000 − $3,500) = $500
Maintenance margin requirement = $400

# LISTED
# PUTS

# FUNDAMENTALS AND TECHNIQUES

PART V

# OVERVIEW

### What

A put option is a mirror image of a call option. Whereas a call is an option to *buy* stock at a specific price, a put is an option to *sell* stock at a specific price.

### Why

Puts are primarily bear market instruments, permitting investors to participate in an anticipated stock price decline without assuming the risks of short selling.

### How

A put option becomes more valuable as the market price of the underlying stock declines. The put gives the holder the right to sell stock at a predetermined (exercise) price regardless of how sharply the stock price may decline. In return for selling this right, the put writer (seller) receives a premium.

# BASIC COMPONENTS

A put option is the mirror image of a call option; its nomenclature, strike price, premium, expiration month, and so on, are the same. The difference is that whereas a call is an option to buy shares of stock at a specific price (the strike price), a put is an option to sell shares of stock at the specified strike price. The put option gives its owner the right to sell 100 shares of an underlying stock at a specified strike price any time before the option expires.

# MIRROR-IMAGE CONCEPT: PUTS VERSUS CALLS

Although puts share some components with calls, the meanings of "in the money" and "out

# put basics

# 14

of the money" are diametrically opposed for puts and calls.

The following illustration shows the miror-image nature of in-the-money and out-of-the-money calls versus in-the-money and out-of-the-money puts.

| Stock Price | Call Strike Price |
|---|---|
| $40 | $35 (in the money) |
| $40 | $40 (on the money) |
| $40 | $45 (out of the money) |

| Stock Price | Put Strike Price |
|---|---|
| $40 | $35 (out of the money) |
| $40 | $40 (on the money) |
| $40 | $45 (in the money) |

## In-the-Money Puts

At expiration of the option, a put is in the money if its strike price is *above* the market price of the underlying stock. The put's value should approximate the difference between the strike price and the market price.

The value of a put at expiration, therefore, hinges on *how much,* if at all, the option allows its holder to sell the stock above its current market price.

*Example:* At October 14, 1977, closing, Eastman Kodak (Eas Kd) had the following price data on its April 70 put:

| Stock | Strike Price | Apr. Put Price | Stock Price |
|---|---|---|---|
| Eas Kd | 70 | 12½ | 58⅛ |

Based on these price data, an Eas Kd April put conveying the right to sell 100 shares of Eas Kd stock at $70 per share had the following value components:

| | |
|---|---|
| Intrinsic value ($70 − $58⅛) | 11⅞ |
| Time value (12½ − 11⅞) | ⅝ |
| Total value | 12½ |

As expiration nears, time value disappears, and the price of the in-the-money put would have been approximately the intrinsic value of ⋅ 11⅞ ($1,187.50 for the 100-share option).

In the put examples, as in the call examples in this book, both commission costs and taxes have been excluded.

## Out-Of-The-Money Puts

If the stock price at expiration is *above* the strike price, the put is out of the money and should expire worthless.

*Example:* At its October 14, 1977, closing Santa Fe International (SAF) and its underlying stock had the following price relationship:

| Stock | Strike Price | October Put Price | Stock Price |
|---|---|---|---|
| SAF Put | 45 | 3/16 | 46½ |

The SAF October 45 put had no intrinsic value since the stock price was *above* the strike price. The 3/16 price tag for the put option was for the remaining time value of 5 days before it expired October 19, 1977.

To summarize, a put is out of the money when the underlying stock price is *above* the strike price and in the money when the underlying stock price is *below* the strike price. A call is the reverse; that is, it is out of the money when the underlying stock is *below* the strike price and in the money when the stock price is *above* the strike price.

## Cost and Leverage Factors

Since an in-the-money put already has some intrinsic value, it generally costs more. It will move more closely with the stock in declining markets. On the other hand, an investor would lose his entire put premium on an advance in the stock.

On the other hand, since an out-of-the-money put has no intrinsic value, it will cost less. In the event of a substantial decline in the stock price, an out-of-the-money put provides greater leverage because of its smaller dollar investment and, of course, because fewer dollars are at risk. However, relative to the in-the-money put, the underlying stock would have to decline a greater percentage before an out-of-the-money put began to gain intrinsic value.

# TWO SIDES
# TO THE GAME

### Buying Side

Just as call options have two sides to the game, put options also involve buying on the one side and selling on the other. On the buying side, a trader buys a call option when he believes the underlying stock will rise in value; and he buys a put option when he thinks the underlying stock will decline in value.

Calls are essentially bull market instruments, permitting investors to participate in the anticipated rise in the price of the underlying stock at a fraction of the cost required for outright stock ownership.

On the other hand, puts are primarily bear market instruments, permitting investors to participate without the undue risk of the short sale of the underlying stock. To go short requires capital the average investor normally does not expose to risk.

A buyer of a call is similar to an owner of 100 shares of stock, with no more risk than the cost of the call; and a buyer of a put is similar to a short-seller, with his entire risk confined to the cost of the put.

The most you can lose when you buy a put option is its total cost. But such a total loss will normally occur only if you continue to hold the option and it expires worthless. If the option is sold prior to its expiration, you should recover part of the premium because of the option's remaining time value.

*Example:* Assume that on July 27, 1977, you paid 2¼ for a December 40 put on Revlon (REV) while the stock was 39¾.

The stock rose to 43¼ as of September 14, 1977, while its December 40 put declined to ⅞. If you had liquidated the put for ⅞ at this point (with three more months remaining until expiration), your loss would have been 1⅜ (2¼ − ⅞) before commissions, instead of a total loss.

### Selling Side

On the selling side, an investor sells (writes) a call option when he thinks the stock will either flat or fall, and sells (writes) a put option when he believes the underlying stock will go up.

From a writer's point of view, puts make option writing a year-round activity, since writers who don't want to sell calls in an up market can then write puts.

# PUT PREMIUMS

How is the price of a put, or the put option premium, arrived at, and what factors cause put prices to increase or decrease? Generally, supply and demand for puts determines put premium levels.

In the listed options market, if a put and a call have the same terms (same underlying stock, expiration date, and strike price) and if the stock is selling at the strike price, the put generally remains priced somewhat lower than the call. One reason for this is that the stock can theoretically move farther to the upside than to the downside, because stock can only decrease by 100 percent but can increase by much more than that.

### Inverse Relationship to Stock Price

Put option premiums, like call option premiums, are influenced by changes in the price of the underlying stock, but the price relationships are exactly opposite. All other factors being equal, as the price of the stock decreases, the put premium tends to increase. This increase occurs because the right the put conveys—the right to sell shares of the stock at a specific price—becomes more valuable as the market price of the underlying stock declines. A call, of course, becomes less valuable as the market price of the underlying stock declines.

*Example:* Assume you buy a put option with a strike price of $60. You have a locked-in right—at any time during the life of the option—to sell the stock at that price regardless of how sharply the market price of the stock declines in the meantime.

Thus, if the market price of the stock drops to $52, the right to sell at $60 could be worth approximately $8 ($60 − $52). Should the stock drop to $50, the right to sell it at $60 could be worth approximately $10 ($60 − $50). And so it would go, with the increased value being reflected in an increased option premium.

The three major factors determining put option premiums are (1) the current market price of the underlying stock relative to the strike price of the option, (2) the length of time remaining until expiration of the option, and (3) the volatility of the underlying stock.

## Underlying Stock Price Relative to the Strike Price

Since the put strike price is a fixed dollar amount, decreases in the market price of the underlying stock tend to result in an increase in the put premium. On the other hand, an increase in the price of the underlying stock tends to reduce the put premium.

At expiration, the put option premium should be approximately the amount that the option strike price is above the then current market value of the underlying stock. If the strike price happens to be below the market price of the stock, the option should expire worthless.

*Example:* On September 13, 1977, Hughes Tool (HT) closed at 35⅞ while its September 40 put was at 4½. Since the September option was to expire four days later, the put price at 4½ reflected mostly its intrinsic value of 4⅛ (40 − 35⅞). The balance, ⅜ (4½ − 4⅛), represented the remaining 4-day time value.

Had the market price of HT been above the put strike price of 40, the put option at expiration would have been worthless.

## Time Remaining until Expiration

A put, like a call, is a wasting asset; its value decreases as its expiration date approaches. An option that is not worth exercising by expiration becomes worthless.

## Volatility of the Underlying Stock

A major factor in the determination of put values is the volatility of the underlying stock. If large swings in the stock's price are common, option buyers will usually pay a larger premium for it, because chances of profit from a large upswing are better. Likewise, the writer will insist on a larger premium for an option on such a stock because chances of substantial loss are increased.

## The Stock Beta

Investors should know and understand the *beta* of the stock underlying the option—that is, the stock's propensity to move with the market, or its price movement volatility. While it is impossible to predict the price movement of a stock accurately, it is possible, based upon its historical performance, to state whether a particular stock is likely to have a large price movement.

Stocks with great movement have high *beta,* and so options on such stocks command high premiums. Conversely, stocks with low *betas* have low premiums. The reasoning is, of course, that a high-*beta* stock has a greater probability of moving faster and farther than a low-*beta* stock.

## OVERVIEW

### What

Two simple strategies each for the put buyer and for the put seller are:

1. For the buyer
   a. Long put
   b. Long put, long stock
2. For the seller
   a. Short put
   b. Short put, short stock

### Why

Put buying offers a desirable alternative to selling stock short because of its two advantages: (1) leverage and (2) limited risk. It is also used as "insurance" to protect a stock position.

Put selling is primarily for (1) generating cash flow and (2) acquiring stock at below market price.

### How

At the relatively small cost of a put, the put buyer achieves the same gain as a short seller without the latter's unlimited risk. The put seller expects to pocket the premium money if and when the stock rises, as anticipated; the rise of the stock renders the put written (sold) worthless.

### Basic Strategies

With the advent of listed puts, possible option strategies increase manyfold through combinations of puts with puts, calls with calls, and calls with puts. We will focus on the simpler put strategies. Essentially, there are four of them: two each from the put buyer's and the put seller's viewpoint.

1. From the put buyer's viewpoint
   a. Buying a put
   b. Buying stock, buying a put
2. From the put seller's viewpoint
   a. Selling a put
   b. Selling stock short, selling a put.

## FROM THE PUT BUYER'S VIEWPOINT

### First Simple Strategy: Buying a Put

The fist simple put strategy is buying puts. When an investor anticipates a stock rising, his simples choices are between stock purchase or call purchase. The call purchase has two advan-

# simple put strategies

# 15

tages: leverage (the possibility of higher percentage returns) and limited downside risk.

Conversely, when an investor expects a stock to go down, his choices are between shorting the stock or buying a put. The put purchase also offers two advantages: leverage (because of the much smaller initial investment) and limited upside risk (versus, theoretically, no limit on the upside exposure for short sellers). As with a call, the risk to the put holder is limited to 100 percent of his initial investment or the premium paid for the put.

*Example:* On September 9, 1977, Honeywell (HON) had the following puts with the strike prices of 40 and 45:

| Strike | Nov | Feb | May | Stock price |
|--------|-----|------|-----|-------------|
| 45 | ¾ | 1⁹⁄₁₆ | 2 | 47⅝ |
| 40 | 3⅛ | 3⅞ | 4⅜ | 47⅝ |

If you were only moderately bearish on HON at 47⅝, you could have bought a put with a strike price of 45 at ¾ for the November option, or at 1⁹⁄₁₆ for the February option, or at 2 for the May option, depending upon the time frame within which you believed the stock decline would take place.

If you were extremely bearish on HON at 47⅝, you could have bought the more expensive strike price at $40 puts for 3⅛ (November) or for 3⅞ (February) or for 4⅜ (May), again depending on the length of the time you believed necessary for the anticipated price decline in the underlying stock to occur.

If a stock rises above the strike price, the holder incurs a loss limited to the money put up for buying the option. Most of the time, however, a holder wouldn't have to suffer a total loss because he might be able to sell the put in the secondary market.

If a stock declines, the put holder may realize a profit by either (1) selling the put in the secondary market, or (2) exercising the put by buying stock at the current market price and delivering it against payment of the strike price. In making a choice between the two alternate courses of action the holder should be guided by such factors as the current premium for the put in the secondary market, applicable commissions, margin requirements, and tax considerations.

## Second Simple Strategy: Buying Stock, Buying a Put

The second simple stategy is to combine buying stock with buying a put. If an investor purchases stock but desires to protect his position against a substantial decline in its market value, he can buy the stock and simultaneously buy a put. Thus, the investor has complete protection against loss, no matter how much the stock might decline, since he can always sell the stock at the strike price (assuming that the strike price is the same as the purchase price of the stock). Just as a call option can guarantee the purchase price of a short position, a put option can guarantee the sale price of a long position.

For this downside protection, the investor pays a price for the put as an insurance or offset against possible correction in the market value of the underlying stock.

*Example:* At October 20, 1977, closing, you could have combined long stock, long put positions on the following four issues and puts:

| Stock | Price | Put | Price |
|-------|-------|-----|-------|
| Amerada Hess (AHC) | 30 | Feb 30 | 1¾ |
| Inexco (INX) | 20⅛ | Feb 20 | 1½ |
| Mesa (MSA) | 39⅛ | Jan 40 | 2⅜ |
| Northwest Industries (NWT) | 51 | Dec 50 | 1⁹⁄₁₆ |

The cost of combining a long stock position and a long put to protect that long stock position is summarized as follows:

| Stock | Cost of Stock | Cost of Put | Total Cost |
|-------|---------------|-------------|------------|
| AHC | 30 | 1¾ | 31¾ |
| INX | 20⅛ | 1½ | 21⅝ |
| NWT | 51 | 1⁹⁄₁₆ | 52⁹⁄₁₆ |
| MSA | 39⅛ | 2⅜ | 41½ |

If the stock price is *above* the strike price of the put option at expiration, the put will be worthless. No one would logically want to exercise a put option to sell stock at the strike price when he could merely go to the open market and sell for a higher price.

On the other hand, if the stock declines well below the strike price of the put option, the increase in the value of the long put position will essentially offset the decrease in the value of the long stock position.

In buying a put simultaneously with stock purchase, the investor does not sacrifice the opportunity to participate in increases in the stock price. Any increase in the price of the stock in excess of the price paid for the option (plus transaction costs), will result in a net gain for the investor.

This strategy also applies to helping protect previously acquired stocks. Thus, the holder of a put is able to (1) protect long-term capital gains in a stock he wishes to hold indefinitely, and (2) freeze a capital gain or loss in a stock in a current year to defer the tax consequences to the succeeding year.

# FROM THE PUT SELLER'S VIEWPOINT

For every buyer of a put option, there must first be a seller, or writer. The following are two simple put strategies from the seller's point of view.

### Third Simple Strategy: Selling a Put

The third simple strategy involving the use of puts is selling (writing) puts.

You sell (write) a put on a stock you believe will rise in value. By writing a put, the seller automatically receives a premium, which varies in amount. In general, the more volatile the underlying stock, the greater the premium. Investors may find writing puts—especially during periods of stable or rising stock prices—can be to their advantage. In simplest terms, put selling offers a method to increase the cash flow for one's investment portfolio.

If, for example, an investor writes a put with a strike price of 60 and receives a premium of $4 a share, that works out to $400 for the 100-share option; if the put is not exercised, the writer is $400 richer. But, of course, it may not

work out that way. Selling put options, just like buying puts, involves its own risks and potential rewards.

*Example:* At October 24, 1977 closing Inexco (INX) had the following puts available with a strike price at 20:

| Strike price | Nov | Feb | May | Stock Price |
|---|---|---|---|---|
| 20 | 1⁵⁄₁₆ | 2 | 2⅜ | 19⅛ |

If you believed that the recent weakness in INX was likely to be only temporary, you could have sold (written) a November 20 put for 1⁵⁄₁₆, or a February 20 put for 2 or a May 20 put for 2⅜, depending on your assessment of how long INX would remain weak. If INX rose in price as anticipated the put you had sold would have become worthless and you would have pocketed the premium received for selling (writing) the put. Or you could have realized a gain, prior to expiration, by closing out your position in the secondary market.

If, on the other hand, the stock price fell below the strike price, you could have been assigned an exercise notice. In that event, you would have been required to purchase the underlying shares at the strike price, which would have been higher than the then current market value. You could have liquidated the position immediately, realizing a loss, or you could have chosen to hold the stock for future recovery.

### Fourth Simple Strategy: Selling Stock Short, Selling a Put

The fourth simple strategy involving the use of puts is combining short stock sale with selling a put on the stock.

Selling stock short is ordinarily considered a speculative investment strategy, but the investor can reduce this risk and earn premium income by hedging through the sale of a put.

If the stock price subsequently declines as expected, the investor can cover his short stock position at a profit and repurchase his put in the secondary market at a loss. If the profit on the short sale exceeds the loss on the put, he realizes a net gain on the transaction. If, instead, the investor waits to receive an exercise notice, he can use the stock "put" to him to cover his short stock position. In this case, his profit is the premium originally received upon sale of the put.

If the stock price rises, the investor is still hedged to a certain degree, since the premium income from the put will partially offset his loss from his short position in the stock. Unlike covered call writing, however, risk is unlimited.

***Example:*** If, on October 4, 1977, you were bearish on Eastman Kodak (EK) at 60⅜, you could have sold EK short at that price and reduced the risk of such a short position by selling an EK April 60 put for 3½.

At October 24, 1977, closing, EK had declined 7¾ points to 52⅝ while the EK April 60 put had risen 4⅝ points to 8⅛. You could have covered your short stock position at a 7¾-point profit ($60⅜ − $52⅝) while repurchasing the put in the secondary market at a 4⅝-point (8½ − 3½) loss. The net result would have been a 3⅛-point gain (7¾ − 4⅝). All calculations exclude transaction costs.

# SUMMARY OF SIMPLE STRATEGIES

## *Simple Buying Strategies*

For the put buyer, the first simple strategy (buying a put) provides a valuable vehicle to participate in the anticipated stock decline. In effect, it offers a limited-risk alternative to shorting the underlying stock itself, which theoretically has unlimited upside exposure.

A put buyer achieves the same gain (less the cost for the put) as a short seller, while limiting risk to no more than the cost of the put, which normally accounts for only a fraction of what it would cost to buy the underlying stock.

Another simple strategy for the put buyer (buying stock, buying a put) is to combine buying a put with owning the underlying stock. In this strategy the put is used to protect a stock position either (1) already owned or (2) being acquired. In the first instance, the put is bought as an insurance against a possible stock-purchase mistake. In the second instance, the put is bought to protect an established stock position with large unrealized taxable gains.

## *Simple Selling Strategies*

For the put seller, the simplest strategy (selling a put) offers a means of generating option-premium income or cash flow for his investment portfolio.

He sells (writes) a put on a stock he believes will rise in value. He expects to benefit from a stock rise that will render the put written worthless, permitting him to keep the option without further obligations.

Another simple strategy (selling stock short, selling a put) for the put seller is to combine selling a put with selling stock short. If the stock price declines as anticipated, he will cover his stock position at a profit, reduced only by the cost of having to buy back the put written at a higher price. If the stock rises instead, the option income will partially offset his loss in the short stock position.

# PUT BUYING

PART **VI**

PART **VI**

/ 85

## OVERVIEW

### What

A put buyer may or may not own the underlying stock. He pays the seller premium money for the right to sell stock.

### Why

Buying puts provides a means of investing small amounts of capital for possible higher returns. Also, along with a stock position, put buying gives some protection for a stock position against possible near-term fluctuations in the marketplace.

### How

Buying puts alone gives a chance to make money on a highly leveraged basis, while limiting loss only to the cost of the put. Buying puts and owning stock simultaneously let a stock profit run at the relatively small cost of a put.

### Three Important Reasons for Buying

Why should you buy the right to sell a security at a given price within a specified period?

There are several important reasons for doing so.

First, if you anticipate a price decline in a particular stock, buying put options provides a way to profit from the decrease. A put buyer is allowed to participate fully in any decline in the price of the underlying security, except for the initial premium paid for the put. It is thus possible to make substantial profits on a relatively small investment.

Second, if you already own the stock and are reluctant to sell it at a particular time, the purchase of puts can provide protection—a hedge—against a substantial decline in its market price.

Third, if you are buying shares of an especially volatile stock, you may also wish to purchase puts as a way to establish a minimum selling price for the stock.

### Risk Limitation

A put buyer is required to pay the entire purchase price of the premium at the time of purchase. The premium paid for a put fluctuates with the market price of the underlying stock and the time remaining until expiration.

Although a put holder anticipates that the

# put buying: why and how

# 16

premium price will rise, it can decline. However, since he is under no obligation to exercise his right to sell the stock to the put contract seller (writer), his loss is limited to the price paid for the put. He will lose his entire investment if he still holds a put when it expires. On the other hand, he may realize his loss at any time prior to expiration date by entering a sell order in the secondary market. Or he can hold the option in the hope that its price will subsequently rise.

## Comparison with Call Buying

In several aspects, the put buyer and the call buyer are similar. First, as in call buying, the most frequent reason for buying puts is in anticipation of a significant movement in the underlying stock during the option's life. The anticipated moves are in opposite directions, however. The call buyer benefits when the price of the underlying stock rises significantly; the put buyer profits when the stock price declines sharply, because the value of a put rises as the stock price declines.

Second, like calls, puts are wasting assets, and time works against the holder. The risk for both the put buyer and the call buyer is limited to the amount paid for the option.

Third, as the case with a call holder, there is some salvage value for the put holder, even if the market should go against him. Instead of allowing his put to expire unexercised, the holder may recapture part of his investment at any time prior to expiration date by entering a sell order in the secondary market.

Put buying is different from call buying in one important aspect: potentially, the call buyer can realize a higher profit than the put buyer. Whereas the reward for the call buyer is *theoretically* unlimited, the potential profitability to the put buyer is limited because the underlying security can decline only to zero. This distinction, however, is more theoretical than practical.

## Covered versus Uncovered Put Buying

A buyer of a put may or may not own the underlying stock. A put buyer who does not own the stock is said to be uncovered whereas one who owns the stock is said to be covered.

1. Uncovered put buying: When the stock is not owned, buying a naked put is the economic equivalent of shorting stock and buying a call, although the leverage is different with the two strategies. The maximum loss for the uncovered buyer is the premium paid. The gain on the position will move point for point with a stock that is falling in price below the exercise price.

2. Covered put buying: In the case where the stock is owned, the buyer of a put is taking out insurance against long position. The investor who buys a put against long stock is in the same economic position as the buyer of a call option. Put buying locks in a sale price but allows unlimited opportunity for gain (less the cost of the put). Purchasing the put permits the investor to ride through a short-term price decline in anticipation of long-term price appreciation.

Put options are bought for a significant number of uses and with varying techniques. The two principal categories of put buying applications are:

1. Long put
2. Long put, long stock

## Uses of Long Put Buying

Simply stated, "long put" is uncovered put buying. A put buyer agrees to pay the put seller a certain amount of money, called the premium, in exchange for the right to sell him (put to him) 100 shares of a specified stock at a specified price at any point over a specified period. Buying puts has the advantage of providing leverage at a limited risk.

Buying puts can provide leverage, a means of investing small amounts of capital with the possibility of high return. Should the price of the underlying stock on which you had bought a put decline over the life of the contract, the option will become more valuable and the premium will increase. It may then be possible for you to sell the option you have bought to another investor at a higher premium than you paid for it.

A put can double or triple in value in a matter of days with only a relatively small percentage decline in the price of the underlying stock.

On the other hand, you can lose the entire premium you pay for the put. However, loss is limited to the cost of your put, and you know the amount of that risk in advance.

*Example:* Assume XYZ stock was selling at 60 when you bought a January 60 put for 5. The following table shows profit and loss results with the stock, at expiration, trading at different price levels:

| Stock Price At Expiration | Put Value At Expiration | Cost of Put | Put Profit or Loss |
|---|---|---|---|
| 45 | 15 | 5 | 10 |
| 50 | 10 | 5 | 5 |
| 55 | 5 | 5 | 0 |
| 60 | 0 | 5 | −5 |
| 65 | 0 | 5 | −5 |
| 70 | 0 | 5 | −5 |

If the underlying stock were to move downward from 60 to 50, the put would have a value of 10, which, less the cost of the put (5), would produce a profit of 5 (disregarding commissions). If the stock should fall to 45, the put value would rise to 15, which, less the cost of the put, would result in a profit of 10.

On the other hand, a loss normally would occur if the stock should advance. The loss, however, would be limited to the cost of the put, regardless of how far the stock might go against you.

## Uses of Long Put, Long Stock Buying

The other principal purpose of put purchase is to protect an existing stock position. Buying a put provides a vehicle with which you can let profits run, while giving you at the same time some protection against possible near-term fluctuations in the marketplace.

Now, what happens if you are wrong and the stock goes up rather than down? The premium you pay, of course, is a loss. However, the put still serves its purpose by protecting you against potential major losses without unduly limiting further possible appreciation in your stock position.

### What

A long put is an outright put purchase without any hedge or cover.

### Why

A long put is used (1) for outright speculation, (2) as a short-sale alternative, and (3) for protection.

### How

The put buyer should have an opinion not only about the *direction* and *extent* of stock market movement, but also about the *timing* of the movement.

While an out-of-the-money put costs less, its chance of becoming profitable is also relatively less. On the other hand, an in-the-money put costs more, but it has a better chance to attain profitability.

The simplest use of a put purchase is for speculative purposes. The buyer hopes for a decline in the price of the underlying security in order for his put to become more valuable. More specifically, put buying should be considered by an investor seeking a highly leveraged, limited risk short position in a stock he believes will decline.

*Example:* Buy XYZ October 50 at 5 when XYZ is 50.

| XYZ Price at Expiration | Put Price at Expiration | Put Option Profit or Loss |
|---|---|---|
| 30 | 20 | +$1,500 |
| 40 | 10 | +   500 |
| 45 | 5 |  |
| 50 | 0 | −   500 |
| 55 | 0 | −   500 |
| 60 | 0 | −   500 |

# long put

# 17

Since XYZ is at the strike price of 50, the price of $5 paid for XYZ Oct 50 is for the time premium.

Assuming that XYZ declines to 50 on the October expiration date, the put holder has the right to sell XYZ at 50, or 10 points above the market price. The put is said to have an intrinsic value of 10 ($50 strike price − $40 market price). As the put cost 5, the profit to the put buyer is 5 (10 − 5) which means a profit of $500 ($5 × 100 shares per contract).

If XYZ is at 45 when the put expires, the put has an intrinsic value of 5 ($50 − $45). That means the put buyer breaks even since the put cost 5.

On the other hand, the put has no intrinsic value if XYZ is 50 or more on expiration date. Thus, any close above 50 for the underlying stock means a loss for the put buyer.

To recapitulate:

1. If the stock price rises: If the stock rises above the strike price, the put will have no value to its holder (buyer). His maximum loss will be limited to the premium paid for the option. He may be able to reduce the loss by liquidating the put in the secondary market prior to expiration.
2. If the stock price drops: If the stock declines below the strike price, the put holder may either (1) sell the put in the secondary market, or (2) exercise the put by buying stock at the current market price and delivering it against payment of the higher exercise price.

# SHORT-SALE ALTERNATIVE

Another simple put application is as an alternative to a short sale. When an aggressive investor expects a stock to drop, he has a choice between shorting the stock and buying a put. Selling short and buying puts are two different means of achieving essentially the same objective. However, put buying has the major advantage over short sale of being a limited-risk way to use leverage.

## Leverage

The put purchase provides leverage for an investor seeking to benefit from a decline in a

stock price. He can do so with an investment equal to only a fraction of the cost required for shorting the stock itself. Moreover, the short seller has to deposit a sizable percentage (currently 50 percent) of the value of the underlying stock shorted to satisfy the margin requirement. To short 100 shares of XYZ at $50, an investor must deposit the 50-percent margin requirement of $2,500. For the put buyer, the $500 option purchase price constitutes his entire cash layout.

Using the above prices for XYZ and its option in the preceding example, Table 17.1 compares a short sale to put buying in terms of dollar and percentage profits and losses.

### TABLE 17.1 COMPARISON OF SHORT-SALE AND PUT-BUYING PROFITS AND LOSSES

| XYZ Price at Expiration | Short Sale | Put Purchase |
|---|---|---|
| 30 | +$2,000 (+ 80%) | +$1,500 (+ 30%) |
| 40 | + 1,000 (+ 40%) | + 500 (+100%) |
| 50 | 0 | − 500 (−100%) |
| 60 | − 1,000 (− 40%) | − 500 (−100%) |
| 100 | − 5,000 (−200%) | − 500 (−100%) |

**Example:** Let's compare a short sale to put buying based on actual stock and put prices. On June 15, 1977 with Avon (AVP) selling at 50¾ a share, Investor A bought an October 50 put for $250. On the same day Investor B sold 100 shares of AVP short at 50¾.

Assume that on September 15, 1977, AVP had declined 10 points, from 50¾ to 40¾, and Investor B could cover his short position at 40¾ (then market price) for a 10-point profit. Meanwhile, Investor A's October 50 put probably would be trading at 11.

Let's compare the relative position of the short seller and the put buyer as follows:

| | Investor B Short Sale | Investor A Put Buying |
|---|---|---|
| 6/15/77 | $5,075.00 | $ 250.00 |
| 9/15/77 | $4,075.00 | $1,100.00 |
| Profit (before transaction costs) | $1,000.00 | $ 850.00 |
| Initial Investment | $2,537.50 (50% margin) | $ 250.00 (put premium) |
| Return on Initial Investment | 39.4% | 340% |
| Leverage | 1 | 8.6 |

The leverage is 8.6 to 1 in favor of the put buyer (340% return versus the short seller's 39.4%).

Had, of course, AVP not declined, or declined less than anticipated, the put buyer could have lost part or even all of the investment.

The following examples show how a put buyer who anticipates a decline in the price of the underlying stock earns a greater percentage return (leverage) on invested funds than if he sold the stock short.

*Example:* On June 17, 1977, General Motors was 69⅛ when an investor bought a GM January 70 put at 5. If, by September 15, 1977, GM had declined about 10 percent to 62, GM Jan 70 would probably be selling around 9, indicating a 4-point profit on the $500 paid for the put.

On the other hand, had GM been sold short at 69⅛, the gain to the short seller would have been $712.50 ($6,912.50 − $6,200) on an investment of $3,456.25 (margin deposit) over the same time period.

The comparison is as follows:

| | Short Sale 100 GM | Jan 70 Put Purchase 1 GM |
|---|---|---|
| 6/17/77 | $6,912.50 | $500.00 |
| 9/15/77 | $6,200.00 | $900.00 |
| Profit (before transaction costs) | $ 712.50 | $400.00 |
| Initial Investment | $3,456.25 (50% margin deposit) | $500.00 (put premium) |
| Return on Initial Investment | 20.6% | 80.0% |
| Leverage | 1 | 3.9 |

Thus, the leverage would be almost 4 to 1 in favor of the put buyer (80% versus the short seller 20.6%).

*Example:* On July 15, 1977, Eastman Kodak (EK) and its January 60 put closed, respectively, at 58⅜ and 4⅝. Assume that an EK October 70 put was bought for $462.50 (4⅝ per share) by one investor while 100 shares of EK were sold short by another investor. About five months later, on December 8, 1977, EK declined to 49¾, while EK January 60 put rose to 10⅛:

| | Short sale 100 EK shares | Put Purchase 1 EK Oct 70 put |
|---|---|---|
| 7/15/77 | $5,837.50 | $ 462.50 |
| 12/8/77 | $4,975.00 | $1,012.50 |
| Gross Profit | $ 862.50 | $ 550.00 |
| Initial Investment | $2,918.75 (50% margin) | $ 462.50 (put premium) |
| Return on Investment | 29.6% | 118.9% |
| Leverage | 1 | 4 |

The "depreciation factor" is designed to calculate by what amount the stock must decline for the percentage gain on the put at expiration to equal the gain on the shorted stock.

We use the following formula for such a calculation:

$$df = \frac{2m - 2}{m - p} - 1$$

where

$df$ = depreciation factor
$m$ = market price of stock
$s$ = put strike price
$p$ = put price

*Example:* On June 21, 1977, Honeywell (HON) was selling at 54 and its February 50 put was trading at 1⅞. Applying the formula, we have:

$m = 54$
$s = 50$
$p = 1.875$

$$df = \frac{2(54) - 50}{54 - 1.875} - 1$$

$$= \frac{58}{52.125} - 1 = 1.1127 - 1 = 0.1127$$

The stock would have to decline 11.27 percent for a put purchase to offer the same percentage gain as shorting the stock.

A decline of 11.27 percent would cause the stock to fall to 47.914 (54 − 11.27% of 54). At that price, the 50 put is worth 2.086 (50 − 47.914) or a gain of 0.211 (2.086 − 1.875) over its 1.875 cost. This, indeed, is an 11.3 percent gain, thereby verifying the formula and providing a quick answer to the short sale versus purchase of a put decision for capital gains.

### Limited Risk

Put buying has another advantage over short sale: Whereas short sale has no limit to its risk on a price surge in the underlying stock, a put purchase has limited risk on the upside.

### No Margin Call

Unlike the short seller, who is subject to margin calls if the underlying security should rise, the put buyer is free from margin calls.

### Salvage Value

A put buyer can lose his entire investment if the price of the stock stagnates or rises during the option's life. However, he may be able to recoup some of his investment by selling the put in the secondary market for whatever time value it has.

The same secondary market provides an outlet for a successful long put to be sold at a profit, or exercised, with the holder buying the stock at the lower market price and selling it at the higher strike price.

There is, of course, no such outlet for short sellers in the form of a secondary market.

### Flexibility in Timing

A short seller may be basically correct in his assessment about a particular stock. However, the stock can go up before it goes down, at which point the short seller may be intimidated into covering the short at a loss.

Since the risk to a put buyer, on the other hand, is limited to the cost of the put, exact timing is not so critical a factor.

Related to the timing factor, a stop-loss order is designed for the primary purpose of protecting a major portion of unrealized profits. However, while the stock may go down to a price level that would activate a stop order, the stock may then turn around and rise to new highs. Put buying provides a means of avoiding this latter possibility and insulating the stock from short-term breaks.

### No Cash Dividend Liability

When a cash dividend is paid on the underlying stock, the short seller incurs a liability for that dividend. However, listed options are not adjusted to reflect ordinary cash dividends.

Does a short seller have any advantage at all over a put buyer? Only one: if the underlying stock stands still, time works against the put buyer, but not necessarily against the short seller.

# PROTECTION

### Shielding Profit

One use of puts is to achieve protection against an anticipated decline in the price of a stock you own and may not wish to sell for any number of reasons. For instance, you may not want to sell a stock you acquired at a price level considerably below its current market value; you are understandably reluctant to realize the large taxable gain that sale of the stock would produce.

One way to resolve this problem is to lock in most of the profit already made by buying a put whose strike price is near the then market value of the underlying security. Should a significant decline ensue, you have the right to sell the shares at the strike price, and thus protect your profit.

### How the Protection Works

By buying a put on such stock any decline in its value should be largely offset by an increase in the value of the option. If the stock price increases, you will benefit from the increase.

*Example:* Assume that on July 15, 1977, you had a substantial paper profit in Santa Fe International (SAF), which was selling at 53½. You were reluctant to sell the stock even though you expected a possible decline in stock prices over the next several months. For protection, you bought an SAF October 55 put at 3¼.

In three months, as of September 14, 1977, SAF had dropped to 44, for a loss of 9½ on the stock. Meanwhile, however, as the stock declined in price, the put rose in value, possibly to the 10⅞ level. The 7⅜-point (10⅞ − 3¼) gain in the put served to offset somewhat the decline in the market value of the stock.

In the event that the anticipated stock price decline doesn't materialize, you lose only the price paid, as insurance, for the put. In the SAF illustration, had the stock not gone down, you would have lost on the put. However, the relatively low cost of a put (3¼) would have been a smaller loss than the indicated 9½-point loss on the stock.

Indeed a stock may rise instead of taking an anticipated downturn. In that eventuality, buying a put serves to retain for the investor the opportunity to benefit from the increase in the price of the stock.

***Example:*** Assume that on June 10, 1977, you owned Revlon (RLM) at 38½ but were reluctant to sell the stock despite your bearish views on the near or intermediate term. You could have bought a September 40 put at 3⅜ for protection.

As of September 14, 1977, RLM, instead of declining, had risen 4¾ to 43¼ from 38½ while its September 40 put dropped 3⁵⁄₁₆ (from 3⅜ to ¹⁄₁₆). On balance, you would have been better off because the 3⁵⁄₁₆-point loss on the put would be more than offset by the 4¾-point gain on the stock.

### Protection for Volatile Stocks

Puts provide a particularly protective useful investment tool in connection with speculative purchase of volatile stocks because such stocks are especially vulnerable to downside correction.

To recapitulate, the use of put options limits risk while reducing a profit oppportunity by only the cost of the put. Of course, expecting a certain stock to go down, an investor could sell the stocks in anticipation of being able to repurchase them later at a lower price. The alternate course of buying puts as an insurance is advantageous, because it involves less guesswork and less need to be precisely right in timing. This gives the investor downside price protection as well as the retention of ownership of the stock and thus the opportunity to profit from subsequent appreciation in the price of the stock.

## WHAT PUTS TO BUY, AND WHEN

The put buyer must make the same decisions as a call buyer regarding which put to purchase. Since, as a call, a put is an asset with a limited life, the put buyer should have an opinion not only about the *direction* and *extent* of stock price movement, but also about the *timing* of that movement. Timing should be a determining factor of whether to purchase a put in the less expensive, near expiration month, or in a more expensive, distant expiration month.

Also to be considered is whether to buy a put in-, out-of-, or at-the-money. This initial cost is larger for in-the-money puts because they have intrinsic value. Out-of-the-money puts cost less because they have no value other than the time value.

### Absolute versus Relative Risks

A put buyer can never lose more than the initial cost of buying the put, regardless of how adversely the price of the underlying security may go against him.

The next example helps to clarify the risk ramifications of in-the-money and out-of-the-money puts.

***Example:*** On June 17, 1977, Honeywell (HON) was selling at 53 and its January 45, January 50 and January 60 puts were selling at ¾, 2 and 8⅝, respectively:

| | |
|---|---|
| Jan 45 | ¾ |
| Jan 50 | 2 |
| Jan 60 | 8⅝ |

With HON at 53, in-the-money HON January 60 had an intrinsic value of 7 points and a time value of 1⅝ (8⅝ − 7). The stock had to move up at least 7 points by expiration date for this option to expire worthless. On the other hand, for an at-the-money or out-of-the-money put to expire worthless, it is only necessary for the underlying security to remain unchanged until expiration date.

On the minus side, absolute risk is larger with in-the-money puts than with at- or out-of-the-money puts because changes in the premium of an in-the-money put are closely correlated with movement in the price of the underlying security. In actuality, the whole amount would not be lost unless the stock were to move up to the strike price of the put or higher.

### Out-of-the-money Puts

While the actual amount of money at risk with the purchase of an out-of-the-money put is relatively small, the risk of total loss is relatively large. This is because the likelihood of sufficient stock movement to make such an option profitable is relatively slim.

Since all of the value of an out-of-the-money option consists of time value, there is relatively little correlation between a move in the price of the underlying security and a change in the price of the option.

### Above or Below Strike Price at Expiration

What happens to a put buyer if the price of the underlying stock on expiration date is (1) below the strike price, or (2) above the strike price?

If the stock were to decline well below the strike price of the put option, the put holder could make a profit. He could buy stock in the open market and then exercise his put to *sell* that stock for a profit at the strike price, which is higher.

On the other hand, if the stock were above the strike price of the put option at expiration, the put would expire worthless. No one would exercise a put option to *sell* stock at the strike price, which is lower than the market price.

# TO SELL OR TO EXERCISE?

The holder of a profitable put can either (1) sell it in the secondary market or (2) buy the underlying security and exercise the put.

Generally, if an in-the-money put is selling for more than its intrinsic value, the put holder will realize more profit by selling his option than by exercising it. The put holder can exercise his option any time during the put's life by simply buying the stock at the lower current market price and selling it at the higher strike price.

The following examples compare these two approaches. The scenario is this: On June 17, 1977, Honeywell (HON) and HON November 60 put were selling, respectively, at 52⅞ and 8. If, On September 15, 1977, HON had dropped 10 percent to 47¾, HON November 60 put might well have been selling around 15.

*Example 1—Exercising the Put:* A stock purchase combined with the exercise of the put would have the following result:

| Cost | | |
|---|---|---|
| Put premium | $ 800.00 | |
| Put commission | 25.00 | |
| Stock purchase | 4,775.00 | |
| Stock commission | 80.00 | |
| Total cost | | $5,680.00 |

| Proceeds | | |
|---|---|---|
| Stock sale | $6,000.00 | |
| Commission | 100.00 | |
| | | $5,900.00 |

| Totals | |
|---|---|
| Proceeds | $5,900.00 |
| Cost | 5,680.00 |
| Net profit | $ 220.00 |

*Example—Selling the Put:* The sale of the put in the secondary market would have resulted in the following:

| Cost | | |
|---|---|---|
| 6/14/77 Put bought | $ 800.00 | |
| commission | +25.00 | |
| Total cost | | $ 825.00 |

| Proceeds | | |
|---|---|---|
| 9/15/77 Put sold | $1,500.00 | |
| commission | −50.00 | |
| | | $1,450.00 |

| Totals | |
|---|---|
| Proceeds | $1,450.00 |
| Cost | 825.00 |
| Net profit | $ 625.00 |

In the preceding example, the profit of $625 realized from the resale of the put on the secondary market is approximately three times the amount ($220) realized from the exercise of the put. There are two reasons for the larger realized profit from the resale of the put: (1) Whatever time value remaining in the option is lost to the put holder when the option is exercised; and (2) option exercising costs much more in commissions than option resale in the secondary market.

Other factors affecting the decision to sell or exercise include transaction costs, margin requirements, and tax considerations.

### Another Alternative

If a put holder remains bearish on the underlying stock, another alternative is to "borrow" shares to deliver against his sales at the exercise price. In this manner, he creates a short position in the underlying stock (which must be appropriately margined) that he hopes to cover profitably by repurchasing the shares at lower prices in the future.

# PUT BUYING AS A TRADING VEHICLE

### Locking in a Short-Sale Profit

After a substantial decline in the underlying security in which an investor has a short-sale profit, he may have difficulty deciding whether to cover the short or maintain the position.

Buying puts provides a means to lock in this profit at a relatively small cost.

*Example:* On June 8, 1977, Eastman Kodak (EK) was selling at 60. Assume that an investor who had shorted EK at 75 earlier might decide to take his 15-point profit even if he felt EK might continue to fall.

One possible put strategy would have been to cover the short and use part of the profits to buy an EK October 60 put for 3⅞. This put strategy would have enabled the short seller to take his profit and still participate in any further decline in the underlying stock, while his risk would have been limited to the cost of the put (3⅞) plus transaction costs.

### Averaging Down on a Short Position

The short seller in the preceding illustration might have decided to add to his short position, instead of taking a 15-point profit.

One possible put strategy would have been to buy EK October 60 at 3⅞, thus doubling his short position with an additional risk of only 3⅞ plus transaction costs.

### Trading for Down Fluctuations

Under the protective umbrella of a put option, one can play the down fluctuations of the underlying stock. This trading technique involves making a number of short-term transactions through buying the stock on dips and then selling the stock out on rallies. There is no limitation to the number of trades that can be made against a particular put during the life of the option.

### Using Puts to Diversify

A bearish investor may use puts as a diversification vehicle. Diversification can be achieved by using some of the funds earmarked for short stock to buy puts instead. Generally, the cost of shorting a certain number of shares is enough to cover many times that number through the use of puts.

In addition to greater diversification with the same amount of funds, such an approach also has several other important advantages: expanded downside leverage; risk limited to the money paid for the puts; and no margin calls if the underlying stock advances.

# ALTERNATIVE RISK-MINIMIZING VEHICLES

Before buying puts, the investor must carefully weigh the cost and attributes of put options against alternative risk-minimizing vehicles. Why, for example, should an investor buy a put when a stop-loss order can provide similar downside protection without cost?

To begin with, let's see how a stop-loss order works. When an investor enters a stop-loss order, he instructs his broker to sell his long position at the market or at a limit—as soon as the stock reaches a predetermined price.

## Disadvantages

Compared to a long put position, a stop-loss order has certain disadvantages:

1. No flexibility: The put holder has more flexibility, since the put gives the holder the option to exercise, liquidate, or allow the put to expire, regardless of the underlying stock's fluctuations during the put's life.

   On the other hand, after a stop-loss order has been entered, it becomes a market order when the price of the underlying stock reaches the stop price. However, the investor has no assurance that the stock will be sold at that exact price. In a sharply declining market, it is possible that the broker will be unable to execute the sell order until the stock has dropped substantially below the specified price. In contrast, the put holder is entitled to receive the contracted price for his stock upon exercise.

2. Untimely "stopped" out: When the price of the stock falls to a predetermined level, your broker must "stop" you out. It often happens, however, that the stock's fall may be only temporary and the stock subsequently goes back up. The investor thus misses out on a large gain if the stock goes down to the stop-loss point and then rebounds to a much higher price. In contrast, the put holder can afford to ride out a temporary storm because he can't lose more than the cost of the put.

3. Trading halt in stock: Execution of a stop-loss order may not be possible during such a market dislocation as a trading halt in the stock.

## Advantages

A stop-loss order has several definite advantages over a long put. First, the former costs no money. Second, it has no fixed expiration date and can be maintained indefinitely, or "good 'til cancelled." Third, it can be used on an odd lot (less than 100 shares) while listed puts generally cover 100-share units.

## Sell-Stop versus Put Purchase

Let's examine another version of the stop-loss order for protection of profit. Assume you have a paper profit of $1,500 in a stock after it had risen from 30 to 45. Further, assume you are concerned about possible erosion of this paper profit. What would you do? You could sell the stock; however, you may be reluctant to do so, either for tax reasons or because you expect the stock may have the potential for further gains.

One alternative is to place a sell-stop order, 5 to 10 percent below the market. This sell-stop order would accomplish the primary purpose of protecting a major portion of the profit. However, while the stock might go down to a price level that would activate a stop order, the stock might then turn around and rise to new highs.

Another alternative would be for you to buy a put; that would provide the best means of avoiding the latter possibility and insulating the stock from short-term breaks.

## OVERVIEW

### What

"Long put, long stock" means simultaneous ownership of both a put and its underlying stock.

### Why

This option strategy is designed primarily for investors who want to limit the downside risk in a stock position during the life of the put.

### How

Under the cover of a protective umbrella (put), an investor may pursue the long-term growth possibilities in a stock position. Any increase in the price of the stock over and above the price paid for the put will result in a net gain.

### Buy a Put, Buy Stock

When an investor simultaneously owns both common stock and a put on the same stock, he is protected against a possible substantial decline in the market value of that stock.

This long-stock, long-put strategy is designed primarily for an investor seeking to limit the downside risk of his long stock position during the life of the put.

For this downside protection, the investor pays the put premium. Any increase in the price of the stock in excess of the price paid for the put will result in a net gain for the investor.

### Instrument for Long-Term Investment Strategies

While options are usually considered short-term investment vehicles, put-buying, like call-writing, may actually allow an investor to pursue long-term investment strategies and to reduce his vulnerability to steep market corrections. For example, by buying puts, investors may maintain an existing position in long-term growth stocks in a depressed market, without being pressed into decisions regarding the disposal of such stocks.

*Example:* Assume that you had bought Mesa Petroleum (MSA) at 29⅜ on October 25, 1976. On August 29, 1977, MSA closed at 42⅜. If you had become concerned about possible erosion of this paper

# long put, long stock

# 18

profit in an uncertain market, one means of defense would have been to buy a January (5-month) 45 put at 4⅜.

If your concern had proved groundless and the stock continued its upward course, you would simply have allowed the put option to expire. Your loss would have been limited to 4⅜, the cost of the premium, and transaction costs.

On the other hand, if the stock had dropped, say to 30, you could have exercised your put option and sold the stock at 45. Instead of having your paper profit completely wiped out, you would keep the bulk of that profit, namely 15⅜ minus 4⅜, paid for the put premium.

# COMPLETE HEDGE

While covered call-writing offers a partial hedge against market decline, put buying provides the *only* method available in the option market whereby an investor can *completely hedge* a long stock position, assuming that the strike price of the put option is the same as the purchase price of the stock. This put hedge provides investors complete protection against loss, regardless of how much the stock might decline.

This put strategy can be used for either of the following:

1. To protect profits in a long stock position already established
2. To hedge new long purchases.

In the first category, an investor is seeking protection for a long position in a stock that he is not considering selling. In the second category, a stock buyer seeks insurance against possible mistakes.

## *Protecting Existing Positions: Safeguarding Unrealized Profits*

Put options can, in two situations, protect unrealized profits in existing positions. First, they can protect long-term capital gains in a stock you wish to hold indefinitely. Second, with a put, you can freeze a capital gain or loss in a stock in the current year and defer the tax consequences to the succeeding year.

If you are correct in your assessment of the underlying security, most of the long-term profits may be retained with the protection of a put. On the other hand, your loss is limited to the cost of the put. Even that loss may be reduced by liquidation of the put in the secondary market while it still had some remaining time value, and by the possibility of offsetting gains in the underlying stock itself.

The following are illustrations of buying puts to protect an unrealized profit in a long position already held. The circumstances are that in mid-1976 an investor bought 100 shares of Pennzoil (PZL) at 24⅞. On January 19, 1977, PZL and its July 35 put closed at 34⅞ and 2½ respectively. He had a 10-point profit in his long position.

While the investor believed that the long-term prospects for the stock were favorable, he wanted to protect his unrealized profit against a possible short-term decline by buying a July 35 put at $250 ($2.50 per share).

***Example:*** **PZL Rises 10 Points:** Say PZL rose to 45 by the end of 1977. The investor fully participated in the advance of his long position. The value of his put, however, declined as the stock advanced. In this event, he could have allowed the put to expire unexercised. Or he could have tried to recapture some of the option premium he paid by liquidating the put in the secondary market. The profit in his long position could not have been reduced by more than the $250 paid for the option (disregarding transaction costs). The relevant data are tabulated as follows:

|  | Stock plus Put | Stock Only |
| --- | --- | --- |
| **Stock Bought Mid-1976** | $2,488 ($1,244 margin) | $2,488 ($1,244 margin) |
| **Stock on 1/19/77** | $3,488 | $3,488 |
| **Put Bought 1/19/77** | $ 250 | |
| **Stock at 1977 Year-end** | $4,500 | $4,500 |
| **Put at 1977 Year-end** | 0 | |
| **Profit** | $1,762 | $2,012 |
| **Profit on Investment** | 141.6% | 161.7% |

***Example:*** **PZL Declines 10 Points:** If the stock were to decline to 25, the investor could have exercised his put by delivering his long stock against payment of the strike price ($35).

In this case his profit would have been the $1,000 attributable to the long position, minus the $250 option premium, amounting to $750 (disregarding transaction costs).

No matter how much the stock might have declined during the life of the put, the investor could have exercised the put and delivered his long stock for $35 per share. He thus effectively locked in a minimum $1,400 profit (disregarding transaction costs).

Following is another illustration for practice purposes. Suppose that on June 3, 1977, Honeywell (HON) was selling at 50¼ and a HON October 50 put was available at 2⅞. If an investor had bought HON earlier at 44 and desired to protect his profits in the long stock position, he could have bought an October 50 put at 2⅞.

Let's see what would have happened if the underlying stock were to have either (1) risen 10 points or (2) declined 10 points.

*Example:* HON Rises 10 Points: Assume HON subsequently rises to 60¼. The put expires and the stock is sold:

| Transaction | Long Stock | Put |
| --- | --- | --- |
| Stock bought (50% margin required) | $2,200 | |
| 6/3/77—Put bought (100% put purchase price required) | | $287.50 |
| 10/21/77—Put expires, stock sold | $6,025 | |
| Profit or loss | $3,825 | −$287.50 |

*Example:* HON Declines 10 Points: Assume HON declines to 40¼, and the put is exercised:

| Transaction | Long Stock | Put |
| --- | --- | --- |
| Stock bought (50% margin required) | $2,200 | |
| 6/3/77—put bought (100% put purchase price required) | | $287.50 |
| 10/21/77—Put exercised | $3,300 | |
| Profit or Loss | $1,000 | −$287.50 |

## Protecting New Purchases: Establishing the Minimum Liquidating Price

When an investor buys stock for appreciation purposes, he can buy puts to limit his risk in that long stock position. This long-stock, long-put strategy establishes a minimum price for the investor upon liquidating his stock regardless of how severely the underlying stock may decline during the put's life.

The maximum loss in this strategy is limited to the cost of the put, less the amount realized, if any, from a closing sale of the put. Profits result if the cost of the put is exceeded by the stock appreciation.

*Example:* On July 15, 1977, ABC Broadcasting (ABC) and its February 45 put had the following price data:

| Strike Price | Put Price | Stock Price |
| --- | --- | --- |
| 45 | 2½ | 45⅞ |

Approximately five months later, on December 8, 1977, ABC had declined 6⅛ (from 45⅞ to 39¾) while its February 45 put had risen 3⅞ (from 2½ to 6⅜).

If you were to go long the stock alone, you would have suffered a 6⅛-point loss.

However, if you had combined a long stock position with a long put, you would have offset the 6⅛-point loss in the stock with a 3⅞-point gain in the put, with an overall loss of only 2¼. To put it in even better perspective, the long put would have eliminated 63.3 percent of the stock loss, leaving only 36.7 percent of the loss unprotected.

# LONG PUT, LONG STOCK VERSUS LONG PUT, LONG CALL

Following is a comparison between long put plus long stock on the one hand, and long put plus long call on the other. The background is that on June 10, 1977, Honeywell (HON) and its August 50 put and August 45 call had the following price data:

| Strike Price | Call Price | Put Price | Stock Price |
|---|---|---|---|
| 45 | 6⅞ | | 51⅜ |
| 50 | | 1⅜ | 51⅜ |

## Long Put, Long Stock

| | |
|---|---|
| Buy 100 shares HON at 51⅜ | $5,138 |
| Buy 1 HON August 50 put at 1 | + 138 |
| Total cost | $5,276 |

This strategy permits retaining unlimited upside potential in the stock position, minus the relatively low cost of the put bought for protecting the stock position. On the downside, this strategy acts to limit possible setbacks in the stock price, while keeping its upside potential in the stock reduced only by the cost of the put.

## Long Put, Long Call

| | |
|---|---|
| Buy 1 HON August 45 call at 6⅞ | $688 |
| Buy 1 HON August 50 put at 1⅜ | +138 |
| Total cost | $826 |

Note that the deep-in-the-money August 45 call is substituted for the long stock. Also note that the long-call, long-put combination costs only a fraction of what a combined long-put, long-stock position would cost.

This relatively low-cost strategy is designed for aggressive investors bullish on HON and seeking upside leverage.

For the investor to break even, the underlying stock has to reach 53¼:

| | |
|---|---|
| HON call strike price | 45 |
| Cost of HON 45 call | +6⅞ |
| Cost of HON 50 put | +1⅜ |
| Upside breakeven point | 53¼ |

The cost of downside protection for this long-put, long-call combination is:

| | |
|---|---|
| Upside breakeven point | 53¼ |
| Put strike price | −50 |
| Cost of downside protection | 3¼ |

# PUT SELLING

# PART VII

## OVERVIEW

### What

Writing a put consists of selling a put option on an underlying stock that the writer expects to rise in price or remain stable.

### Why

Income from premium dollars or the ultimate acquisition of stock at a price below the current market price are the objectives.

### How

The investor enters an order to sell a put option on a stock that he expects to rise or at least remain stable. This strategy is best suited to stocks that are not volatile.

When one sells (writes) a put, he is selling to another the right to sell a stock at the exercise price within a specified period of time. The seller (writer) must stand ready to buy the stock at the exercise or strike price any time during the option's life. Unlike the call writer, who must deliver stock and receive payment, the put writer delivers cash to pay for the stock purchase. For selling this right, he receives a premium.

Put option writers accept market risks on the downside. They take the risk that the stock may go down more than the value of the premium received during the option's life.

On November 8, 1977, Avon (AVP) closed at 45 when its July 45 put was available at 3. If on that day you sold an AVP April 45 put and collected $3 per share (or $300 on a 100-share put contract) in premium money, you were a seller (writer) of an AVP Apr 45 put at 3.

One possible motive for that transaction was your expectation that AVP would probably remain stable or rise in price during the life of the put contract. If the stock had risen, you could have realized a gain by closing out your position in the secondary market. If the stock had remained above the strike price, the put would have expired, and the premium money would have been yours without further obligation.

put selling basics

19

# THE PUT SELLER'S OBLIGATIONS

The put writer remains obligated until the option is liquidated, either through exercise, expiration, or a closing purchase transaction.

## The Exercise Notice

If a put-covered stock falls below the exercise price, the writer may be assigned an exercise notice. In that event, he is required to buy the stock at the exercise price, which would be higher than the then market price.

While the put holder (buyer) normally will exercise only if the market price of the stock is below the exercise price, the put seller should be prepared to buy the underlying stock at any time during the option's life. After the stock has been "put" to the writer through exercise, the writer can immediately liquidate the stock and realize the loss or hold the stock for possible future recovery.

## Closing Purchase Transaction

The put writer need not remain obligated to buy the underlying stock throughout the option's life. He may cancel his obligation through a closing purchase transaction.

In a closing transaction, the option writer cancels his obligation by buying a put identical to the one previously sold. He will realize a profit if the cost of the put is less than the price at which he originally sold it. He will incur a loss if the cost of the put is greater than the price received.

# COVERED VERSUS UNCOVERED PUT WRITING

The popular notion is that selling puts is speculative and, consequently, inappropriate for conservative investors. Actually, the word "conservative" carries different meanings for different individuals with varying investment motivations and objectives. Whether a certain option strategy is conservative or not depends on the individual investor's assessment of its relative risk and potential reward.

## Short Put versus Short Put, Short Stock

There are two types of put selling (writing): covered and uncovered. An uncovered seller takes a simple short-put position while a covered seller combines a short-put position with a short-stock position.

The seller of an uncovered put is at risk if the price of the underlying stock declines, since he must, upon exercise, purchase the underlying stock at the exercise price, which will be above the current market price.

Even a covered put seller is substantially at risk. The term "covered" put writing is a sort of misnomer, because a covered put writer is only partially covered, as his short position in the underlying stock is not completely hedged. If the stock price rises substantially, the writer may be forced to cover his short position by buying in the stock at a price much higher than the price at which he made his short sale.

## Uncovered Put Selling

Strange as it may seem, selling an uncovered (naked) put places the seller in precisely the same economic position as a conservative covered call writer. However, the leverage is different with these two strategies.

Assuming that the premiums for both a put and a call with the same exercise price and expiration dates are identical, the maximum downside risk is the same for both the covered call writer who holds the underlying stock and the uncovered put writer who does not hold the stock.

The maximum risk for a call writer who buys a stock at 40 and receives a premium of 4 is 36 (40 − 4 excluding commissions). The maximum exposure for an uncovered put writer who writes a put at 40 is likewise 36: the 40 he agrees to buy the stock for if exercised, minus 4 he receives for writing the put.

Let's use an illustration to compare a naked put writer to a covered call writer.

*Example:* Assume XYZ is selling at 70, and its January 70 call and January 70 put are both trading at 4 ($400).

Investor A buys 100 shares of XYZ at 70, and writes a January 70 call at 4 ($400). If XYZ stands still, or rises only moderately, he will earn $400; if it falls, he will lose the amount of the decline, less $400.

Investor B sells a *naked* January 70 put at 4 ($400). If the stock stands still or rises, he will make $400. If the stock falls, he will lose the amount of that decline, less $400.

The following also illustrate how uncovered put writing has essentially the same economic characteristics as those for covered call writing. The data are these: On November 8, 1977, Avon (AVP) had a July 45 put available at 3 when the stock was 45:

| Strike Price | Put Price | Stock Price |
|---|---|---|
| 45 | 3 | 45 |

Assume on that day you wrote a July 45 put, for which you received $300 (commissions excluded). Now let's see how the passage of time, and changes in the price of the underlying stock might have produced a number of results.

*Example:* *The Stock Declined:* If the stock had declined and the put had been exercised, your account would have been charged $4,500 for the purchase of 100 shares of AVP. However, your actual cost would have been reduced to $4,200:

| | |
|---|---|
| Stock purchase cost ($45 × 100 shares) | $4,500 |
| Put premium received ($3 × 100 shares) | −300 |
| Actual stock cost (before commissions) | $4,200 |

*Example:* *The Stock Rose:* If the stock had risen and the put had expired, you would have pocketed $300 in put premium money without further obligations.

*Example:* *You Closed Out before Expiration:* If, instead of waiting for an exercise by the other party (put holder), you closed out your written position by purchasing a July 45 put (identical to the one previously written), you would make money if the new put were to cost less than the one previously written. You would lose money if the new put were to cost more than the old one.

At the end of the option contract period, the approximate value of the put is the amount the exercise price is above the stock price. In the AVP illustration (with an exercise price of 45 for the put), the put should have been worth 4 if the stock traded at 41 but worthless if the stock traded above the exercise price of 45.

The essential characteristics of uncovered put writing are the same as those of covered call writing. Just as for the covered call writer, the uncovered put writer benefits if the underlying stock rises, although the latter achieves the result without owning the stock. If the stock rises sufficiently for the call holder to exercise the option, the covered call writer sells his shares, whereas the uncovered put writer, with no exercise occurring, does not buy the stock.

In a declining market, the covered call writer usually holds onto his stock, while the uncovered put writer usually acquires the stock. The option money received from writing either the call or the put has the effect of reducing the cost basis in both situations. Both writers are adversely affected if the stock has a significant decline.

## Risk versus Reward Potential

Let's use another illustration to compare, in more detail, an uncovered put writer with a covered call writer in terms of risk versus reward potential. The facts are as follows:

For this illustration we will select a put and a call with *identical* premiums on a stock with the same exercise price and expiration month as follows:

**November 28, 1977, closing prices**

Continental Oil (CLL) 29⅛
CLL July 30 call 2
CLL July 30 put 2

*Example:* *Risk-and-Reward Potential for Covered Call Writer:* Assume you bought 100 shares of CLL at 29⅛ and wrote a July 30 call for $200 ($2 × 100 shares). If CLL stood still or rose slightly, you would earn $200. If CLL declined, you would lose the amount of the decline, less the call option premium ($200) received.

*Example:* *Risk-and-Reward Potential for Uncovered Put Writer:* Assume you wrote a CLL July 30 put for $200 ($2 × 100 shares). If the stock rose or remained unchanged, you would earn $200. If the stock fell, you would lose the amount of the decline, less the put premium ($200) received.

So you see that both the economic risk and potential reward of writing an uncovered put is essentially the same as writing a covered call.

## Differences

What are the differences, then, between uncovered put writing and covered call writing?

1. Psychological factor: One major difference is essentially psychological. Since the covered call writer already owns the stock, he is likely to be continually aware of the diminished value of his ownership if the stock suffers a sharp decline. On the other hand, since the put writer would not own the stock until an exercise took place, it could come as a shock to him, when the exercise happens, to pay $4,500 on a given day for 100 shares of stock worth only $3,500 on the open market.
2. Initial cash outlay: The covered call writer would have an immediate charge in his account due to the purchase of stock. On the other hand, a debit would not be created for the uncovered put writer unless the put were exercised.
3. Cost factors: Cost factors tend to be lower for the uncovered put writer because there may be no stock commissions to pay. In the margin account there would be no interest to pay.
4. Return on capital: The uncovered put writer would also tend to have lower margin requirements to back up the position. This could result in a greater return on the capital utilized.

# HOW TO CHOOSE WHICH PUT TO WRITE

One writes (sells) a put option:

1. To earn income and enhance his return on investment
2. To acquire stock at a cost below its current market value

## Choice of Exercise Price

The choice of exercise price will depend upon an investor's view of the underlying stock. If he is bullish, an investor might choose a put with a high exercise price and a larger premium, in anticipation of a rise in the stock value above the exercise price, in order to earn a greater return. Conversely, an investor might select a put with a lower exercise price so as to lessen the likelihood of exercise, or to acquire the stock at a lower cost in the event the put is exercised.

Let's compare what would happen to the put writer if the price of the underlying stock is below or above the strike price at expiration.

If the price of the stock subsequently declines below the strike price at expiration and the put is exercised, the put writer would be obligated to acquire the stock at the exercise price (higher than the then market price) less the premium received.

The result of this is to lower the effective price of the stock. His cost of acquiring the stock would be the exercise price less the put premium received.

**Example:** *Stock below Strike Price at Expiration:* On March 16, 1977, Xerox (XRX) and its October 50 put closed at 50 and 4½ respectively. Assume that an investor sold a XRX October 50 put for $450 (4½ per share).

Near expiration, had XRX fallen below the strike price of 50, the option would likely have been exercised and the investor would have had to buy 100 shares of XRX at $50 a share (higher than the market price).

If XRX had declined to $47, he would have had to pay $5,000 (plus transaction costs) for stock currently worth $4,700 in the market. His cost of acquiring the stock, however, would have been reduced to 45½ a share, reflecting the $4½ per share premium. Were the stock decline substantial—for example, to $40 a share—the put seller would have been required to buy stock at $50 a share, incurring an unrealized loss (disregarding transaction costs) of $1,550 ($2,000 paper loss in his stock position offset in part by the $450 premium received).

It is apparent that puts should be written only on stocks that option writers would be willing to own.

If, on the other hand, the stock rises, as expected, above the strike price at expiration, and the option expires or is repurchased, the put writer will not acquire the stock. However, he will be compensated by an earned premium.

*Example:* *Stock above Strike Price at Expiration:* If XRX in the preceding example had risen above the strike price of $50 by expiration, the option would probably have expired and the put writer would have earned the $450 premium.

The put writer bases his transaction (writing) on his anticipation that the premium income (less transaction costs) will not be exceeded by the downside risk of the underlying stock.

# PUT WRITING MARGINS

The concept of covered writing is different for puts than it is for calls. The put option writer will generally write against a cash margin. The put must be margined in the same manner as an uncovered call—that is, at 30 percent of the value of the underlying security (1) *plus* the amount that the put is in the money, or (2) *less* the amount the put is out of the money.

## Margin Exceptions

The above margin requirement must be met unless one of the following conditions exists:

1. For margin purposes, a short put is considered to be covered only when the writer has, in his account, a long put on the same underlying security with a strike price equal to or greater than that of the short put.
2. No margin is required of the writer if he has a letter of guarantee from an exchange-approved bank stating that funds in the aggregate amount of the strike price are on deposit at the bank.

*Note:* The Option Clearing Corporation will not accept bank guarantee letters on short stock positions. It is, therefore, up to each individual firm to decide whether it will accept a bank guarantee letter in satisfaction of the firm's margin requirement.

*Warning:* A put option writer holding margin will be subject to additional margin calls in a declining market, and be liable to pay for the stock in the event of exercise.

The importance of this warning cannot be overemphasized. Some investors fail fully to understand put margining and thereby fail to keep an adequate cash reserve behind each put they have written.

# OVERVIEW

### What

Also called "naked" put selling, short put amounts to selling puts against cash.

For selling a put, an investor takes the risk that the stock might go down more than the premium he receives from selling the put.

### Why

An investor sells a put primarily to receive the option money, in the expectation that the put written will expire worthless if the stock is trading above the put's exercise price. One may also write a put in a stock one wishes to buy at a lower price.

### How

In return for having received the option money, the seller remains obligated to buy stock at the exercise price any time during the life of the option, should an exercise take place. He would either earn the premium if the stock goes up, or buy the stock (at below-market price) if the stock goes down.

What is a short put? It is naked or uncovered put writing as opposed to covered put writing. Whereas covered put writing covers a short put (an obligation to buy 100 shares of a specific stock at a specific price) with a short stock, naked put writing is not backed by a short stock but by cash or buying power reserves. Essentially, short put amounts to writing (selling) puts against cash.

### Known versus Unknown Risk

By writing a put and collecting the premium, you become obligated to purchase the stock from a holder of the option if and when he decides to exercise his right to sell the stock. The price you will pay for the stock—if the put is exercised—is the exercise price specified in the option. This price will be higher than the market price.

Unlike the uncovered call writer, whose risk is unknown, an uncovered put writer knows his downside risk. The worst that can happen to him is that he would be required to buy the stock at the strike price. His effective cost of the

# short put

# 20

stock will be the exercise price less the premium received from writing the option.

### Financial Preparedness

Since the possibility of being put is always present, the put writer is strongly advised to have enough reserve cash to pay for the delivery of the stock should the put option be exercised.

Writing puts on extremely volatile stocks can be quite dangerous. Since the put writer is responsible for paying the exercise price for the stock, the results can be disastrous if the underlying stock has dropped precipitously. Always prepare for the worst!

# STEP-BY-STEP WRITING PROCEDURE

Generally you write (sell) a put on a stock that you expect to rise or, at the least, remain stable. If the stock stays above the exercise price, you will retain the option money received for writing the put.

Let's set out some data to explain the step-by-step procedure of a typical put sale. On November 25, 1977, Honeywell (HON) traded at $49\frac{1}{2}$ when its May 50 put was priced at $3\frac{3}{4}$:

| Strike Price | May 50 Put Price | Stock Price |
|---|---|---|
| 50 | 3¾ | 49½ |

**Example:** *Initial Put-Writing Positon:* Enter an order with your broker to sell (write) one HON May 50 put at 3¾ ($375) and thus establish your initial position:

Sell 1 HON May 50 put at     3¾ ($375)

**Example:** *Initial Margin Requirement:* The initial put-writing margin requirement for most brokers is 30% of the stock value, *less* the difference between the stock price and the exercise price if the stock sells above the exercise price, or *plus* the difference if the stock sells below the exercise price *reduced* by the amount of the put option received. The calculation is:

| | |
|---|---|
| 100 shares HON × 49½ strike price = $4,950 | |
| 30% of $4,950 | $1,485 |
| ½ (50 strike price − 49½ stock price) | + 50 |
| | $1,535 |
| Put premium | $−375 |
| Initial margin required | $1,160 |

The securities in the margin account may provide the collateral (initial margin) required to write a put.

### Maintenance Margin Requirements

Maintenance margin requirements increase or decrease as the stock declines or rises.

If the stock declines, maintenance margin requirements will increase.

The requirement increases $70 for each point decline in the stock, without considering the put premium received.

If the stock rises, maintenance margin requirements decrease $70 for each point rise in the stock, with a $250 minimum.

### Potential Results at Different Stock Price Levels

Table 20.1 shows a hypothetical put-writing position at expiration, with the stock at different price levels:

**TABLE 20.1 PUT WRITING OUTCOME AT EXPIRATION**

| Stock Price Levels | May 50 Put Value | Gain/Loss on the put |
|---|---|---|
| 52 | 0 | $375 |
| 51 | 0 | 375 |
| 50 | 0 | 375 |
| 49½ | 0 | 375 |
| 48 | $200 | 175 |
| 47 | 300 | 75 |
| 46¼* | 375 | 0 |
| 45 | 500 | −125 |
| 44 | 600 | −225 |
| 43 | 700 | −325 |

* Breakeven level (with put bought to close out position)

### Option Profit Levels

A put decreases in value as the stock increases in value.

As you can see from Table 20.1, if the stock is trading above the put's exercise price at expiration, the put will expire worthless. You benefit from retaining the put premium received from writing the put.

### When and How to Close Out

If the stock declines sharply below the exercise price, consider closing out your put option to prevent exercise. You may terminate your option obligation at any time as long as the put holder (buyer) hasn't exercised the option.

You close out by purchasing a put identical to the one previously sold. If the closing costs are higher than the premium originally received, a loss will occur. On the other hand, a gain will result if closing costs are lower than the premium received.

If the put holder exercises the option (with the exercise price higher than the stock price), you will acquire the stock. However, the effective cost for your stock acquisition will be the exercise price, *less* the option premium received as follows, using HON data from above:

| | |
|---|---|
| Exercise price on HON May 50 put | 50 |
| Put premium | −3¾ |
| Stock cost before commissions | 46¼ |

No exercise will take place unless the exercise price is above—perhaps substantially above—the stock's current market value. If no exercise takes place, you will have earned premium income as a return on the cash in your investment account.

# PUT SELLING TO EARN PREMIUM INCOME

One reason for writing put options is to increase the cash flow from an investment portfolio. Option premiums can add substantially to income from dividends and other sources.

For premium income, you would generally write puts in advancing markets just as you would write calls in declining markets. In other words, you sell a put on a stock you believe will rise in price.

You may realize premium income in either of two ways. One way is for the underlying stock to advance and the put to expire worthless. Another way is to repurchase the put on the secondary market at a profit.

The put seller earns the premium income when the price of the underlying stock is either (1) flat or has a moderate rise or (2) has a significant rise. In the first instance, the put will expire worthless. In the second instance, the put could be repurchased at a lower price than the price paid. In either case, a profit will result.

On the other hand, a decline in the price of the underlying stock would cause a rise in the value of the option and a probable loss. Either the put must be repurchased at a higher price in the secondary market to terminate the obligations, or the stock "put" by the put holder taken at a price higher than the market price.

### Worthless Expiration

Let's see how a short put works for you in producing premium income by expiring worthless.

Anticipating a flat or moderate rise in the underlying stock, the uncovered put writer sells a put option, seeking to profit from a dissipation of the option time value. In other words, the put writer expects the following two developments: (1) failure of the underlying stock to decline much below the exercise price, and (2) dissipation of the option's time value. His bet is that the put option written will not be exercised, expiring worthless.

*Example:*  On June 8, 1977, when Eastman Kodak (EK) was selling at 60, an EK January 60 put could be written for 4⅞. If on expiration date EK were above the exercise price of 60, the put would have expired worthless, and the put writer would have retained the premium originally received.

### Profitable Repurchase At Secondary Market

Sometimes you needn't wait until the expiration of the option to realize profits, if the underlying stock should rise as anticipated. With an increase in the price of the stock, the value of the put you have sold would decline. Thus, you could buy an identical put option (closing transaction) in the secondary market at a lower cost than you received from the sale of the put (opening transaction).

*Example:* In the preceding example on EK, if the stock had subsequently risen to 64, EK June 60 might have been selling for 1⅜, at which point it could have been repurchased for a profit of 3½ points (4⅞ − 1⅜) before transaction costs:

| | |
|---|---|
| EK January 60 put repurchased at | 4⅞ |
| EK January 60 put originally sold at | 1⅜ |
| Profit | 3½ |

With the passage of time, sometimes even a relatively small rise, or no action in the price of the underlying stock, produces a profit for the put writer due to the fact that options are wasting assets.

# PUT SELLING TO ACQUIRE STOCK BELOW MARKET PRICE

Sometimes you can get away with not paying the existing market price of a stock you would like to own. Put writing provides a possible means to buy a certain stock at below market.

## Establishing An Effective Cost

Here's how it works. A put written on an underlying stock permits you to acquire that stock if the put is exercised and put to you. Your cost of owning the stock is the exercise price, less the premium received for writing the put. Stated in another way, by writing a put option you establish your effective cost of the stock—if the option is exercised—at the exercise price minus the premium received for writing the option.

On the other hand, if the put is not exercised, you will not acquire the stock but will still retain the premium.

Here is an illustration of this buy-below-the-market method of writing (selling) an option against *cash*.

*Example:* On June 22, 1977, Santa Fe International (SAF) was selling at 53¼. Say that you wanted to buy SAF but felt the stock was priced too high. You would not buy SAF unless it dropped to the 48 level. With this view, you bought a SAF January 50 for 2⅛.

If the stock had fallen below the strike price of 50, the put holder most probably would have exercised the option and put the stock to you. In that event the effective cost to acquire SAF would have been 47⅞ (50 − 2⅛) plus commissions. The put premium of 2⅛ received would have had the effect of reducing your purchase price by that amount.

On the other hand, if SAF had risen in price, the put would not have been exercised. Although you would not have acquired the stock, you would have retained the premium.

Since the put seller may be forced to buy the stock if the put is exercised, he should only sell a put in stocks he would in any event be willing to own. Thus, one of the key considerations in put writing is whether the put writer desires to own the underlying stock and, if so, at what price.

## Another Method of Lowering Purchase Price

Another option strategy to lower the effective cost of acquiring a particular stock is one involving writing puts with different strike prices or different expiration months.

*Example:* On November 10, 1977, you might have wanted to acquire 200 shares of Santa Fe International (SAF) at a price lower than its then market price (49).

One SAF July put with an exercise price of 45 (out of the money) might have been written for a premium of 2¼, and another SAF July put with an exercise price of 50 (in the money) might have been written for a premium of 4⅝. The average premium would then be 3⅞:

| | |
|---|---|
| SAF July 45 put | 2¼ |
| SAF July 50 put | +4⅝ |
| Average purchase price (divide by 2) | 3⁷⁄₁₆ |

Let's see what would happen to you as the put writer if the underlying stock should (1) go up; (2) remain unchanged; or (3) go down.

1. The Stock Rises: Should the stock go up, you would not acquire the stock but would be able to retain the entire premium amount of $6\frac{7}{8}$.

    Failure to acquire stock doesn't mean you can't subsequently use the cash in your account—which has now been increased by the option premium ($6\frac{7}{8}$)—to purchase the stock in the market. As long as the market price of the stock is less than $42\frac{7}{8}$ ($49 - 6\frac{7}{8}$) a share, you would be better off having written the option (rather than buying the stock without obtaining option premiums as a means of reducing your purchase price).

2. The Stock Remains Unchanged: Should the stock remain unchanged at 49, the put with the exercise price of 50 would be exercised, giving you an effective purchase price for 100 shares of $45\frac{3}{8}$ (exercise price of 50 less the premium of $4\frac{5}{8}$). The remaining put would expire worthless, allowing you to retain the $2\frac{1}{4}$ in premium.

3. The Stock Goes Down: Should the stock fall below 45, then you would have to buy 100 shares at 50 and 100 shares at 45, for an average price of $47\frac{1}{2}$ as follows:

| | |
|---|---|
| Buy 100 shares at | 50 |
| Buy 100 shares at | +45 |
| | 95 |
| Average purchase price (divide by 2) | $47\frac{1}{2}$ |

On the other hand, the average premium of $3\frac{7}{16}$ would lower the effective purchase cost to $44\frac{1}{16}$ ($47\frac{1}{2} - 3\frac{7}{16}$), which is $4\frac{15}{16}$ points ($49 - 44\frac{1}{16}$) below the initial market price of 49.

### Investment Flexibility

Although put writing obligates you to purchase the underlying stock if and when the option is exercised, this obligation can usually be terminated at any time prior to exercise simply by buying in the put—that is, by purchasing an identical put, and thereby offsetting the obligations of the one previously written.

Whether this results in a profit or a loss will depend on whether the premium paid (to buy in the option) is lower or higher than the premium originally collected.

In either case, the opportunity to offset an outstanding option results in investment flexibility—the opportunity to change your mind if and when circumstances change.

*Example:* Assume that on June 10, 1977, you collected $3\frac{1}{4}$ per share on writing a December 55 put option on Northwest Industries (NWT), which was selling at 57, indicating that you probably would be willing to own NWT shares if they could be purchased at $51\frac{3}{4}$ ($55 - 3\frac{1}{4}$).

On September 14, 1977, NWT declined to $52\frac{1}{2}$. Since the option still had about three more months remaining until expiration, its holder might not yet have exercised it. Meanwhile, if you as the put writer decided that you were no longer interested in owning NWT stock, or at least not at the exercise price of 55, you could terminate your obligations under the option by buying in the put previously written.

If the then put price was less than $3\frac{1}{4}$ per share, you would realize a profit, exclusive of commissions and taxes. If it was more than $3\frac{1}{4}$, you would incur a loss.

Since an offsetting NWT December 55 put could be bought at 4, you would have suffered a loss of $\frac{3}{4}$ ($4 - 3\frac{1}{4}$) before transaction costs:

| | |
|---|---|
| NWT December 55 put bought back at | 4 |
| NWT December 55 put originally sold at | $-3\frac{1}{4}$ |
| Loss | $\frac{3}{4}$ |

### In-the-Money versus Out-of-the-Money Put Writing

For an easy explanation of the relative pros and cons of in-the-money versus out-of-the-money put writing, let's take a look at the following three July puts of Mesa Petroleum (MSA) on November 11, 1977, when MSA closed at $40\frac{7}{8}$:

| Strike Price | Put Price | Stock Price |
|---|---|---|
| 35 (out of the money) | $1\frac{3}{8}$ | $40\frac{7}{8}$ |
| 40 (near the money) | $2\frac{3}{4}$ | $40\frac{7}{8}$ |
| 45 (in the money) | $5\frac{1}{4}$ | $40\frac{7}{8}$ |

Normally a 45 put, being in the money 4⅛ (45 − 40⅞) with the stock at 40⅞, is most likely to be exercised, unless the underlying stock rises above the strike price of 45 before expiration. While the risk of exercise is greater with in-the-money puts, they offset such risk by providing more premium income.

In the case of high-volatility stocks such as MSA, however, the chance of rising above the strike price of 45 is real, with the resultant possibility that the put buyer may not exercise the option.

Normally, a 35 put, being out of the money 5⅞ (40⅞ − 35) with the stock trading at 40⅞, is most unlikely to be exercised, unless the stock declines below the strike price of 35. Thus, writing out-of-the-money puts reduces the risk of exercise, but, at the same time, the premium income is usually less too.

## MULTIPLE-EXERCISE-PRICE PUT WRITING

### Different Exercise Prices

You may write puts with different exercise prices instead of writing puts with a single exercise price. The following data will be used.

On November 25, 1977, Mesa Petroleum (MSA) had the following January 40 and 45 puts when the stock was 44:

| Strike Price | Put Price | Stock Price |
|---|---|---|
| 40 (out of the money) | 1¾ | 44 |
| 45 (in the money) | 3⅞ | 44 |

Assume you sold a 40 put for 1¾ and a 45 put for 3⅞:

| | |
|---|---|
| Sell January 40 put at | 1¾ |
| Sell January 45 put at | +3⅞ |
| Total premium received | = 5⅝ |
| Average premium (divide by 2) | = 1¹³⁄₁₆ |

Next, let's see how you would be doing if the stock should (1) rise; (2) stand still; or (3) decline.

***Example:*** *The Stock Rises in Price:* Should the stock rise above the higher strike price of 45, you would pocket the entire premium of 5⅝ without further obligations.

***Example:*** *The Stock Remains Unchanged:* If the stock should stand still at 44, (1) the 40 put would expire worthless, permitting you to retain the premium of 1¾ on the 40 put without further obligations. Then, (2) the 45 put would be exercised, forcing you to buy 100 shares of stock at an effective purchase price of 41:

| | |
|---|---|
| Buy stock at exercise price of 45 | 45 |
| Premium received from writing the 45 put | −4 |
| Effective purchase price | 41 |

***Example:*** *The Stock Falls in Value:* Should the stock decline below the lower strike price of 40, you would be compelled to buy 100 shares at 45 and another 100 shares at 40, for an average price of 42½:

| | |
|---|---|
| Buy 100 shares at | 45 |
| Buy 100 shares at | +40 |
| Total purchase price | 85 |

$$\text{Average purchase price} = \frac{85}{2} = 42\frac{1}{2}$$

The average purchase price of 42½, however, would be reduced by the average premium received—to 39¹¹⁄₁₆:

| | |
|---|---|
| Average purchase price | 42½ |
| Average premium received | − 2¹³⁄₁₆ |
| Average effective cost | 39¹¹⁄₁₆ |

Thus, the average effective cost of 39¹¹⁄₁₆ would be 4⁵⁄₁₆ below the initial market price of 44:

| | |
|---|---|
| Initial market price | 44 |
| Average effective cost | −39¹¹⁄₁₆ |
| Effective cost advantage | 4⁵⁄₁₆ |

## HOW TO MEASURE VOLATILITY

When you select a stock to write puts, you should be aware of its volatility history, because its tendency to move wildly could spell disaster for you. Volatility is a statistical measure of a stock's tendency up and down, based on its price history.

A stock's price movement volatility, as mentioned earlier, is also called *beta,* which is its propensity to move with the market. Generally, a stock with a higher *beta* will most likely move *up* or *down* faster and further than one with a low *beta.*

It is impossible, at least for the short duration of a stock option, for anyone to accurately predict the price movement of the stock. However, based on its historical performance, it is possible to predict whether a particular stock is likely to have a large or small price movement. Certain stocks have always moved up or down sharply relative to the market as a whole, and these stocks are very likely to do so again.

## Which Direction? To What Extent?

Perhaps the most important questions for a buyer or seller of an option (whether call or put) are whether its underlying stock will go up or down during the period of the option and by how much. The behavior of the stock price movement in the past is invaluable in determining the answer to these questions. And the stock with the likelihood of greatest movement (either up or down) has the highest *beta.* Generally, the buyer (whether call or put) should seek a stock with a relatively high *beta.* Generally, the seller (whether call or put) should seek a stock with a relatively low *beta.*

# MEANS OF DEFENSE

Most options are written by sellers who have or will immediately establish a concurrent stock position to offset the option in the event that it is exercised. This means of defense is available both to call and put sellers (writers):

Short put, short stock (sale of put versus short position in the stock)

Short call, long stock (sale of call versus long position in the stock)

Some writers prefer selling options without the protection of an offsetting stock position in their accounts. They believe that the odds are on their side. Historically, only one-third of all options written were ever exercised, and only 20 percent were fully profitable for the buyers. This means that two-thirds of the time, a naked option writer would have profited by keeping all or part of the premium he received without undertaking a stock position during the life of the option contract.

## Basic Rules

What are the possible defenses for put option writers to minimize exposure?

1. Sell put options only against cash and only on securities for ownership.
2. Use only a fraction of your funds in any single put option writing situation.
3. Place a ceiling on the number of put options sold to expire in any one month. This spreads risk and evens out fluctuations.

There are also several specific defense strategies for the put option writer if the underlying security upon which he has issued a put option has declined in price.

## Defense 1: Naked Call Writing

One possible recourse open to the writer who remains bullish about the stock in spite of its price decline is to write a naked call option at the price to which the stock has declined.

## Defense 2: Selling Stock Short

Another possible recourse is to sell the stock short at a price to which the stock has declined.

## Defense 3: Selling Stock Short Plus Call Buying

A third possible defense is to sell the stock short at the price to which it has declined, and to purchase an above-the-market call at the original strike price for the remaining period of the put option. This defensive strategy is to limit loss of the premium paid for the above-the-market call, as well as to prevent substantial loss. This strategy is suited primarily for professional investors.

To recapitulate, writing (selling) puts generates premium income; also it offers the possibility of acquiring shares of stock below the current market price.

In the first instance, if the underlying stock goes down instead of up as anticipated, the put holder exercises the option. Thus, the put writer must be prepared for the possibility of paying far more for the stock than its current market price. This fact is one of the most important in evaluating the risks of put writing. In the second instance, a rise in the price of the underlying stock compensates the put writer with the opportunity to buy the underlying stock at a price below the market price. Puts should be written only on stocks the writer would like to own, albeit at a lower price. If the stock does not go up, the put writer is compensated with the premium.

# OVERVIEW

### What

"Short put, short stock" is an option strategy that combines selling a put with selling short on the underlying stock.

### Why

With this "dual-short" strategy, if the stock price declines as anticipated, the investor can cover his short stock position at a profit, repurchase his put at a loss, and have an overall gain for the two transactions.

### How

This dual position is protected on the upside only to the extent of the premium money received. A loss occurs if the stock rises substantially instead declining.

# HEDGED PUT WRITING

As distinct from uncovered put writing, covered put writing combines short-put and concurrent short-stock positions. Actually, the term "uncovered" put writing is a sort of misnomer, because a covered put writer is only partially covered; his short position in the underlying stock is not completely hedged.

This position is protected on the upside only to the extent of the amount of the premium received from the sale of the put. If the underlying stock rises substantially, the covered put writer may be forced to cover his short position by buying in the stock at a price much higher than the price at which he made his short sale.

### High-Risk Bear Strategy

The short-put, short-stock stategy is to short the stock and write a put against the short stock position. This is a bearish put strategy, and a highly risky one because it carries with it the possibility of unlimited losses if the stock rises in price. Therefore, it is suitable only for a sophisticated investor able and willing to assume a large risk. Note that a put writer is not required to deposit margin if he has a corresponding short position in the underlying security.

Let's see how this short-put, short stock strategy works when the underlying stock (1)

short put,
short stock

21

declines, as expected, and (2) rises instead of declining.

### The Stock Declines

If the stock price declines, as anticipated, the investor can cover his short stock position at a profit and repurchase his put in the secondary market at a loss. He will realize a gain if the profit on the short stock sale exceeds the loss on the put sale. He will experience a loss if the profit from the short stock sale is less than the loss from the put sale.

*Example:* On September 2, 1977, Eastman Kodak (EK) traded at 61⅜ when its April 60 put was 3½. An investor sold 100 shares of EK short at 61⅜ and simultaneously sold an April 60 put for 3½ ($350).

As of November 25, 1977, EK had declined to 53 while its April 60 put had risen to 7½.

The investor could have realized a gain of 4⅜ by covering his short stock position at a 8-point profit and repurchasing the put in the secondary market at a 4-point loss:

| | Stock | Put |
|---|---|---|
| **9/2/77** | | |
| **Stock sold short at 61⅜** | $6,137.50 | |
| **9/2/77** | | |
| **Put sold at 3½** | | $350.00 |
| **11/25/77** | | |
| **Stock covered at 53** | $5,300.00 | |
| **11/25/77** | | |
| **Put repurchased at 7½** | | $750.00 |
| **Gain or loss** | $ 837.50 | −$400.00 |
| | −400.00 | |
| **Net gain before commissions** | $ 437.50 | |

Or, he could have waited to receive an exercise notice, using the stock put to him to cover his short stock position. In that event, his profit would have been the premium originally received upon sale of the put.

### The Stock Rises

If the stock rises instead, the investor is still hedged to a degree because the premium income from the put partially offsets his loss from his short position.

*Example:* On September 2, 1977, Santa Fe International (SAF) traded at 46⅝; its April 50 put was 5½. An investor, applying the "short put, short stock" approach, takes these steps:

| | |
|---|---|
| Sells 100 shares of SAF short at | 46⅝ |
| Sells one SAF April 50 put at | 5½ |

As of November 28, 1977, SAF had risen sharply to 53½; its April 50 put had dropped to 1⅞. The investor could have taken an aggregate 3¾-point loss by covering the stock at a 6⅞-point loss and repurchasing the April 50 put at a 3⅛-point gain:

| | Stock | Put |
|---|---|---|
| **9/2/77** | | |
| **Stock sold short at 46⅝** | $4,662.50 | |
| **9/2/77** | | |
| **Put sold at 5½** | | $500.00 |
| **11/28/77** | | |
| **Stock covered at 53½** | $5,350.00 | |
| **11/28/77** | | |
| **Put repurchased at 1⅞** | | −$187.50 |
| **Gain or loss** | $ 687.50 | $312.50 |
| | −312.50 | |
| **Net loss before commissions** | −$ 375.00 | |

Thus, the investor would have offset his short-sale loss of $687.50 with a put-sale gain of $312.50, resulting in a net loss of $375 before commissions. A short seller not using the risk-reducing factor of the premiums received from writing a put would have suffered his entire short-sale loss without any offsetting gain.

# HOW TO SELECT
# THE STRIKE PRICE

Options of different strike prices provide investors with considerable flexibility in tailoring a strategy that best conforms to their specific market view and investment objectives.

Here is a summary of how investors use options (1) at the money, (2) in the money, or (3) out of the money when they establish a concurrent short-put, short-stock position.

## At the Money

On November 8, 1977, Avon (AVP) traded at 45 when its July 45 put was 3:

| Strike Price | Put Price | Stock Price |
|---|---|---|
| 45 | 3 | 45 |

Let's use these data for three possibilities: the stock (1) remained unchanged; (2) declines; or (3) rose.

*Example:*  *The Stock Remained Unchanged:* The maximum profit would have occurred if the stock had been unchanged at expiration date. The investor would have been even in the short-stock position and the 45 put would have expired worthless, permitting the investor to retain the entire premium money of $300 ($3 × 100 shares).

*Example:*  *The Stock Demand:* If the stock had dropped 5 points, to 40, the put holder would have exercised his option. The investor would have used the stock thus acquired upon exercise to close out the short position. The 5-point gain from the short sale would have been partly offset by the 3-point loss in the put sale.

*Example:*  *The Stock Went Up:* If the stock had risen, say 5 points, to 50, the 5-point loss in the short-stock position would only have been offset to the extent of the 3-point premium received from the put sale.

## In the Money

An in-the-money put can be used if the investor anticipates that the stock will be strong over the near term and is concerned primarily with as much upside protection as possible.

*Example:*  On November 25, 1977, General Motors (GM) traded at 66 when its July 70 put was 6¼:

| Strike price | Put Price | Stock Price |
|---|---|---|
| 70 | 6¼ | 66 |

If the investor were to have sold 100 shares of GM at 66 and, simultaneously, one GM 70 put for 6¼, his potential results would have been as follows. If the stock had closed below the strike price of 70 at expiration, the put holder would have exercised his option. The effective purchase price for the investor would then have been the exercise price (70), less the premium (6¼), amounting to 63¾ (70 − 6¼).

This put would have provided upside protection since the investor would not have lost money unless the stock sold above 72¼ at expiration:

|  |  |
|---|---|
| Stock price | 66 |
| Put premium | +6¼ |
|  | 72¼ |

## Out of the Money

*Example:*  On November 25, 1977, Eastman Kodak (EK) traded at 53 when its July 50 put was 2½:

| Strike price | Put Price | Stock Price |
|---|---|---|
| 50 | 2½ | 53 |

The investor would not have had to buy the stock unless it declined below 50 at expiration. If this had happened and the put was exercised the effective purchase price would have been 47½:

|  |  |
|---|---|
| Put strike price | 50 |
| Put premium | −2½ |
|  | 47½ |

He would have lost money at any stock price levels above 55½:

|  |  |
|---|---|
| Stock price | 53 |
| Put premium | +2½ |
|  | 55½ |

Very little upside protection would have been provided by the sale of this put.

# OVERVIEW

### What

"Short put, long stock" involves selling a put against a stock which the investor either owns or would like to own at a price lower than the current market price.

### Why

The put seller is bullish to neutral on the underlying stock, which is expected to rise in value.

### How

If the stock appreciates, as anticipated, the put seller keeps the premium money without further obligations. As long as the stock remains stable or rises, he will pocket the money.

### Writing with or without Stock Ownership

An investor may write puts against a long stock position he either (1) already has or (2) wouldn't mind having at a lower price.

In the first instance, he is bullish on the market in general and on the underlying stock in particular. He believes that the put will most likely not be exercised—that the underlying stock will appreciate and be above the exercise price at expiration. Writing puts against stock owned can be one way to increase the cash flow on a position being held for long-term appreciation. As long as the stock remains at the same price or goes up, the writer will keep the premium.

In the second case (item 2 above), the investor is bullish to neutral on the underlying stock and considers the sale of a put as an alternative to the use of a limit buy order. (A limit buy order is an order authorizing a broker to buy a certain stock at a certain price lower than the market price.) If the stock were to go lower, he wouldn't mind buying 100 shares. If the stock were to go higher, he would keep the premium.

### Double Leverage

The writer of a put with a long position in the stock must be very confident about the price action of the stock, since the position has leverage both on the upside and on the downside.

# short put, long stock

# 22

On the upside, profit accrues from the stock going up and from the premium for selling the put. However, when the stock declines, the value of the investor's position will drop twice as fast as the stock price.

Let's illustrate how a short-put, long-stock position would do either (1) when the underlying stock rises as anticipated, or (2) when the stock declines instead of rising as anticipated.

## Upside Double Leverage

Double leverage on the upside will result if the underlying stock rises as anticipated.

*Example:* On September 2, 1977, Santa Fe International (SAF) traded at 46⅜ when its April 50 put was 5½:

| Strike Price | Put Price | Stock Price |
|---|---|---|
| 50 | 5½ | 46⅜ |

If an investor assumed the following short-put, long-stock position:

Long 100 shares of SAF at = 46⅜
Short 1 SAF April 50 put at = 5½

As of November 25, 1977, SAF had risen to 53½ and its April 50 put had declined to 1⅞. The investor benefited from the upside double leverage, including (1) a 7⅛-point profit accrued from the long stock position's having risen in price and (2) a 3⅝-point gain resulting from the short put position's having diminished in value:

| | Long Stock | Short Put |
|---|---|---|
| **9/2/77 Stock bought** | 46⅜ | |
| **9/2/77 Put sold** | | 5½ |
| **11/25/77 Stock value** | 53½ | |
| **11/25/77 Put value** | | −1⅞ |
| **Gain or loss** | 7⅛ | 3⅝ |

## Downside Double Leverage

Double leverage on the downside will occur if the underlying stock declines instead of rising.

*Example:* On September 2, 1977, Reserve Oil & Gas (RVO) traded at 17 when its February 20 put was 3¼. An investor had assumed the following short-put, long-stock position:

Long 100 shares of RVO at = 17⅜
Short 1 RVO February 20 put at = 3¼

As of November 25, 1977, RVO had declined to 14½ while its February 20 put had risen to 5¼. The investor would have suffered from a downside double leverage from (1) a 2⅞-point loss on the long stock position and (2) a 2-point erosion on the short put position:

| | Long Stock | Short Put |
|---|---|---|
| **9/2/77 Stock bought** | 17⅜ | |
| **9/2/77 Put sold** | | 3¼ |
| **11/25/77 Stock value** | 14½ | |
| **11/25/77 Put value** | | 5¼ |
| **Gain or loss** | −2⅞ | −2 |

# PUT SPREADING

## PART VIII

## OVERVIEW

### What

Put spreading is the simultaneous purchase and sale of puts of different series within the same class.

### Why

A spreading position is to reduce the risk inherent in a single long or short put position. However, the same action that reduces a spreader's risk also lowers the profit potential.

### How

Spreads between two options sometimes deviate from their normal patterns for short periods of time. Thus, a spreader may be able to capture such value or price discrepancy either due to temporary deviation from normal patterns, or from other market forces.

## BASIC CONCEPTS

Put spreading is the simultaneous purchase and sale of puts of different series within the same class. The same types of spreads may be used with puts as with calls. Let's review the basic concept of spreading, which is common to puts and calls alike.

Spreading is essentially a hedging strategy. Its concept was borrowed from the commodity futures markets. Essentially, spreads are an application of the century-old arbitrage technique in the field of commodity options, utilizing the basic concepts of price differentials and time dissipation of premium.

The primary reason for entering into a spread position is to reduce the risk inherent in a single long or short position. However, the same action that reduces a spreader's risk also lowers his potential profits. Thus, spreading is a tradeoff between risk reduction and profit-potential limitation.

### Dollar Difference

Simply stated, spreading is the simultaneous purchase and sale of options on the same stock. A spread is the dollar difference between the buy and sell premiums. Its object is to capture the difference in premiums between the long option and the short option.

# put spreading: why and how

# 23

*Example:* On November 11, 1977, Honeywell (HON) had the following February 45 and February 50 puts when the stock was 47¾:

| Strike price | Feb | Stock price |
|---|---|---|
| 45 | 1⅛ | 47¾ |
| 50 | 3⅜ | 47¾ |

You could have bought a HON February 50 put at 3⅜ and sold a HON February 45 put at 1⅛:

| | |
|---|---|
| Buy HON February 50 put at | 3⅜ |
| Sell HON February 45 put at | 1⅛ |
| Dollar difference (spread) | 2¼ |

The spread (2¼) is the dollar difference between the buy and sell put-option premiums. An option is said to be long when you buy it; an option is said to be short when you sell it.

## Relative versus Absolute Differences

A spreader is less concerned with high or low option premium levels than with the extent of spread between the premium paid and the premium received in establishing the spread position.

When a particular put sells at an excessive premium, the other related puts will also usually sell at proportionately high premiums. These premiums will tend to balance each other.

By entering into a spread transaction rather than purchasing a put, an investor generally does not have to pay an extra amount when puts are selling at exceptionally high premiums. This enables the spreader to trade in the more volatile issues without paying high premiums.

## Simultaneous Long and Short

Spreads are actually two separate option contracts in one transaction. Although composed of individual options, a spread option order cannot be executed at all unless both sides of the order are executed. This is because the two-orders-in-one is entered as a unit order.

All forms of spreading have at least one thing in common: they contain simultaneous long and short positions on the same option with different strike prices and/or different expiration months.

## Debit and Credit Defined

The spread is expressed as a debit if the cost of the long put is *more* than the proceeds of the put sold.

*Example:* On November 11, 1977, Avon (AVP) had the following July 45 and July 50 puts when the stock was 47⅜:

| Strike Price | Put Price | Stock Price |
|---|---|---|
| 45 | 2⅛ | 47⅜ |
| 50 | 4¾ | 47⅜ |

If you had bought an AVP July 50 put at 4¾ and sold an AVP July 45 put at 2⅛ you would have had a debit of 2⅝:

| | |
|---|---|
| Buy AVP July 50 put at | 4¾ |
| Sell AVP July 45 put at | 2⅛ |
| Debit | 2⅝ |

The spread is termed a credit if the cost of the long put is less than the proceeds of the put sold.

*Example:* On November 11, 1977, General Motors (GM) had the following May 60 and May 70 puts when the stock was 67⅛:

| Strike Price | Put Price | Stock Price |
|---|---|---|
| 60 | 1⅞ | 67⅛ |
| 70 | 5½ | 67⅛ |

If you had sold GM July 70 at 5½ and bought GM July 60 at 1⅞, you would have had a credit of 3⅝:

| | |
|---|---|
| Sell GM July 70 at | 5½ |
| Buy GM July 60 at | 1⅞ |
| Credit | 3⅝ |

A spread is said to be even when the cost of buying an option and the cost of selling an option are equal.

# SPREAD CONSTRUCTION

Since options normally carry three different expiration months and often multiple strike prices, a great variety of spreading combinations is typically available in many put classes.

In addition, different ratios of long to short may be devised to fit the individual investor's expectations and objectives. Different spreads involve different degrees of risk and are among the most complicated of option transactions.

The two principal forms of spread technique are the price spread and the time spread.

## Put Price Spread

Also called a "money" or "vertical" spread, a price spread is the purchase of a listed option and sale of a listed option having the same expiration month but different strike prices. In a put price spread, the two puts have different strike prices but the same expiration month.

*Example:* On November 14, 1977, ABC Broadcasting (ABC) had the following May 40 and 45 puts when the stock was 42⅛:

| Strike Price | May Put Price | Stock Price |
|---|---|---|
| 40 | 2¼ | 42⅛ |
| 45 | 5 | 42⅛ |

You would have established a put price spread if you had bought an ABC 45-strike price put and sold a 40-strike price put as follows:

| | |
|---|---|
| Buy 45-strike price put at | 5 |
| Sell 40-strike price put at | 2¼ |
| Debit | 2¾ |

## Put Time Spread

Also called a "calendar" or "horizontal" spread, a time spread is the purchase of a listed option and the sale of a listed option having the same strike price but different expiration months. In a put time spread, the two puts have different expirations but the same strike price.

*Example:* On November 14, 1977, IBM had the following January and April puts with the strike price of 260 when the stock was 258¼:

| Strike Price | Jan | Apr | Stock Price |
|---|---|---|---|
| 260 | 6½ | 9⅛ | 258¼ |

You would have established a put time spread if you had bought April 260 at 9⅛ and sold January 260 at 6½:

| | |
|---|---|
| Buy April 260 put at | 9⅛ |
| Sell January 260 put at | 6½ |
| Debit | 2⅝ |

## Value Deviation

Spreads between two options sometimes deviate from their normal patterns for short periods of time, especially when a new strike price is added to the existing strike prices or when a new expiration month is added to the current expiration months.

When new expiration months or strike-price options are first available, there may be a preponderance of either buyers or sellers. Consequently, the price of such options is out of balance; the other outstanding options remain at their normal price levels. The investor who is familiar with the spread pattern of a particular issue can profit from spreads that deviate from their normal patterns for short periods of time.

## Potential Risk and Reward

Before an investor enters into a spread, he should carefully read and thoroughly understand the Options Clearing Corporation's prospectus. Next, he should review the possible risk as well as the potential reward with his broker.

The appeal of option spreading has been greatly enhanced by the adoption of margin rules that require a relatively small cash outlay to enter into a position. After the initial spread is paid for, no additional costs or additional margin is required. In the preceding IBM illustration, the cost of spreading is limited to the 2⅝ debit plus commissions.

However, although the risk of any spread is known and limited, it can be considerable. Spreading transactions can produce losses of up to 100 percent of the amount invested, although gains of 200 percent or more are possible.

### Important Commission and Tax Factors

Attracted by high profit potential and definable risk, many investors have jumped into spreading without fully understanding all the pitfalls.

First, commissions on spreads are high because each spread involves at least two option contracts and, more often than not, a closing (liquidating) transaction before expiration. A closing transaction then involves at least two additional option contracts. Thus, the initiation of a spread and its subsequent liquidation involves a minimum of four contracts. The commissions might very well dissipate substantial gains from the spread.

Second, an investor should consult his tax advisor before entering into spread positions because tax treatment of various possible results of a spread position may be advantageous or disadvantageous.

# PUT SPREAD MARGINS

### General Put Margin Requirements

Spreads can be executed only in margin accounts. A position is considered a spread for margin purposes if both options are of the same class and if the long option expires no earlier than the short option. A $2,000 minimum initial margin requirement applies to spreads. In addition, the long option must be paid for in full.

The margin required on a put spread position is the *lesser* amount as calculated by the following rules:

Rule 1: The amount by which the strike price of the short put exceeds the strike price of the long put.

Rule 2: The amount required to margin the short put, namely, 30 percent of the margin value of the underlying security *plus* the amount in the money or *minus* the amount out of the money, with a minimum of $250 per contract.

The following illustrations will help you to calculate put spread margins.

*Example—Out-of-the-Money Margin Calculation*
On November 15, 1977, Northwest Industries (NWT) had the following June 45 and 50 puts when the stock was 53¼:

| Strike Price | June Put Price | Stock Price |
|---|---|---|
| 45 | 1 | 53¼ |
| 50 | 2½ | 53¼ |

Assume an investor sold a June 50 put for 2½ and bought a June 45 put for 1

| | |
|---|---|
| Sell June 50 at | 2½ |
| Buy June 45 at | 1 |
| Credit | 1½ |

Margin is calculated below. Based on rule 1:

| | |
|---|---|
| Difference in strike prices (50 − 45) | $500.00 |
| Premium received | −150.00 |
| Margin | $350.00 |

Based on rule 2:

| | |
|---|---|
| 30% of $5,324 stock value | $1,597.20 |
| Out-of-the-money amount of the short option ($5,324 − 5,000) | −324.00 |
| | $1,273.20 |
| Premium received | −150.00 |
| Margin | $1,123.20 |

The lesser of the above two, $350.00 under rule 1 or $1,123.20 under rule 2, is obviously $350.00. This amount would have been required of this investor in addition to the $150.00 premium received.

If, however, there were other securities or cash in his account, the margin requirement would have been $1,850.00 ($2,000.00 less the $150.00 premium received).

The long put ($100) would, in any case, have had to be paid in full.

***Example:*** *In-The-Money Margin Calculation*
On November 15, 1977, General Motors (GM) had the following July 60 and 70 puts when the stock was 66⅝:

| Strike Price | July Put Price | Stock Price |
|---|---|---|
| 60 | 2 | 66⅝ |
| 70 | 6 | 66⅝ |

Assume an investor sold GM July 70 for 6 and bought GM July 60 for 2:

| | |
|---|---|
| Sell July 70 at | 6 |
| Buy July 50 at | 2 |
| Credit | 4 |

Margin is calculated as follows. Based on rule 1:

| | |
|---|---|
| Difference in strike prices (70 − 60) | $1,000.00 |
| Premium received | −400.00 |
| Margin | 600.00 |

Based on rule 2:

| | |
|---|---|
| 30% of $6662.50 stock value | $1,998.75 |
| In-the-money amount of the short option ($7,000 − $6662.50) | +337.50 |
| Margin | $1,661.25 |

Under rule 1 we have calculated $600.00. Under rule 2 the amount is $1,661.25; so the lesser is clearly $600.00.

### What

Also called a "horizontal" or "calendar" put spread, a put time spread involves the purchase of a put and the sale of a put having the same strike price but different expiration months.

### Why

A spreader may gain in two ways. First, a spread will widen if the stock price approaches the strike price of the options.

### How

Spreading widens or narrows with (1) the passage of time and (2) movement in the price of the underlying stock.

The spread between two options tends to be greatest when the stock is trading at the exercise price.

### Different Expiration Months

As with call time spreads, put time spreads involve options of different expiration months but the same strike price. You can use time spreads either for bullish or bearish purposes.

In a bull put time spread, you sell (short) a put for the further month and buy a put for the closer month. Conversely, in a bear put time spread, you buy the further put and sell (short) the closer put.

Time spreads carry built-in protection. In fact, the principal use of the time spread is to give the trader a degree of protection in the event that his judgment on the near-term movement of the underlying stock is incorrect.

put time spreads

24

## How To Widen The Spread

As with call time spreads, the theory of put time spreads is that, as time passes, the spreads will widen, and widening spreads provide a profitable opportunity for spreaders. A widening spread means a widening difference between the increased value of a spread and what it originally costs an investor to establish the spread. As time passes, the distant spread will become the nearby spread.

*Example:* Assuming XYZ has the following puts with the strike price of 100 when the stock trades at 100:

|  | Feb. | May | Aug. | Stock Price |
|---|---|---|---|---|
| Strike Price 100 | 4 | 7 | 9 | 100 |

Note that the difference between the near (February) put and the middle (May) put is 3 (7 − 4) while the difference between the middle (May) put and the far (August) put is 2 (9 − 7).

The investor might buy the August for 9 and sell the May for 7 to establish the following spread with a 2-point debit:

| | |
|---|---|
| Buy August 100 put at | 9 |
| Sell May 100 put at | 7 |
| Debit | 2 |

If, at February expiration, XYZ remains at 100, the relationship between the May and the August premium might approximate the above relationship between the February and the May premium. Their spread might then widen to 3, and the spreader might liquidate his position at a 1-point profit, that being the difference between the widened 3-point spread and the original 2-point spread:

| May Put | | August Put | | Credit/(Debit) |
|---|---|---|---|---|
| Sold at | 7 | Bought at | 9 | (2) |
| Bought at | 4 | Sold at | 7 | 3 |
| Profit | 3 | Loss | −2 | 1 |

Assuming that the stock is standing still at expiration, the spread will widen over time. However, instead of standing still the stock could either go up or down. If it rose, say, to 110, both puts would narrow and the spreader would lose money. Also, if the stock declined, say to 90, both puts would be selling near their intrinsic value of 10. Again, the spread would narrow and the investor would lose money.

## Time Passage

As time passes, assuming no movement in the price of the underlying stock, a spread tends to widen. That is, the spread between the two most distant expiration months will be less than that between the two nearby expiration months.

The ideal point to initiate a put time spread is just before the time value begins to diminish rapidly, which is approximately 4 to 6 weeks before expiration. Initiating at that point allows the spreader to take advantage of the drop in premium value and, at the same time, obtain a further-out put that will lose its time value at a much slower pace.

## Stock-Price Movement

The spread between two options tends to be greatest when the underlying stock is trading at the exercise price. The spread between options tends to narrow as the underlying stock moves, in either direction, away from the exercise price.

If the anticipated price movement in the underlying stock does not occur at expiration, the spread will suffer a loss. Therefore, it is important to have an opinion on the likely direction of the stock (bullish, bearish, or neutral).

## Two Ways to Profitability

A spreader may gain in two ways. First, a spread will widen if the stock price approaches the strike price of the options. (On the other hand, a loss will result from a spread narrowing if the stock moves away from the strike price in either direction.)

Second, the spread will also widen if the short put expires unexercised (or is repurchased for a small amount), leaving the long put held for a possible rise in value.

*Example:* Based on the preceding spread example on XTZ:

| | |
|---|---|
| Buy August 100 put at | 9 |
| Sell May 100 put at | 7 |
| Debit | 2 |

If the stock stands still at expiration the spread will widen to 3, allowing the spreader to liquidate his position at a 1-point profit (3 − 2).

If, however, the near (May) put expires worthless, the spreader will earn 7 (May put premium), thereby reducing the cost of his August put to 2 (9 − 7). He could realize a nice profit if the stock were to rise in value in the next three months. If not, the most he could lose would be the cost of the spread (2).

Generally, the movement in the price of the underlying security has a greater impact on the spread than does the passage of time.

### *Keys to Sound Spreading*

Since successful time spreading depends upon faster shrinkage in the value of the short option than in the long option, to be effective, time spreads generally require a short option with a large time value.

A narrow spread premium differential is another prerequisite to sound time spreading. Spread differential is the difference between the premium you pay for the long position and what you receive for the short one.

In the above illustration of XYZ, the spread debit or differential is 2. All things being equal, one spread with a debit of 1½ would be more desirable than another spread with a debit of 2.

In entering a time spread order, it is important to obtain the best possible spread difference. Even a small fraction is vital because it usually accounts for a high percentage of the investment.

## PRINCIPAL APPROACHES TO PUT TIME SPREADS

Put time spreads can be used when you are bullish or bearish or when you expect the stock to remain flat or neutral. In other words, there are three principal approaches to put time spreading, namely:

1. Neutral, using at-the-money puts
2. Bullish, using in-the-money puts
3. Bearish, using out-of-the-money puts.

### *Neutral Approach: Using At-the-Money Puts*

A neutral put time spread strategy using at-the-money put options is designed for investors who believe that a particular security will not move appreciably over the near term.

This strategy is based on the theory that as the far spread becomes the nearby spread with the passage of time, the difference between the premiums of the two options will widen.

***Example:*** On December 6, 1977, ABC Broadcasting (ABC) had the following near-the-money put options when the stock traded at 40:

| | Feb | May | Aug | Stock Price |
|---|---|---|---|---|
| Strike Price 40 | 1 15/16 | 2¾ | 2⅞ | 40⅛ |

A neutral put time spread might have been set up with a ⅛-point debit:

| | |
|---|---|
| Buy August 40 at | 2⅞ |
| Sell May 40 at | 2¾ |
| Debit | ⅛ |

It's important to sell a large-value, closer-by put (relative to the further-out put being bought) in order to make such a spread feasible.

If, at February expiration, ABC had remained unchanged at 40, the relationship between the May put and the August put might have approximated that between the February put and the May put. As indicated below, the spread might then have been sold at a 11/16-point profit:

| | May Put | Aug Put | Credit/(Debit) |
|---|---|---|---|
| **Sold** | 2¾ | Bought 2⅞ | (⅛) |
| **Bought** | 1 15/16 | Sold 2¾ | 13/16 |
| **Profit** | 13/16 | (⅛) | 11/16 |

## Bullish Approach: Using In-the-Money Puts

An investor bullish on a particular security over the near term might consider using in-the-money put options in a put time spread.

This strategy is based on the theory that the spread tends to widen as the stock price approaches the strike price of the options.

**Example:** On June 14, 1977, ABC Broadcasting (ABC) had the following in-the-money put options when the stock traded at 43½:

|  | Aug | Nov | Feb | Stock Price |
|---|---|---|---|---|
| **Strike Price 50** | 6½ | 7 | 7¼ | 43½ |

A bullish put time spread could have been stuctured by buying ABC February 50 at 7¼ and selling ABC November 50 at 7, resulting in a debit of ¼:

| | |
|---|---|
| Buy February 50 at | 7¼ |
| Sell November 50 at | 7 |
| Debit | ¼ |

If, by November expiration, the stock had risen from 43½ to 50, the November 50 put would have expired worthless. Meanwhile, the February 50 put would have reflected some time value and might have sold at around 2½. Thus, the spread would have widened, with a profit of 2¼ (before transaction costs) to the investor:

| Nov 50 Put | | Feb 50 Put | | Credit/(Debit) |
|---|---|---|---|---|
| **Sold** | 7 | **Bought** | 7¼ | (¼) |
| **Expired** | 0 | **Sold** | 2½ | 1¾ |
| **Profit** | 7 | **Loss** | −4¾ | 2¼ |

The premature exercise problem for in-the-money puts is far more serious than for in-the-money calls. It is not unusual to see distant in-the-money puts exercised; this rarely occurs with distant in-the-money calls.

**Example:** *Rolling a Bullish Put Time Spread:* In the situation set up in the preceding example, the spreader might have constructed a bullish put time spread by utilizing the near and middle (August-November) puts instead of the middle and far (November-February) puts:

| | |
|---|---|
| Buy November 50 at | 7 |
| Sell August 50 at | 6½ |
| Debit | ½ |

This spread would have been set up with a debit of ½.

If the stock had gone up from 43½ to 50 just prior to the August expiration, the following relative price structure might have emerged:

|  | Aug | Nov | Feb | Stock Price |
|---|---|---|---|---|
| **Strike Price 50** | ½ | 3 | 5 | 50 |

The August put could have been repurchased for ½ at a 6-point profit:

| | |
|---|---|
| Short position: August 50 | 6½ |
| Repurchased position: August 50 | ½ |
| Profit | 6 |

The spread could then have been reestablished by selling the November put at 3.

If the underlying stock remained unchanged at 50 through the November expiration, the November put would have expired worthless. Reflecting its remaining time value, the February put might have been selling at 3½. If the February put had then been sold, the following would have been the profit/loss picture:

| Aug 50 | | Nov 50 | | Feb 50 | | Credit/(Debit) |
|---|---|---|---|---|---|---|
| **Sold** | 6½ | | | **Bought** | 5 | 1½ |
| **Bought** | ½ | **Sold** | 3 | | | 2½ |
| | | **Expired** | 0 | **Sold** | 3½ | 3½ |
| **Profit** | 6 | **Profit** | 3 | **Loss** | −1½ | 7½ |

## Bearish Approach: Using Out-of-the-Money Puts

If a trader expects the underlying stock to go down toward the expiration of the short put, he should initiate a put time spread using a strike price lower than the stock price. In contrast, as illustrated above, when a trader expects the underlying stock to rise toward the expiration of the short put, he should initiate a put time spread using a strike price higher than the stock price.

Following is an illustration on the bearish time spreading strategy utilizing out-of-the-money puts.

*Example:* Assuming that XYZ had the following out-of-the-money puts when the stock traded at 55:

|  | Aug | Nov | Feb | Stock Price |
|---|---|---|---|---|
| **Strike Price 50** | 2 | 4 | 5½ | 55 |

A bearish put time spread might be set up with a 1½-point debit:

| | |
|---|---|
| Buy February 50 put at | 5½ |
| Sell November 50 put at | 4 |
| Debit | 1½ |

If the investor's market assessment had proved correct and the stock declined to the strike price of 50 at November expiration, the November 50 put would expire worthless, while the February 50 put might be trading at 7, creating the following profit/loss picture:

| | Nov 50 | | Feb 50 | Credit/ (Debit) |
|---|---|---|---|---|
| **Sold** | 4 | **Bought** | 5½ | (1½) |
| **Expired** | 0 | **Sold** | 7 | 7 |
| **Profit** | 4 | **Profit** | 1½ | 5½ |

In other words, with the passage of time, and as the stock price declined to the strike price of the put option, the spread would widen from 1½ to 7 points, indicating a 5½-point profit on the spread transaction.

If the investor's market assessment had proved wrong and the stock advanced to 60, the November option would still expire worthless, while the February option would be given some value because of its remaining time. While it's possible that the original 1½-point spread might remain essentially unchanged, the spread would probably not have widened to a point where a profit would occur for the spreader.

## Bearish Put Time Spread versus Bearish Call Time Spread

Bearish put time spreads generally are more frequently used than bearish call time spreads, for two reasons. First, since bearish put time spreads typically are structured with out-of-the-money options, the chance of exercise is less than with bearish call time spreads, where in-the-money options are used.

Second, an out-of-the-money put tends to have a larger time value than an in-the-money call. The key to profitable time spreading (whether call or put) depends, to a great extent, on the diminishing time value of the short option.

Note that all our illustrations on put time spreads (bullish, bearish, or neutral) involve buying the further-out options and selling the closer-by options. Put time spreads that involve selling the further-out options and buying the closer-by options are seldom used. For one thing, they require much higher margin requirements. For another, the passage of time tends to work against such spreads.

## OVERVIEW

### What

Also called a "vertical" or "money" spread, a put price spread involves the purchase or sale of puts having the same expiration month but different strike prices.

### Why

A price spread is set up with the expectation that the spread will narrow so that it can be bought back for less than it was originally sold.

### How

Like call spreads, put price spreads can be used both for bullish and bearish purposes. In a bullish put price spread, you sell the higher strike price and buy the lower strike price. In a bearish put spread, you do the reverse.

### Vertical Structure

A put price spread consists of two puts that have the same expiration month but different strike prices. Listed options data are shown in vertical lines in daily newspaper option price tables; hence, the name. Following is an example of such a vertical listing on the June puts of Northwest Industries (NWT) with the strike prices of 50 and 55 on November 14, 1977:

| Strike Price | June | Stock Price |
|---|---|---|
| 50 | 3 | 52 |
| 55 | 5 | 52 |

Like call price spreads, put price spreads can be used both for bullish and bearish purposes.

Essentially, a bull put spread is long the less expensive put and short the more expensive put. Conversely, a bear put spread is long the more expensive put and short the less expensive put. In other words, a bullish approach calls for selling a put with a higher strike price and buying a put with a lower strike price. A bearish approach is the converse.

Call and put price spreaders differ in their attitude toward exercise. Whereas a bull spreader in puts is hurt by exercise, a bull spreader in calls welcomes exercise. Conversely,

# put sprice spreads

a bear spreader in puts welcomes exercise, but a bear spreader in calls does not.

# BULLISH APPROACH: SELL HIGHER STRIKE, BUY LOWER STRIKE

## Risk in One-Sided Simple Buying

If an investor were bullish on a certain stock he might consider writing (selling) a put with the expectation that the stock would go up and the option premium would be retained. There is considerable risk in this one-sided simple selling, however. If the underlying stock should decline, the investor might have to buy the stock back at a price much higher than the original market price.

## Risk-Reducing Element

To reduce the risk in this situation, the investor might also buy a put with a lower strike price.

**Example:** XYZ had the following puts when the stock traded at 45:

| Strike Price | Put Price | Stock Price |
| --- | --- | --- |
| 40 | 3 | 45 |
| 45 | 6 | 45 |

An investor who was bullish on XYZ and who only wrote a put might select the at-the-money 45 put because its price would have the highest correlation with a move in the underlying stock. This simple-selling strategy would be based on the expectation that the underlying stock would go up, the 45 put would expire worthless, and the put premium of 6 would be retained. The seller's maximum profit would be 6 (the premium received).

However, if the stock should fall from 45 to zero, theoretically possible, there would be a risk of 39:

| | |
| --- | --- |
| Stock price | 45 |
| Put premium received | −6 |
| Theoretical risk | 39 |

To reduce the risk inherent in this situation, the investor might consider buying a lower-strike-price 40 put at 3 to establish the following bullish price spread:

| | |
| --- | --- |
| Sell July 45 put at | 6 |
| Buy July 40 put at | 3 |
| Spread credit | 3 |

This spread would be set up with the expectation that the spread would narrow so that it would be bought back for less than it was originally sold.

Let's analyze the above spread from the viewpoint of potential profit versus potential risk. On one side of the scale, the potential profit would now be limited to the spread credit of 3 (the difference between the sell premium of 6 and the buy premium of 3) instead of the premium of 6 received under the simple-selling strategy.

On the other side of the scale, the potential risk would now be limited to 2:

| | |
| --- | --- |
| Difference in strike prices (45 − 40) | 5 |
| Spread credit received | −3 |
| Potential risk | 2 |

The potential profit of 3 versus the potential risk of 2 would be considered an acceptable risk/reward ratio, a concept explained in the following section.

The maximum profit for the spread would occur when the underlying stock at expiration went beyond the higher strike price of 45, rendering both puts worthless. The spread would have thus narrowed to zero, and the spreader would realize the maximim gain of 3 (6 − 3).

On the other hand, if the stock should fall below the lower strike price of 40 at expiration, the long 40 put would expire worthless, while the short 45 put would be selling at its intrinsic value of 5 (45 − 40). The spread would have widened to 5 points and the spreader would realize the maximum potential loss of 2:

| | |
| --- | --- |
| Short put value | 5 |
| Spread credit originally received | −3 |
| Maximum potential loss | 2 |

# HOW TO CALCULATE THE POTENTIAL SPREAD PROFIT/RISK

### Calculation of Potential Spread Profit

In our previous illustration on XYZ, the maximum potential spread profit equals the spread credit (the differential between the sell and buy premiums):

| | |
|---|---|
| Sell premium | 6 |
| Buy premium | 3 |
| Maximum potential profit | 3 |

### Calculation of Potential Spread Risk

The maximum potential spread risk is equal to the strike differential (the difference between the strike prices) *less* the spread credit.

In other words, the sum of the maximum potential profit and the maximum potential risk equals the strike differential. Thus, the greater the maximum potential spread profit, the less the maximum potential spread risk.

### How to Maximize Spread Profit/Risk

In order to maximize the potential spread profit, experienced traders do not consider *selling* a price spread unless they can sell it at a credit of no less (preferably more) than 60 percent of the difference between the strike prices. In our XYZ illustration, the spread credit of 3 is equal to 60 percent of the strike differential of 5 and is, thus, in line with the foregoing spread selling guideline.

By the same token, experienced traders do not *buy* a price spread unless they can buy it at a debit of no more (preferably less) than 40 percent of the strike differential (the difference between the strike prices). Buying price spread is a bearish strategy, to be discussed in a later section.

### Calculation of the Spread Breakeven Point

The spread breakeven point is the price at which the underlying stock may sell on the last option trading day and return your initial investment (potential spread risk). It is computed by adding the potential spread risk to the strike price of the long option.

The above rules regarding (1) selling a spread at a credit of no less than 60 percent of the spread or (2) buying a spread at a debit of no more than 40 percent of the spread apply both to a 5-point spread and to a 10-point spread.

### 5-Point Spread Calculations

In a 5-point spread, the maximum potential profit plus the maximum potential risk totals 5 points. In our above XYZ illustration, the maximum potential profit is 3 and the maximum potential risk is 2 (5 − 3). If the maximum potential profit were 3½, the maximum potential risk would be 1½ (5 − 3½), as calculated below.

1. Calculation of potential profit:

| | |
|---|---|
| Sell premium | 4 |
| Buy premium | −½ |
| Potential spread profit | 3½ |

2. Calculation of potential risk:

| | |
|---|---|
| Spread differential (45 − 40) | 5 |
| Potential profit | −3½ |
| Potential spread risk | 1½ |

3. Calculation of breakeven point:

| | |
|---|---|
| Strike price of the long option | 40 |
| Potential risk | +1½ |
| Breakeven point | 41½ |

### 10-Point Spread Calculations

In a 10-point spread, the maximum potential profit plus the maximum potential risk totals 10 points. In order to maximize the potential spread, experienced traders do not sell a price spread at a credit of less than 60 percent (or 6 points) of a 10-point spread or buy a price spread at a debit of more than 40 percent (or 4 points) of a 10-point spread.

Assuming the following XYZ 70-60 put price spread:

| | |
|---|---|
| Sell XYZ 70 put at | 9 |
| Buy XYZ 60 put at | 3 |
| Credit | 6 |

The maximum profit, risk and break-even are calculated below:

1. Calculation of potential profit:

| | |
|---|---|
| Sell premium | 9 |
| Buy premium | −3 |
| Potential spread profit | 6 |

2. Calculation of potential risk:

| | |
|---|---|
| Spread differential (70 − 60) | 10 |
| Potential profit | −6 |
| Potential spread risk | 4 |

3. Calculation of breakeven point:

| | |
|---|---|
| Strike price of the long option | 60 |
| Potential risk | +4 |
| Breakeven point | 64 |

# BEARISH APPROACH: BUY HIGHER STRIKE, SELL LOWER STRIKE

If an investor were bearish on a certain stock, he might buy a put with the expectation that if the anticipated decline in the price of the underlying stock should take place, the value of the put would rise.

Assume XYZ had the following June puts when the stock traded at 50:

| Strike Price | Put Price | Stock Price |
|---|---|---|
| 45 | 3 | 50 |
| 50 | 5 | 50 |

The investor who was bearish on the stock and who only bought a put might select the at-the-money 50 put for 5 because its price would have the highest correlation with a move in the underlying stock. The risk of this simple-buying strategy would be limited to the purchase premium of 5, while its maximum profit potential would be 45 (the difference between the stock price of 50 and the purchase premium of 5 if the stock should decline to zero, a theoretical possibility).

## Risk/Reward Potential

To reduce his capital commitment as well as his maximum potential risk, the investor might consider selling a put with a lower strike price. In our above illustration, he might sell the 45 put for 3, thereby reducing his maximum risk from 5 to 2 (5 − 3):

| | |
|---|---|
| Buy XYZ 50 put at | 5 |
| Sell XYZ 45 put at | 3 |
| Debit | 2 |

In effect, he would be establishing a 50 − 45 bearish price spread at a debit of 2. While his maximum potential risk would now be limited to the initial 2-point debit, his maximum potential profit would now be limited to 3:

| | |
|---|---|
| Difference between the strike price (50 − 45) | 5 |
| Initial spread debit | −2 |
| Potential spread profit | 3 |

The potential spread profit of 3 would amount to 60 percent of the 5-point spread and is thus in line with the spread-buying guideline's buying at a debit of no more than 40 percent of the spread.

## How to Widen a Bear Put Price Spread

A bear put price spread should be structured with the objective of its widening to a point where it can be sold at a profit. This outcome will occur if the anticipated decline in the price of the underlying stock takes place.

*Example:* Assume XYZ had the following August puts when the stock traded at 100:

| Strike Price | Put Price | Stock Price |
|---|---|---|
| 100 | 9 | 100 |
| 90 | 5 | 100 |
| 80 | 2 | 100 |

Further, assume an investor initiated the following bear put price spread:

| | |
|---|---|
| Buy August 100 put at | 9 |
| Sell August 90 put at | 5 |
| Debit | 4 |

The spread was set up at a 4-point debit (40% of the 10-point spread) with the expectation that the underlying stock would decline.

If the spreader's assessment is correct and the stock declines to the strike price of 90 or lower by August expiration, the August 90 put would expire worthless and the August 100 put would be selling at its intrinsic value of 10 points. The spread would widen to 10 as follows:

| | |
|---|---|
| The long put (August 100) worth | 10 |
| The short put (August 90) worth | 0 |
| | 10 |

The spreader would have a profit of 6:

| | |
|---|---|
| Spread widened to | 10 |
| Spread originally bought at a debit of | −4 |
| Spread profit | 6 |

With the spread trading at any price below 90, the two puts would rise in value point for point with the stock decline.

If the spreader's assessment of the underlying stock's outlook were wrong, and if the stock did not decline below 100 by August expiration, both puts would expire worthless, and the spread would have narrowed to zero, with a maximum loss of 4 points (the initial spread debit).

# HOW TO ROLL A BEAR PUT PRICE SPREAD

The bear put price spreader in the foregoing illustration can consider rolling down to a new position if the spread becomes profitable before August expiration. Here are the data for the original put price structure, when the stock traded at 100:

| Strike Price | Put Price | Stock Price |
|---|---|---|
| 100 | 9 | 100 |
| 90 | 5 | 100 |
| 80 | 2 | 100 |

The bear put price spread was:

| | |
|---|---|
| Buy August 100 put at | 9 |
| Sell August 90 put at | 5 |
| Debit | 4 |

Following is the new bear put price spread structure, when the stock declined from 100 to 90:

| Strike Price | Put Price | Stock Price |
|---|---|---|
| 100 | 10 | 95 |
| 90 | 4 | 94 |
| 80 | 2 | 95 |

If the spreader decides to liquidate his spread position, he can do so, since the spread has widened to 6 points (10 − 4) from the original 4-point spread.

The spreader might consider rolling down his position by buying the August 90 put for 4 in a closing transaction, and selling the August 80 put for 2 in an opening transaction. Doing so would allow the in-the-money August 100 put to continue its upside profitability.

If the stock declined to 80 at the August expiration, the August 80 put would expire worthless, and the August 100 put would be selling at its intrinsic value of 20 (100 − 80).

The following shows these rolling-down transactions:

| Aug 100 | | Aug 90 | | Aug 80 | | Credit/ (Debit) |
|---|---|---|---|---|---|---|
| Bought | 9 | Sold | 5 | | | (4) |
| | | Bought | 4 | Sold | 2 | (2) |
| Sold | 20 | | | Expired | 0 | 20 |
| Profit | 11 | Profit | 1 | Profit | 2 | 14 |

This rolling transaction would result in a profit of 14 points. Compare this profit with the much smaller maximum profit potential of 6 points without the rolling operation.

There is considerable risk, however, in rolling a bearish put price spread. The primary risk is that the underlying stock might reverse its course and go back up, leading to the dissipation or even disappearance of the profit in the August 100 put. Should this occur, the relatively small profit remaining in the August 90 and August 80 puts would provide the only offsetting factor.

# OTHER
# MULTIPLE OPTIONS
# AND MARGINS

PART **IX**

### What

A straddle is the purchase or sale of both a call and a put with the same strike price and the same expiration month on the same underlying stock.

### Why

Straddles provide both the buyer and the seller an opportunity to make money. Besides, neither investor need know the direction of the stocks on which they structure straddles!

### How

For a straddle buyer to profit from his transaction, he needs only a sufficient fluctuation in the stock price, regardless of its direction. Straddle works best for buyers of volatile stocks, which are likely to fluctuate. The straddle seller makes money if the fluctuations in price remain narrow.

The advent of listed puts has made the straddle an increasingly used strategy. A straddle is the purchase or sale of both a call and a put with the same strike price and the same expiration date on the same underlying stock.

While calls and puts can be used together in various combinations, the straddle is probably the most common of them.

### No Need to Know Market Direction

Why have straddles developed into a major trading tool? Simply stated, straddles provide traders on both sides an opportunity to make money, and straddle investors need not know the direction of the market. For a straddle buyer to profit from the transaction, only a sufficient fluctuation in the price of the stock is necessary, regardless of its direction. For a straddle seller to benefit from the transaction, it

straddles

26

is necessary for the price fluctuation to stay narrow.

As a rule, the sale (writing) of straddles is advisable when it seems likely that the price of the stock will fluctuate within narrow bounds.

On the other hand, the purchase of straddles is advisable if the price of the stock seems to show a definite trend. In this event, the investor expects one side of the straddle to produce a profit and the other side to provide insurance against a sudden and unexpected reversal of the trend.

### *Straddle Premium*

Since it is very unusual for straddle holders to fail to liquidate at least one side of a straddle option profitably, straddle writers generally obtain larger premiums than call or put writers. Straddle premiums are approximately 70 percent higher than call premiums that cover the same time period.

The generally strong demand for straddles also contributes to their high premiums.

Of course, the generally higher premiums for straddle options mean correspondingly larger losses should they fail to work out. Insufficient movement in the price of such stocks causes the straddle to fail and straddle buyers to lose the bulk of their premium money.

### *Upper And Lower Profit Levels*

To illustrate the method of calculating the upper and lower profit levels of a long straddle position, we use an ABC example, the basics of which are as follows:

On November 8, 1977, ABC Broadcasting (ABC) had the following May 40 call and put when the stock was 39½:

| Option | May 40 | Stock Price |
|---|---|---|
| Call | 2⅝ | 39½ |
| Put | 3 | 39½ |

A May 40 straddle could have been structured thus:

| | |
|---|---|
| Buy ABC May 40 Call at | 2⅝ |
| Buy ABC May 40 Put at | 3 |
| Straddle cost | 5⅝ |

***Example:*** *Calculating Profit on the Call Side:* The straddle would have become profitable when the stock moved above 45⅝:

| | |
|---|---|
| Strike price | 40 |
| Cost of straddle | +5⅝ |
| | 45⅝ |

***Example:*** *Calculating Profit on the Put Side:* The straddle would have become profitable when the stock moved below 34⅜:

| | |
|---|---|
| Strike price | 40 |
| Cost of straddle | −5⅝ |
| | 34⅜ |

In other words, the straddle buyer would have been profitable when the underlying stock rose above 45⅝ or declined below 34⅜.

On the other side of the trade, the profit or loss position for the straddle seller (writer) is just the opposite. He would have become profitable if the stock stayed within the range of 34⅜ to 45⅝, which is appropriately called his zone of profitability.

In other words, a straddle seller (writer) realizes a profit as long as the price of the underlying stock remains within a narrow range, or more specifically, within a range of the exercise price plus or minus the total premiums involved.

## LONG STRADDLE

### *Volatility*

The single most important rule for a straddle buyer to remember is that the underlying stock has to be sufficiently volatile to make his straddle buying (long straddle) position profitable. A straddle will be profitable for the buyer if the stock moves far enough in *either* direction. His maximum risk is limited to the amount of his initial investment.

## Other Key Criteria

In addition to volatility, straddle buyers should look for the following criteria in stocks to underlie straddles:

1. Stocks that sell at high price/earnings ratios
2. Stocks that sell for a high dollar price per share
3. Stocks that sell close to the high for the current year.

## Advantage of Far Expiration Month

In selecting the expiration month for buying straddles, middle or far expiration months are desirable to give the underlying stock time to experience several substantial fluctuations in either direction during the life of the straddle. (Of course, time advantage usually means a higher price.)

The more frequent such fluctuations, the more trading opportunities the straddle holder has.

## Basic Straddle Analysis

In order to help understand the straddle more fully, let's work through an example.

**Example:** Assume XYZ is at 50 when you establish a long straddle position by buying a 3-month call at 3 and a 3-month put at 2:

| | |
|---|---|
| Buy XYZ 50 call at | 3 |
| Buy XYZ 50 put at | 2 |
| Straddle cost | 5 |

If XYZ rose to 60, the straddle buyer would have a $5-per-share gain from the call side ($500 per 100-share contract):

| | |
|---|---|
| 50 call's gain (60 − 50) | 10 |
| Straddle cost | 5 |
| | 5 |

If XYZ rose further, to 70, the straddle buyer would gain $15 per share ($1,500 per contract) from the call side:

| | |
|---|---|
| 50 call's gain (70 − 50) | 20 |
| Straddle cost | 5 |
| | 15 |

On the other hand, if XYZ declined, from 50 to 40, the straddle still would have a gain of $5 per share, this time from the put side:

| | |
|---|---|
| 50 put's gain (50 − 40) | 10 |
| Straddle cost | 5 |
| | 5 |

If XYZ declined further, to 30, the straddle would gain $15 per share, also from the put side:

| | |
|---|---|
| 50 put's gain (50 − 30) | 20 |
| Straddle cost | 5 |
| | 15 |

Only if the stock stood still or remained substantially unchanged would the straddle buyer suffer a loss; in our example, the loss would be $3 per share on the call side and $2 per share on the put side.

Profit and loss on this straddle at expiration are as follows:

| Stock Price at Expiration | Call Profit or Loss | Put Profit or Loss | Straddle Profit or Loss |
|---|---|---|---|
| 30 | −$ 300 | +$1,800 | +$1,500 |
| 40 | −$ 300 | +$ 800 | +$ 500 |
| 50 | −$ 300 | +$ 200 | −$ 500 |
| 60 | +$ 700 | −$ 200 | +$ 500 |
| 70 | +$1,700 | −$ 200 | +$1,500 |

Note that the straddle buyer profits if the underlying stock moves far enough in *either* direction—up or down. He will incur a loss if XYZ stands still; however, his loss will be limited to his two option purchase premiums, totaling $500. The maximum loss is predetermined.

# SHORT STRADDLE

A short straddle is a combination of one call and one put written on the same stock at the same strike price with the same expiration date.

*Example:* On December 7, 1977, Honeywell (HON) had the following August 45 call and put when the stock traded at 45:

| Strike Price | Call Price | Put Price | Stock Price |
|---|---|---|---|
| 45 | 4⅝ | 3 | 45 |

A short straddle would have been established if an investor had sold both an August 45 call and an August 45 put:

| | |
|---|---|
| Sell August 45 call at | 4⅝ |
| Sell August 45 put at | 3 |
| Total premiums | 7⅝ |

The straddle was sold (written) with the expectation that the underlying stock would not move significantly either up or down.

## Calculation of Profit Parameters

The following is a simple method for calculating the profit parameters of a short straddle position:

1. Straddle proceeds:

| | |
|---|---|
| Call premium | 4⅝ |
| Put premium | 3 |
| Total proceeds | 7⅝ |

2. Upside profit parameter:

| | |
|---|---|
| Strike price | 45 |
| Straddle proceeds | +7⅝ |
| | 52⅝ |

3. Downside profit parameter:

| | |
|---|---|
| Strike Price | 45 |
| Straddle proceeds | −7⅝ |
| | 37⅜ |

4. Profitability zone: 52⅝ to 37⅜

You can figure out the potential profit zone of a straddle you are planning to sell simply by using the straddle strike price plus or minus the total premiums you would receive for selling the straddle. The straddle seller will remain profitable as long as the underlying stock stays within a range of the exercise price *plus* (for the upside limit) or *minus* (for the downside limit) the total premiums received.

Even if the stock in the example above had moved 4 points up or down, the premiums received would still have provided a sufficient cushion to result in an overall profit.

If the stock had risen rose 4 points, from 45 to 49, the call would have been exercised at a 4-point loss (49 − 45) for the straddle writer. But the 7⅝-point total premiums received would have more than covered the 4-point loss, resulting in an overall profit of 3⅝ (7⅝ − 4).

On the other hand, if the stock had declined 4 points, from 45 to 41, the put would also have been exercised, at a 4-point loss to the straddle seller. Here, too, however, the 7⅝ total premiums received would still have provided a gain of 3⅝.

## Whipsaw

Straddle sellers should be aware of the risk of major market moves in *either* direction. Even more dangerous, though, is the situation where the underlying stock both rises *and* declines during the life of the options.

Unhedged (uncovered) straddle sellers must always be aware of this possibility, called a "whipsaw" (a sharp price movement in one direction quickly followed by a sharp reversal in the opposite direction) and should at all times be prepared to have to buy *and* sell the underlying stock at the option holders' discretion.

If, in the HON illustration, the stock had initially dropped 7 points, from 45 to 38, the put might have been exercised, delivering a 7-point loss to the straddle writer. If the stock had subsequently reversed its course and had risen to 52, the call might also have been exercised, resulting in a second 7-point loss to the straddle seller. The total loss of 14 points would only be partially offset by the 7⅝-point premium cushion, resulting in an overall loss of 6⅜ (14 − 7⅝).

# BULLISH VERSUS BEARISH APPROACH

An investor may buy or sell a straddle with a strike price *below* the stock price to give a bullish bias to the straddle position. On the other hand, he may buy or sell a straddle *above* the stock price to give a bearish bias to the straddle position.

A straddle position is considered bullish when it takes only a relatively small up-move for the straddle buyer to break even. A straddle position is considered bearish when it requires only a relatively small down-move for the straddle buyer to break even.

## Bullish Approach: Using Out-of-the-Money Puts

Generally, an out-of-the-money put, with its strike price *below* the stock price, is used to structure a bullish straddle. Several examples illustrate bullish techniques. The basic scenario follows.

Assume XYZ had the following May calls and puts when the stock traded at 50:

| Strike Price | Call Price | Put Price | Stock Price |
|---|---|---|---|
| May 45 | 6 | 2 | 50 |
| May 50 | 3 | 4 | 50 |
| May 60 | 1 | 11 | 50 |

An investor established a bullish straddle buying position by using the May 45 call and put:

| | |
|---|---|
| Buy May 45 call at | 6 |
| Buy May 45 put at | 2 |
| Straddle cost | 8 |

**Example:** *Calculation of Straddle Buyer's Position:* The call side becomes profitable at 53:

| | |
|---|---|
| Strike price | 45 |
| Straddle cost | +8 |
| | 53 |

The put side becomes profitable at 37:

| | |
|---|---|
| Strike price | 45 |
| Straddle cost | −8 |
| | 37 |

The straddle buyer's position would become profitable with the stock trading above 53 or below 37.

Since the underlying stock would have to make only a 2-point (4%) up-move, from 50 to 52, for the straddle buyer to break even, the straddle is considered a bullish one. On the other hand, the stock would have to decline 13 points (26%), from 50 to 37, before the straddle would break even.

**Example:** *Calculation of Straddle Seller's Position:* The profitability zone for the straddle seller is the reverse of that for the buyer. The seller becomes profitable with the stock trading between 37 and 53 and loses money at any stock price either *above* or *below* that range.

## Bearish Approach: Using In-the-Money Puts

Generally, an in-the-money put (with a strike price *above* the stock price) is used in constructing a bearish straddle.

Using the put price data from the preceding XYZ example, let's follow an investor who establishes a bearish straddle buying position by using the in-the-money May 60 call and put as follows:

| | |
|---|---|
| Buy May 60 call at | 1 |
| Buy May 60 put at | 11 |
| Straddle cost | 12 |

**Example:** *Calculation of Straddle Buyer's Position:* The call side becomes profitable at 72:

| | |
|---|---|
| Strike price | 60 |
| Straddle cost | +12 |
| | 72 |

The put side becomes profitable at 48:

| | |
|---|---|
| Strike price | 60 |
| Straddle cost | −12 |
| | 48 |

The straddle buyer is in a profitable position with the stock trading *above* 72 and *below* 48.

Since the underlying stock would have to make only a 2-point (4%) down-move, from 50 to 48, for the straddle buyer to break even, the straddle is considered a bearish one. On the other hand, the underlying stock would have to make a 12-point (24%) up-move, from 50 to 72, for the straddle to break even.

**Example:** *Calculation of Straddle Seller's Position:* As compared with the straddle buyer's position, the straddle seller's is just the reverse. He is in a profitable position with the stock trading between 48 and 72; he would lose money at any stock price either *above* or *below* that range.

# SHORT STRADDLE, LONG STOCK

## With or Without a Related Stock Position

The foregoing discussion of short straddle assumes no long or short related stock existing at the time the straddle is sold (written). However, the sale of a straddle may be done with or without a long or short related stock position. The sale of a straddle obligates the seller to sell 100 shares of the underlying stock at the strike price.

A straddle seller with a long position in the underlying stock is usually motivated by one of two beliefs. One is based on an extremely bullish view of the underlying stock, permitting the sale of a very expensive call. It is equivalent roughly to two covered writes. The other is based on the straddle seller's willingness either to sell his existing stock position at a higher price or buy additional stock at a lower price.

Many straddle sellers own the underlying stock as a means of generating premium income. Let's compare the risk-and-reward possibilities of the sale of a straddle alone with the combination of a straddle seller with a long position in the underlying stock.

## Short Straddle Alone

To illustrate, assume the following May calls and puts on XYZ when the stock traded at 50:

| Strike Price | Call Price | Put Price | Stock Price |
|---|---|---|---|
| May 45 | 6 | 2 | 50 |
| May 50 | 3 | 4 | 50 |
| May 60 | 1 | 11 | 50 |

A straddle seller sold a May 50 call and a May 50 put:

| | |
|---|---|
| Sell May 50 call | 3 |
| Sell May 50 put | 4 |
| Straddle credit | 7 |

He would make money between 57 and 43:

1. Upside profit level:

| | |
|---|---|
| Strike price | 50 |
| Straddle credit | +7 |
| | 57 |

2. Downside profit level:

| | |
|---|---|
| Strike price | 50 |
| Straddle credit | −7 |
| | 43 |

The profits and losses at various stock prices at expiration are tabulated thus:

| Stock price | Call | Put | Premium Received | Profit or Loss |
|---|---|---|---|---|
| 35 | 0 | −15 | 7 | −8 |
| 40 | 0 | −10 | 7 | −3 |
| 43 | 0 | −7 | 7 | 0 |
| 45 | 0 | −5 | 7 | 2 |
| 50 | 0 | 0 | 7 | 7 |
| 55 | −5 | 0 | 7 | 2 |
| 57 | −7 | 0 | 7 | 0 |
| 60 | −10 | 0 | 7 | −3 |
| 65 | −15 | 0 | 7 | −8 |

The maximum profit for the straddle seller occurs with the stock at expiration trading at the strike price of 50. Both the call and the put investor has written are rendered worthless at 50, enabling the seller to retain the entire premium of 7 without further obligation.

If, at expiration, the stock moves away from the strike price (either up or down), the straddle seller's profit diminishes. If the stock rises to 55, for instance, the call would be exercised by the holder at a 5-point loss to the straddle seller, but the premium received (7) would provide a cushion, and the seller's overall profit would be 2 (7 − 5). The upside breakeven point exists at 57 when a 7-point loss on the call would be offset by the 7-point premium cushion.

If the stock declines to 45, the put will be exercised at a 5-point loss to the straddle seller; however, the 7-point premium cushion would more than cover the call loss, with an overall gain of 2 (7 − 5) for the straddle seller. The downside breakeven point exists at 43, beyond which any further stock decline would result in an overall loss.

## Combining a Short Straddle with Long Stock

The inclusion of the stock makes the combination profitable at 46½:

| | |
|---|---|
| Strike price | 50 |
| Straddle premiums: | |
| Call 3 | |
| Put 4 | |
| 7 | |
| *Less* Average premium (7 ÷ 2) | −3½ |
| Point of profit | 46½ |

The maximum profit of 7 would be realized at any price above the strike price of 50, as indicated in the following profit-or-loss results:

| Stock Price Levels | Call | Put | Profit or Loss | Premiums Received | Stock Profit or Loss | Total Profit or Loss |
|---|---|---|---|---|---|---|
| 35 | 0 | | −15 | 7 | −15 | −27 |
| 40 | 0 | | −10 | 7 | −10 | −13 |
| 45 | 0 | | −5 | 7 | −5 | −3 |
| 46½ | 0 | | −3½ | 7 | −3½ | 0 |
| 50 | 0 | | 0 | 7 | 0 | 7 |
| 55 | −5 | | 0 | 7 | 0 | 7 |
| 60 | −10 | | 0 | 7 | 10 | 7 |
| 65 | −15 | | 0 | 7 | 15 | 7 |

The breakeven point for this position occurs at 46½ when the 3½ point loss *each* on the short put and the long stock would be just offset by the 7-point premium cushion.

On the downside, this short-straddle, long-stock combination would lose money twice as fast as the sale of the straddle alone, because both the short put and the long stock would be moving against this investor.

## How to Reduce the Risk in a Short Straddle

How to reduce the risk in a short straddle? Through the purchase of a call at a higher strike price and a put at a lower strike price. The following data apply:

On December 12, 1977, Mesa Petroleum (MSA) had the following May calls and puts when the stock traded at 40:

| Strike Price | Call Price | Put Price | Stock Price |
|---|---|---|---|
| 35 | | 1¼ | 40 |
| 40 | 4½ | 2⅞ | 40 |
| 45 | 2⁵⁄₁₆ | | 40 |

*Example:* *Short Straddle Alone:*
An investor sells a MSA 40 straddle alone:

| | |
|---|---|
| Sell May 40 call at | 4½ |
| Sell May 40 put at | 2⅞ |
| Credit | 7⅜ |

Such a short straddle with a 7⅜-point credit would be profitable between the following two parameters:

1. Upside profit level:

| | |
|---|---|
| Call strike price | 40 |
| Straddle credit | +7⅜ |
| | 47⅜ |

2. Downside profit level:

| | |
|---|---|
| Put strike price | 40 |
| Straddle credit | −7⅜ |
| | 32⅝ |

Thus, the straddle would be profitable between 47⅜ and 32⅝.

The disadvantage of a short straddle alone is the potentially unlimited loss on the call if the underlying stock rises, and a virtually unlimited potential loss on the put if the stock falls. The next example shows a limited potential loss.

***Example:*** *Short Straddle, Long Call, Long Put:* To limit the risk in a short straddle, an investor could buy a call at a higher strike price and a put at a lower strike price than the straddle strike price:

| | |
|---|---|
| Buy May 45 call at | 2 5/16 |
| Sell May 40 call at | 4½ |
| Sell May 40 put at | 2⅞ |
| Buy May 35 put at | 1¼ |
| Credit | 3 9/16 |

Sell premiums of 7⅛ (4½ + 2⅞), *less* buy premiums of 3 9/16 (2 5/16 + 1¼), result in an overall credit of 3 9/16 for the entire position.

The addition of the out-of-the-money put and the out-of-the-money call in the preceding example has limited the potential loss, regardless of how far up or down the stock might move. In return for limiting the risk, the investor has paid two additional commissions and narrowed his profit range.

# HOW TO CALCULATE STRADDLE MARGINS

## *Margin on a Long Straddle*

A long straddle involves a long call and a long put. Both options must be paid for in full, and neither will have loan value in a margin account.

***Example:*** On December 12, 1977, Mesa Petroleum (MSA) had the following July 40 call and put when the stock traded at 40:

| Strike Price | Call Price | Put Price | Stock Price |
|---|---|---|---|
| 40 | 4½ | 2⅞ | 40 |

If you had no cash or other securities in your cash or margin account, and if you bought a July 40 call and a July 40 put, you would have to deposit $738, per the calculation below, as full payment for the call and the put:

| | |
|---|---|
| Buy July 40 call (4½ × 100 shares) | $450 |
| Buy July 40 put (2⅞ × 100 shares) | $288 |
| Total payment required | $738 |

## *Margin on a Short Straddle*

A short straddle involves a short call and a short put. The required margin will be the uncovered short requirement on the call or the put, whichever is *greater.*

***Example:*** On December 12, 1977, Northwest Industries (NWT) had the following March 55 call and put when the stock traded at 55½:

| Strike Price | Call Price | Put Price | Stock Price |
|---|---|---|---|
| 55 | 3 | 2 13/16 | 55½ |

If you had no cash or securities in your cash or margin account, and if you bought a March 55 call at 3 and a March 55 put at 2 13/16, the required margin would be the *greater* of the following two computations:

1. Call computation

| | |
|---|---:|
| 30% of stock price (55½) | $1,665 |
| Call in-the-money amount (55½ − 55) | + 50 |
| Margin requirement | $1,715 |
| Premium received (3 + 2¹³⁄₁₆) | 581 |
| Margin call | $1,134 |

2. Put computation

| | |
|---|---:|
| 30% of stock price (55½) | $1,665 |
| Put-out-of-the-money amount (55½ − 55) | − 50 |
| Margin requirement | $1,615 |
| Put-out-of-the-money amount (3 + 2¹³⁄₁₆) | −581 |
| Margin call | $1,034 |

The *greater* of the above two computations is $1,134, the margin call that must be met.

# OVERVIEW

### What

A combination is either the purchase or the sale of puts and calls on the same underlying stock with different strike prices and the same or different expiration months.

### Why

Combination strategy offers the potential of increased leverage to the buyer and additional income to the seller.

### How

For a combination buyer to have a profitable outcome requires a substantial move in the underlying stock. While the buyer should look for volatile stocks to give him a greater chance for large stock movement, the seller should seek stocks known for their lack of volatility.

### Objectives of Combinations

A combination is either the purchase or the sale of puts and calls on the same underlying stock with different strike prices and the same or different expiration months. The combination strategy offers the potential of increased leverage to the buyer and additional income to the seller (writer).

The most important factor in the success of any of these combinations is the selection of the underlying stock.

### Importance of Volatility

Often, a substantial move in the underlying stock is required for a particular combination to become profitable. Some knowledge of the degree of volatility in the stock provides the key to whether or not you should enter into an option combination strategy.

Should the buyer and the seller of combination options look for the same characteristics in selecting a combination? Definitely not! The buyer should look for volatile stocks. The seller should seek the opposite—stocks known for a

# combinations
# 27

lack of volatility. The seller wants a fairly neutral situation, a static stock expected to show little or no movement in either direction.

It is equally important to the buyer or the seller of combination options to examine the historical price behavior of the underlying stock to see if it is capable of substantial moves. Like the buyer, the seller should weigh positions to conform with a judgment on market direction in general and the direction of the underlying stock in particular. Most major brokerage houses keep records of the volatility of the most commonly held and frequently traded stocks.

Margin requirements must be considered when evaluating the potential return on any combination position. Commission costs also alter the outcome somewhat.

## Broad versus Narrow Definition

In a broad sense, combination option is anything that is not covered by the terms "put," "call," "spread," or "straddle," as currently defined on the listed option exchanges. The term "combination option" came into existence because the word "spread," as used in the OTC option market, has taken on a new meaning in the listed option market. The most common combination option is probably what in the past was referred to as a spread: an option transaction where traders buy or sell, one call and one put on the same underlying stock with either different strike prices, and/or different expiration months.

In the OTC option markets, in addition to spreads, there are other multiple options, including "strips" and "straps." A strip involves one call and two puts. A strap involves one put and two calls. Strips and straps account for a very small percentage of the OTC option market.

# COMBINATION BUYING

## Combination on the Same Expiration Month

This strategy involves the simultaneous purchase of a put and a call. Each of the options would have a different strike price.

For example, if the underlying stock is 50 and the stock has 45, 50, and 55 options, the combination buyer would purchase a 55 call and a 45 put. The purpose of combination buying is to trade one side against the other. Generally, the cash outlay should be small.

## Long Call, Long Put (with Different Strike Prices)

The following is an illustration on combination buying of a put and a call that have different strike prices but the same expiration month.

**Example:** On November 17, 1977, Santa Fe International (SAF) had the following April calls and puts when the stock was 50:

| Call Strike Price | April Call Price | Stock Price |
|---|---|---|
| 45 | 6⅞ | 50 |
| 50 | 3¾ | 50 |
| 55 | 1¾ | 50 |

| Put Strike Price | April Put Price | Stock Price |
|---|---|---|
| 45 | 1⁵⁄₁₆ | 50 |
| 50 | 3⅜ | 50 |
| 55 | 6¾ | 50 |

An investor bought an April 55 call at 1¾ and an April 45 put at 1⁵⁄₁₆.

| | |
|---|---|
| Buy April 55 call at | 1¾ |
| Buy April 45 put at | 1⁵⁄₁₆ |
| Total cost | 3¹⁄₁₆ |

Since both the call and the put are out-of-the-money, the investor would require a relatively small cash outlay of 3¹⁄₁₆. The total risk never could be more than the total cost of 3¹⁄₁₆ for the combination buying position.

If the underlying stock moved enough to make the position profitable, the leverage factor could be dramatic. At expiration, the combination buyer would make money if the stock were either above 58¹⁄₁₆ or below 41¹⁵⁄₁₆.

The call side would become profitable if the stock rose above the call strike price *plus* the cost of the two options:

| | |
|---|---|
| Call strike price | 55 |
| Cost of the two options | +3¹⁄₁₆ |
| | 58¹⁄₁₆ |

The call would have intrinsic value with the stock above the call strike price of 55, in addition to overcoming the cost of the two options.

The put side would become profitable if the stock fell below the put strike price minus the cost of the two options:

| | |
|---|---|
| Put strike price | 45 |
| Cost of the two options | −3¹⁄₁₆ |
| | 41¹⁵⁄₁₆ |

The put would become valuable when the stock declined below the put strike price of 45, in addition to overcoming the cost of the two options.

Maximum risk of 3¹⁄₁₆ would occur at any stock price between 41¹⁵⁄₁₆ and 58¹⁄₁₆.

The potential for movement in the underlying stock is all-important when buying a combination. Volatility is the key word here.

Even though the actual dollars involved are relatively small, a 16 percent move on the upside (from 50 to above 58¹⁄₁₆) and a 16 percent move on the downside (from 50 to below 41¹⁵⁄₁₆) would be necessary for this combination posi-

tion to become profitable. The need for volatility is obvious.

Naturally, large sudden moves in the underlying stock prior to expiration also can provide momentary profits in the option even though the parameters (58¹⁄₁₆ and 41¹⁵⁄₁₆) were not breached.

It also follows that the longer the option time period, the more opportunity for changes in the price of the underlying stock. However, the longer-term option will invariably cost more, and this must be weighed against the potential for increased profits.

Combination options are normally done with both sides out of the money. There are occasional instances, however, where either or both sides may be in the money.

## Step-by-Step Procedure

The following illustration will examine in detail the step-by-step combination buying procedure.

***Example:*** On November 18, 1977, Revlon (REV) had the following June call and put when the stock traded at 43:

| | Strike price | Option price | Stock price |
|---|---|---|---|
| **Call** | 45 (out of the money) | 2 | 43 |
| **Put** | 40 (out of the money) | 2⅛ | 43 |

Notice that both the call and the put were out of the money.

Assuming the following initial combination position:

| | |
|---|---|
| Buy 1 June 45 call (2 × 100 shares) | $200.00 |
| Buy 1 June 40 put (2⅛ × 100 shares) | $212.50 |
| Total cost and risk | $412.50 |

What you are shooting for is a sharp stock price movement in either direction. A sharp up-move should cause a rise in the value of the purchased call; a large down move will increase the value of the purchased put.

Approximately where the call and the put would trade at expiration date, based on various stock price levels, are shown following:

| Stock Price | June 45 Call | June 40 Put | Combination Cost | Profit or Loss |
|---|---|---|---|---|
| 28 | 0 | $+1,200 | $412.50 | $787.50 |
| 31 | 0 | + 900 | 412.50 | 484.50 |
| 34 | 0 | + 600 | 412.50 | 187.50 |
| 37 | 0 | + 300 | 412.50 | −112.50 |
| 40 | 0 | 0 | 412.50 | −412.50 |
| 45 | 0 | 0 | 412.50 | −412.50 |
| 48 | $+ 300 | 0 | 412.50 | −112.50 |
| 51 | + 600 | 0 | 412.50 | 187.50 |
| 54 | + 900 | 0 | 412.50 | 484.50 |
| 57 | +1,200 | 0 | 412.50 | 787.50 |

We summarize the above tabulation into the following "value at expiration":

| | Put | Value | Zone | | No | Value | Call | Value | | Zone |
|---|---|---|---|---|---|---|---|---|---|---|
| Option Value | 12 | 9 | 6 | 3 | 0 | 0 | 3 | 6 | 9 | 12 |
| Stock Value | 28 | 31 | 34 | 37 | 40 | 45 | 48 | 51 | 54 | 57 |

# BASIC APPROACHES

Once a combination buying position is established, there are two basic approaches to take. One is to lift a leg (either call or put) to generate enough profit to cover the cost of the combination, and hold the other "free" leg to wait for an opportune time. The other approach is to stay with both legs to wait for a major stock move.

## Leg-Lifting Approach

If either the call or the put side becomes sufficiently profitable to recoup the entire cost of the combination, liquidate the profitable side by lifting a leg. The investor holds the remaining option at virtually no cost in expectation that a decent profit will result.

*Example:* On July 28, 1977, Honeywell (HON) had the following February 60 call and February 50 put when the stock traded at 51⅛:

| | Strike Price | Option Price | Stock price |
|---|---|---|---|
| **Call** | 60 | 1¼ | 51⅛ |
| **Put** | 50 | 2½ | 51⅛ |

An investor bought the following combination:

| | |
|---|---|
| Buy February 60 call at | 1¼ |
| Buy February 50 put at | 2½ |
| Total cost | 3¾ |

As of November 8, 1977, HON had declined to 45½ when its February 50 put had risen to 4⅞, which was more than the entire cost of the combination originally bought at 3¾. If the investor had liquidated his February 50 put at 4⅞ by lifting the put leg, which would result in a 1⅛-point profit (4⅞ − 3¾), the remaining option (Feb 60 call) would have been held at no cost to him, and could have risen in value if the stock subsequently recovered.

### Aiming-at-High Approach

The alternative approach would be for the investor to stay with both sides of the combination, hoping for a major move (up or down) in the price of the underlying stock.

### Bullish versus Bearish Approach

To explain the bullish versus the bearish approach in combination buying, let's again use the Santa Fe International (SAF) and its April option price data as of November 17, 1977:

| Strike Price | Call Price | Put Price | Stock Price |
|---|---|---|---|
| 45 | 6⅞ | 1⁵⁄₁₆ | 50 |
| 50 | 3¾ | 3⅜ | 50 |
| 55 | 1¾ | 6¾ | 50 |

1. Original position: Assuming the following original combination-buying position:

| | |
|---|---|
| Buy 55 call at | 1¾ |
| Buy 45 put at | 1⁵⁄₁₆ |
| Total cost | 3¹⁄₁₆ |

The call profit level is calculated thus:

| | |
|---|---|
| Call strike price | 55 |
| Combination cost | +3¹⁄₁₆ |
| Above | 58¹⁄₁₆ |

Put profit level is calculated thus:

| | |
|---|---|
| Put strike price | 45 |
| Combination cost | −3¹⁄₁₆ |
| Below | 41¹⁵⁄₁₆ |

2. Bullish approach: If an investor were somewhat partial to an up-move in the stock, the original combination buying position could be tilted upward in various ways. One way would be to buy a call with the strike price near the stock price, while buying the same put:

| | |
|---|---|
| Buy 50 call at | 3¾ |
| Buy 45 put at | 1⁵⁄₁₆ |
| Total cost | 5¹⁄₁₆ |

Call profit level:

| | |
|---|---|
| Call strike price | 50 |
| Combination cost | +5¹⁄₁₆ |
| Above | 55¹⁄₁₆ |

Put profit level:

| | |
|---|---|
| Put strike price | 45 |
| Combination cost | −5¹⁄₁₆ |
| Below | 39¹⁵⁄₁₆ |

3. Bearish approach: If, on the other hand, an investor were partial to a down-move in the stock, he could buy a put with the strike price near the stock price and use the original call strike price at 55:

| | |
|---|---|
| Buy 55 call at | 1¾ |
| Buy 50 put at | 3⅜ |
| Total cost | 5⅛ |

Call profit level:

| | |
|---|---|
| Call strike price | 55 |
| Combination cost | +5⅛ |
| Above | 60⅛ |

Put profit level:

| | |
|---|---|
| Put strike price | 50 |
| Combination cost | −5⅛ |
| Below | 44⅞ |

To summarize the above:

1. Original position
   (A) Call profit above    58¹⁄₁₆
   (B) Put profit below    41¹⁵⁄₁₆
2. Bullish approach
   (A) Call profit above    55¹⁄₁₆
   (B) Put profit below    39¹⁵⁄₁₆
3. Bearish approach
   (A) Call profit above    60⅛
   (B) Put profit below    44⅞

## *Combination Buyer without Stock Position*

The buyer of a combination option without a position in the underlying stock generally holds the view that the stock is likely to make a major move on either the upside or the downside or both. Like the straddle buyer, the combination buyer either takes the posture that the anticipated move in the underlying stock will be more than enough to cover the cost of the premiums paid for the two options or utilizes the combination position as a trading umbrella.

## *Combination Buyer with Stock Position*

A combination buyer who owns the underlying stock considers the long put as insurance for the long stock position on the downside and the long call as added leverage on the upside.

## *Combination Buyer with a Short Stock Position*

The combination buyer may be short the underlying stock and consider the long call as insurance on the upside and the long put as added leverage on the downside.

## *Variable Ratio Combination Buying*

Instead of buying one call and one put, an investor could orient his position in the desired direction by varying the purchasing ratio (adding calls or puts).

A bullish investor may buy two calls and one put. Conversely, a bearish investor may buy two puts and one call. Let's compare the following three:

1. One call to one put combination buying
2. Two calls to one put combination buying
3. Two puts to one call combination buying.

The following data apply:

On November 25, 1977, Eastman Kodak (EK) had the following July call and put when EK traded at 53:

| | Strike Price | Option Price | Stock Price |
|---|---|---|---|
| **Call** | 60 (out-of-the-money) | 2⅜ | 53 |
| **Put** | 50 (out-of-the-money) | 2½ | 53 |

***Example****—One Call to One Put Combination Buying*

| | |
|---|---|
| Buy one 60 call at | 2⅜ |
| Buy one 50 put at | 2½ |
| Total cost | 4⅞ |

The call side would have become profitable if the stock had risen above 64⅞:

| | |
|---|---|
| Call strike price | 60 |
| Combination cost | +4⅞ |
| | 64⅞ |

The put side would have become profitable if the stock had fallen below 45⅛:

| | |
|---|---|
| Put strike price | 50 |
| Combination cost | −4⅞ |
| | 45⅛ |

***Example****—Two Calls to One Put Combination Buying*

| | |
|---|---|
| Buy two 60 calls (2 × 2⅜) | 4¾ |
| Buy one 50 put | 2½ |
| Total cost | 7¼ |

The call side would have become profitable if the stock had risen above 63⅝:

| | |
|---|---|
| Call strike price | 60 |
| Combination cost ÷ 2 | +3⅝ |
| | 63⅝ |

The combination cost of 7¼ would have allowed profitability above 63⅝ (two calls at 60, plus 3⅝ each). For each 1-point move above 63⅝, the investor would have made 2 points.

The put side would have become profitable if the stock had fallen below 42¾:

| | |
|---|---|
| Put strike price | 50 |
| Combination cost | −7¼ |
| | 42¾ |

*Example—Two Puts to One Call Combination Buying*

| | |
|---|---|
| Buy two 50 puts (2 × 2½) at | 5 |
| Buy one 60 call at | 2⅜ |
| Total cost | 7⅜ |

The call side would have become profitable if the stock had risen above 67⅜:

| | |
|---|---|
| Call strike price | 60 |
| Combination cost | +7⅜ |
| | 67⅜ |

The put side would have become profitable if the stock had fallen below 46⁵⁄₁₆.

| | |
|---|---|
| Put strike price | 50 |
| Combination cost ÷ 2 | −3¹¹⁄₁₆ |
| | 46⁵⁄₁₆ |

The combination cost of 3¹¹⁄₁₆ would have allowed a profit on the puts below 46⅝ (two puts at 50, less 3¹¹⁄₁₆ each).

To summarize:

1. One call to one put buying:
   - (A) Call profit above    64⅞
   - (B) Put profit below    45⅛
2. Two calls to one put buying:
   - (A) Call profit above    67¼
   - (B) Put profit below    42¾
3. Two puts to one call buying:
   - (A) Call profit above    67⅜
   - (B) Put profit below    42⅝

# COMBINATION SELLING

## Short Call, Short Put (with Different Strike Prices)

Combination selling involves the simultaneous sale of a call and a put. Each of the options has a different strike price. The seller is, in effect, selling a straddle where the call and the put have different strike prices but generally the same expiration month.

## Seeking a Static Stock

In selecting a combination, the seller should look for exactly the opposite of what the buyer would seek. The seller would want a fairly neutral or static stock that is expected to show little movement in either direction.

The objective for a combination seller is income or cash flow. He takes in option money when a combination writing position is initiated. This money constitutes the maximum profit that may be obtained, provided that all options written expire worthless.

## With or without Related Stock Position

The seller of a combination option may do so with or without a related stock position. A combination seller *without* a related stock position is said to be an uncovered combination seller. A combination seller *with* a related stock position is said to be a covered combination seller.

## Uncovered Combination Seller

A combination seller with no position in the underlying stock believes that the stock will remain static or move so little that both options will expire worthless. Since an uncovered combination seller does not own the underlying stock and is naked, it would be desirable for him to write shorter term options in order to minimize the potential for fluctuation in the underlying stock.

*Example:* On November 17, 1977, Santa Fe International (SAF) had the following April calls and puts when the stock was 50:

| Call Strike Price | April Call Price | Stock Price |
|---|---|---|
| 45 | 6⅞ | 50 |
| 50 | 3¾ | 50 |
| 55 | 1¾ | 50 |

| Put Strike Price | April Put Price | Stock Price |
|---|---|---|
| 45 | $1\frac{5}{16}$ | 50 |
| 50 | $3\frac{3}{8}$ | 50 |
| 55 | $6\frac{3}{4}$ | 50 |

An investor sold an April 55 call at $1\frac{3}{4}$ and an April 45 put at $1\frac{5}{16}$:

| | |
|---|---|
| Sell April 55 call at | $1\frac{3}{4}$ |
| Sell April 45 put at | $1\frac{5}{16}$ |
| Total income | $3\frac{1}{16}$ |

These options would have expired worthless if the underlying stock had stayed within the $16\frac{1}{8}$-point range ($58\frac{1}{16} - 41\frac{15}{16}$):

1. Upper profit level:

| | |
|---|---|
| Call strike price | 55 |
| Option income | $+3\frac{1}{16}$ |
| | $58\frac{1}{16}$ |

2. Lower profit level:

| | |
|---|---|
| Put strike price | 45 |
| Option income | $-3\frac{1}{16}$ |
| | $41\frac{15}{16}$ |

This $16\frac{1}{8}$-point range is called the "profit zone" (or "safety zone") for the seller. If the stock should rise above $58\frac{1}{16}$ or fall below $41\frac{15}{16}$, the seller must close the position out. Exercises must be avoided, because they create commission expenses on the underlying stock. Any closing that costs more than the $3\frac{1}{16}$ option money received would result in a loss.

Unexpected events may cause large moves in the underlying stock, and the risk can be point for point beyond the profit zone. Thus, the seller must pay even greater attention to the position than the buyer. The seller must weigh positions to conform with a judgment on market direction. As a result, the profit zone may be altered.

## Bullish Approach: Using a Put Closer to Being In The Money

The foregoing combination writing position on Santa Fe International (SAF), based on the November 17, 1977, price data, can be altered by using either a call or a put that is closer to being in-the-money.

If the put is closer to being in-the-money than the call, the combination seller's position will work better if the stock rises.

The November 17, 1977, SAF price data are as follows:

| Strike Price | Call Price | Put Price | Stock Price |
|---|---|---|---|
| 45 | $6\frac{7}{8}$ | $1\frac{5}{16}$ | 50 |
| 50 | $3\frac{3}{4}$ | $3\frac{3}{8}$ | 50 |
| 55 | $1\frac{3}{4}$ | $6\frac{3}{4}$ | 50 |

*Example:* If, instead of selling the 45 put for $1\frac{5}{15}$, the seller had sold the 50 put for $3\frac{3}{8}$, the combination would have been sold for $5\frac{1}{8}$-point premiums:

| | |
|---|---|
| Sell April 55 call at | $1\frac{3}{4}$ |
| Sell April 50 put at | $3\frac{3}{8}$ |
| Total income | $5\frac{1}{8}$ |

The profit zone for the combination seller would have been between the following two parameters:

1. Upside profit level

| | |
|---|---|
| Call strike price | 55 |
| Premium income | $+5\frac{1}{8}$ |
| | $60\frac{1}{8}$ |

2. Downside profit level

| | |
|---|---|
| Put strike price | 50 |
| Premium income | $-5\frac{1}{8}$ |
| | $44\frac{7}{8}$ |

3. Profit range: Between $60\frac{1}{8}$ and $44\frac{7}{8}$

## Bearish Approach: Using a Call Closer to Being In the Money

*Example:* If, instead of the 55 call for $1\frac{3}{4}$, the investor had sold the 50 call for $3\frac{3}{4}$, the combination would have been sold with $5\frac{1}{16}$-point premiums:

| | |
|---|---|
| Sell April 50 call at | $3\frac{3}{4}$ |
| Sell April 45 put at | $1\frac{5}{16}$ |
| Total income | $5\frac{1}{16}$ |

The profit zone for the combination writer would have been between the following two parameters:

1. Upside profit level

Call strike price at     50

Premium income at     $+5\frac{1}{16}$

$\overline{55\frac{1}{16}}$

2. Downside profit level

Put strike price at     45

Premium income     $-5\frac{1}{16}$

$\overline{39\frac{15}{16}}$

3. Profit range: Between $55\frac{1}{16}$ and $39\frac{15}{16}$

To summarize, the different profit ranges were as follows:

Original profit zone = $58\frac{1}{16}$ to $41\frac{15}{16}$

Zone for bullish approach (put closer to being in the money) = $60\frac{1}{8}$ to $44\frac{7}{8}$

Zone for bearish approach (call closer to being in the money) = $55\frac{1}{16}$ to $39\frac{15}{16}$

## Covered Combination Seller

A combination seller with a related long position in the underlying stock generally is willing to sell his long position at the strike price of the call plus the two premiums received or to add to his existing position through the exercise of the put if the stock declines.

## Combination Seller With Short Stock Position

A combination seller with a short position in the underlying stock generally is willing to let his short be covered by the exercise of the put plus the premium if the stock depreciates; and he is willing to short additional shares if the underlying stock appreciates in price.

## Varied Ratio Approach

Like the combination buyer, the combination seller may fine-tune his position in the desired direction by adding puts or calls.

**Example:** Based on the November 17, 1977, April option price data on SAF:

| Strike Price | Call Price | Put Price | Stock Price |
|---|---|---|---|
| 45 | $6\frac{7}{8}$ | $1\frac{5}{16}$ | 50 |
| 50 | $3\frac{3}{4}$ | $3\frac{3}{8}$ | 50 |
| 55 | $1\frac{3}{4}$ | $6\frac{3}{4}$ | 50 |

Instead of selling the one-to-one combination outlined below—

Sell 1 April 55 call at     $1\frac{3}{4}$

Sell 1 April 45 put at     $1\frac{5}{16}$

Credit     $\overline{3\frac{1}{16}}$

If the combination seller were bullish, he could have sold two April 55 calls and only one April 45 put, as follows:

Sell 2 April 55 calls @ $1\frac{3}{4}$ at     $3\frac{1}{2}$

Sell 1 April 45 put     $1\frac{5}{16}$

Credit     $\overline{4\frac{13}{16}}$

The credit of $4\frac{13}{16}$ would have allowed the straddle seller to remain profitable between the following two parameters:

1. Upside profit level

Call strike price at     55

Credit ($4\frac{13}{16} \div 2$)     $+2\frac{13}{32}$

$\overline{57\frac{13}{32}}$

2. Downside profit level

Put strike price     45

Credit     $-4\frac{13}{16}$

$\overline{40\frac{13}{16}}$

This profit range of $57\frac{13}{32}$ to $40\frac{13}{16}$ for the two-call, one-put combination selling compares with the profit range of $58\frac{1}{16}$ to $41\frac{15}{16}$ for the one-call, one-put combination selling illustrated above.

## Evaluating Each Component

Combinations offer infinite possibilities to enable investors to meet various goals. Just remember to evaluate each component of the combination for its risks, as well as for its potential reward.

# COMBINATION VERSUS STRADDLE

| Buy April 50 call at | 3¾ |
|---|---|
| Buy April 50 put at | 3⅜ |
| Total cost | 7⅛ |

## *Relative Dollar Risks*

A combination usually involves a put and a call of different strike prices, both out of the money, as shown following, based on the previous November 17, 1977, SAF price data:

| April 55 call | 1¾ |
|---|---|
| April 45 put | 1⁵⁄₁₆ |
| Total premium | 3¹⁄₁₆ |

Since, with the stock trading at 50, both the April 55 call and the April 45 put were out of the money, their combination would have cost less than a straddle on the same stock and would, therefore, have had less dollar risk.

## *Combination Buying versus Straddle Buying*

Let's compare the above combination with the purchase of a straddle, using the April 50 call and the April 50 put as follows:

The total cost of 7⅛ also represents the maximum dollar risk, versus the much smaller dollar risk of 3¹⁄₁₆ for the combination. The 10-point difference between the strike prices of the call and put had the effect of substantially reducing the combination's maximum dollar risk relative to the straddle.

However, while the maximum dollar risk on the combination has been reduced, the area in which some loss would occur has been widened.

## *Combination Sale versus Straddle Sale*

Even though the sale of a combination generates a smaller premium for the seller than the sale of a straddle on the same underlying stock, the underlying stock must make a greater move in either direction for his opponent to become profitable.

# OVERVIEW

### What

Put margins are minimum deposits an investor is required by the regulatory bodies to place with his broker in order to trade in puts.

### Why

Margin requirements are essentially safeguards to insure that only financially eligible persons are permitted to engage in the various put-related transactions.

### How

Different margin requirements exist for (1) long put, (2) long put, long stock, (3) short put, (4) short put, short stock, (5) put spread, (6) straddle, and (7) combination. (Extensive coverage can be found in the respective chapters on each of these topics.)

## Summary of Put Margin Requirements

1. Long put: Must be paid for in full.
2. Long put, long stock:
   a. Cash account: Both the stock and the put must be paid for in full.
   b. Margin account: The put must be paid for in full, and 50 percent margin is required for the stock.
3. Short put: Must be margined as an uncovered call.
4. Short put, short stock:
   a. No margin required for put.
   b. 50 percent margin required for stock.
5. Put spread: *Lesser* of the following two:
   a. Excess of short-option exercise price over long-option exercise price.
   b. Margined as an uncovered short.
6. Straddle
   a. Long call, long put: Both call and put must be paid for in full.

# put margins

# 28

b. Short call, short put: The uncovered short requirement on the call or the put, whichever is *greater*.

7. Combination: 30 percent of stock value *plus* the amount by which either or both positions are in the money. No credit is allowed if the call and/or the put are in the money.

## *Minimum Margin Requirements*

The New York Stock Exchange and the option exchanges have coordinated margin requirements for puts so that member firms can set uniform standards for their customers. These exchange requirements are *minimum* margins (brokerage firms are prohibited from requiring *less* from their clients). Typically, many firms require more than the minimum margins used in the examples throughout this book.

Many of the put margins described below are similar to the margin requirements for calls. The illustrations assume an option to be for 100 shares of the underlying stock. For simplicity, the illustrations disregard minimum account equity requirements, which currently mean $2,000 equity in a margin account.

## LONG PUT

A long put must be paid for in full and has no loan value in a margin account. Long call requirements are identical.

*Example:* On November 28, 1977, Westinghouse (WX) had a July 20 put available at 2¹⁄₁₆ when the stock traded at 19.

If an investor had bought 1 WX July 20 put for 2¹⁄₁₆ and had had no cash or other securities in his cash or margin account, he would have been required to deposit $206.25 ($2.0625 × 100) as full payment for the put.

## LONG PUT, LONG STOCK

### *Initial Margin Requirement*

1. Margin account: Under Federal Reserve Board rules, the initial margin required for a long-put, long-stock position in a margin account is the initial margin requirement (currently 50 percent) on the stock position. The option must be paid for in full.
2. Cash account: In a cash account, both the stock and the put must be paid for in full.

### *Maintenance Margin Requirement*

The exchange maintenance requirement is 25 percent of the market value of the stock, with no "mark-to-the-market" provision for the put. "Marking to the market" means that each day your broker will recompute your margin requirement, and if your account requires more money, you must supply it immediately.

Note that a rapid decline in the price of the stock can require a maintenance call, even though the customer's maximum risk may be the price of the put.

*Example:* On November 8, 1977, Avon (AVP) traded at 45 when its July 45 put was 3.

If an investor in a margin account bought 100 shares of AVP for 45, and 1 AVP July 45 put for 3 (long put, long stock), the downside risk in this position would have been limited to the cost of the put (3) because, during the life of the put, he had the right to "put" (sell) his stock at the exercise price of 45 (at the money).

## SHORT PUT

A short put must be margined in the same manner as an uncovered call. The requirement calls for 30 percent of the value of the underlying stock *plus* the amount that the put is in-the-money or *less* the amount that the put is out-of-the-money, with a minimum $250 margin requirement per contract.

**Example:** *In the Money:* On November 28, 1977, Honeywell (HON) traded at 48 when its August 50 put (in the money) was 4¾:

| Strike Price | Put Price | Stock Price |
|---|---|---|
| 50 | 4¾ | 48 |

With no cash or securities in his margin account, an investor sold a HON August 50 put for 4¾. The margin requirement was:

| | |
|---|---|
| 30% of stock value (48) | $1,440 |
| In-the-money amount (50 − 48) | +200 |
| Margin requirement | $1,640 |
| Put premium received (4¾) | −475 |
| Margin call | $1,165 |

**Example:** Out-of-the-Money: HON's August 45 put (out of the money) was priced at 2¼ when the stock was trading at 48:

| Strike Price | Put Price | Stock Price |
|---|---|---|
| 50 | 2¼ | 48 |

If the investor from the preceding example had sold a HON August 45 put or 2¼, the margin requirement would have been:

| | |
|---|---|
| 30% of stock value (48) | $1,440 |
| Out-of-the-money amount (48 − 45) | −300 |
| Margin requirement | $1,140 |
| Put premium received (2¼) | −225 |
| Margin call | $ 915 |

# SHORT PUT, SHORT STOCK

## Initial Margin Requirement

The initial margin requirement for a short-put, short-stock position in a margin account is currently 50 percent on the short stock position and no margin required on the short put.

**Example:** On November 28, 1977, Hughes Tool (HT) traded at 34⅞ when its June 35 put was 3:

| Strike Price | Put Price | Stock Price |
|---|---|---|
| 35 | 3 | 34⅞ |

Assuming an investor with no cash or other securities in his margin account sold short 100 shares of HT for 34⅞, and sold 1 HT June 35 put for 3, his initial margin requirement would have been:

| | |
|---|---|
| 50% of short-sale stock price (34⅞) | $1,743.75 |
| Put premium received (3) | −300.00 |
| Margin call | $1,443.75 |

## Maintenance Margin Requirement

Except for low-priced stocks (below $5 per share), the minimum maintenance margin requirement is 30 percent of the market value of the short-stock position, with no additional margin requirement for the put.

In computing this 30 percent, the value given to the underlying stock may not be less than the exercise price of the short put even though the stock price may be below the exercise price of the put.

**Example:** Using the preceding illustration on Hughes Tool, the equity in this investor's account after the $1,443.75 margin call had been met would have been $1,743.75.

If HT had risen 10 points, from 34⅞ to 44⅞, equity in the account would have decreased, by the $1,000 loss in the short-stock position, to $743.75:

| | |
|---|---|
| Equity in the account | $1,743.75 |
| Loss in the short-stock position | −1,000.00 |
| | $ 743.75 |

At this time, the maintenance margin requirement would have been recalculated:

| | |
|---|---|
| 30% of the stock value (44⅞) | $1,346.25 |
| Equity in the account | −743.75 |
| Maintenance call | $ 602.50 |

Thus, the investor would have been called upon to come up with an additional margin call of $602.50.

On the other hand, if HT had declined below the exercise price of 35, the market value of the stock could not have been calculated, for margin purposes, at less than the put's exercise price (35). Thus, the maintenance margin would not have fallen below $1,050 (30 percent of $3,500).

# PUT SPREAD MARGINS

## General Spread Margin Rules

A put spread is the simultaneous purchase and sale of puts of different series within the same class. Spreads can be executed only in margin accounts.

A position is considered a spread, for margin purposes, (1) if both the long and short positions are of the same class, and (2) if the long option expires no earlier than the short option.

In addition to the $2,000 minimum initial margin that applies to spreads, the long option must be paid for in full.

## Margins for Put Spreads

The margin required on a put spread position is the *lesser* of the following:

1. The amount by which the exercise price of the short option is above the exercise price of the long option
2. The amount that would be required to margin the short position if it were an uncovered short, namely, 30 percent of the stock price *plus* the amount the short put is in the money, or *minus* the amount the short put is out of the money, with a minimum $250 per contract.

**Example:** *In the Money*
On November 28, 1977, Honeywell (HON) had the following August 45 and August 50 puts when the stock traded at 48:

| Strike Price | Put Price | Stock Price |
| --- | --- | --- |
| 45 | 2¼ | 48 |
| 50 | 4¾ | 48 |

Assuming an investor sold 1 August 50 put or 4¾ and bought 1 August 45 put for 2¼, the required margin would have to be calculated first by determining the amount in rule 1:

| | |
| --- | --- |
| Difference in exercise prices (50 − 45) | $500 |
| Premium received | −475 |
| Margin call | $ 25 |

Calculating for rule 2:

| | |
| --- | --- |
| 30% of the stock price (48) | $1,440 |
| In-the-money amount of short option | +200 |
| Margin required | $1,640 |
| Premium received | −475 |
| Margin call | $1,165 |

Since the required margin is the *lesser* of these amounts, the $25 margin under rule 1 would have been required of this investor in addition to the $475 premium received.

If, however, the investor had no cash or other securities in the account, the margin call would have been for $1,525:

| | |
| --- | --- |
| Minimum margin requirement | $2,000 |
| Premium received | −475 |
| | $1,525 |

**Example:** *Out of the Money*
On November 18, 1977, Revlon (REV) had the following March 35 and 40 puts when the stock traded at 43:

| Strike Price | Put Price | Stock Price |
| --- | --- | --- |
| 35 | ⁷⁄₁₆ | 43 |
| 40 | 1½ | 43 |

An investor having sold 1 March 40 put for 1½ and 1 March 35 put or ⁷⁄₁₆, to determine the margin requirement, the amount under rule 1 had to be calculated first:

| | |
| --- | --- |
| Difference in exercise prices (40 − 35) | $500 |
| Premium received | −150 |
| Margin call | $350 |

Calculation of the rule 2 amount yielded:

| | |
|---|---:|
| 30% of the stock price (43) | $1,290 |
| Out-of-the-money amount of short option | −800 |
| Margin required | $ 490 |
| Premium received | −150 |
| Margin call | $ 340 |

Since the required margin is the *lesser* of the above, the $340 margin under rule 2 was required, in addition to the $150 premium received.

If, however, the investor had had no cash or other securities in the account, the margin call would have been $1,850:

| | |
|---|---:|
| Minimum margin requirement | $2,000 |
| Premium received | −150 |
| | $1,850 |

# STRADDLE MARGINS

A straddle is the purchase or sale of both a call and a put with the same strike price and the same expiration date on the same underlying stock.

## *Long Call, Long Put*

If a straddle involves a long call and a long put, under regulatory rules, both the call and the put must be paid for in full and neither will have loan value in a margin account.

*Example:* On November 29, 1977, IBM had the following April 260 call and put when the stock traded at 262¾:

| Option | Strike Price | Option Price |
|---|---|---|
| **Call** | 260 | 12¼ |
| **Put** | 260 | 7¾ |

If an investor who had no cash or other securities in his cash or margin account bought 1 IBM April 260 call for 12¼ and 1 IBM April 260 put for 7¾, he would have been required to deposit $2,000 as full payment for the call and the put:

| | |
|---|---:|
| Buy April 260 call (12¼ × 100 shares) | $1,225 |
| Buy April 260 put (7¾ × 100 shares) | 775 |
| Total premiums required | $2,000 |

## *Short Call, Short Put*

If a straddle involves a short call and a short put, the required margin is the uncovered short requirement on the call or the put, whichever is *greater*.

*Example:* On November 28, 1977, Eastman Kodak (EK) had the following July 50 call and put when EK traded at 53:

| Option | Strike Price | Option Price | Stock Price |
|---|---|---|---|
| **Call** | 50 | 6½ | 53 |
| **Put** | 50 | 2½ | 53 |

If an investor who had no cash or securities in his margin account sold 1 EK July 50 call for 6½ and 1 EK July 50 put for 2½ when the stock traded at 53, the required margin would have been the *greater* of the following two computations:

1. Call computation:

| | |
|---|---:|
| 30% of stock price (53) | $1,590 |
| Call in-the-money amount (53 − 50) | +300 |
| Margin requirement | $1,890 |
| Premium received (6½ + 2½) | −900 |
| Margin call | $ 990 |

2. Put computation:

| | |
|---|---:|
| 30% of stock value (53) | $1,590 |
| Put out-of-the-money amount (53 − 50) | −300 |
| Margin requirement | $1,290 |
| Premium received (6½ + 2½) | −900 |
| Margin call | $ 390 |

The *greater* of the call computation ($990) and of the put computation ($390) is $990, the margin call that would have been issued.

# COMBINATION MARGINS

## *Short Call, Short Put with Different Exercise Prices*

A combination is either the purchase or the sale of both puts and calls with different strike prices and the same or different expiration months on the same underlying security.

The required margin for a combination is 30 percent of the market value of the underlying stock *plus* the amount by which either or both of the positions are in the money. No credit is allowed if the call and/or the put are out of the money.

*Example:* On November 8, 1977, Avon (AVP) had the following April 40 call and April 50 put when AVP traded at 45:

| Option | Strike Price | Option Price | Stock Price |
|--------|-------------|--------------|-------------|
| **Call** | 40 (in the money) | 4 | 45 |
| **Put** | 50 (in the money) | 5 | 45 |

If an investor had sold two April 40 calls and two April 50 puts, the required margin would have been:

| | |
|---|---|
| 30% of the stock price (2 × 45) | $2,700 |
| Put in-the-money amount (2 × 5) | +1,000 |
| Call in-the-money amount (2 × 5) | +1,000 |
| Margin requirement | $4,700 |
| Premiums received (2 × 9) | −1,800 |
| Margin call | $2,900 |

The rationale behind the margin requirement reflecting both the in-the-money amount and the out-of-the-money amount is that if both sides were to be exercised there would be a 10-point risk in each of the two options. This risk, therefore, must be built into the margin requirement.

# TAXES AND STRATEGY SELECTION

section three

# TAX
# CONSIDERATIONS

PART

Investors in the options market must weigh the implications of income-tax exposure when designing their options strategies. The following chapters describe this critically important factor, federal income taxation of trading in listed options.

The character of income realized in connection with puts and calls depends on the character of the underlying property in the hands of the investor. When the underlying property (stock) is a capital asset to an investor (the usual situation), the option is treated as a capital asset and any gain or loss is a capital gain or loss.

The following material is intended primarily for the options investor for whom the option and the underlying stock are (or would be, if acquired) capital assets. The rules described may not apply to brokers or dealers in securities or options, nor to others in special tax categories or complex situations. Further, each investor's individual tax circumstances may make normally desirable tax results less attractive, or vice versa, in any given case. Consequently, investors are urged always to consult their own tax advisors.

The basic scenario for the individual who invests in options is as follows. Gains and losses from the sale or exchange of capital assets are either long term or short term depending on the holding period of the asset. The dividing line between long-term and short-term treatment is twelve months. Tax consequences to the investor are usually deferred until the option position is terminated. In the following pages, specific situations and strategies are covered in detail.

### 1976 and 1978 Tax-Law Changes

With the great growth of the options markets, substantial changes with respect to puts and calls in the tax law and in Internal Revenue Service (IRS) interpretations of the rules have occurred. The present material is intended to reflect both the changes in law and those in interpretation. The tax rules described in these chapters encompass the changes made by the Tax Reform Act of 1976 and the Revenue Act of 1978.

Although the Tax Reform Act of 1976 eliminated many tax-motivated options strategies, careful tax planning remains an important aspect of successful options trading. In fact, the

# tax planning for options

29

Revenue Act of 1978 heightened the importance of careful tax planning by increasing the difference in the after-tax profitability of short-term and long-term gains. Careful planning can result not only in increased after-tax profits but also in the avoidance of tax pitfalls.

Perhaps the single most important tax-law change is that, pursuant to Internal Revenue Code Section 1234 (as amended by the Tax Reform Act of 1976), an option writer no longer has an ordinary gain or loss upon entering into a closing purchase transaction for options written on or after September 2, 1976.

As most investors are aware, long-term capital gains receive favored tax treatment under the Internal Revenue Code; the Revenue Act of 1978 substantially increased that favored treatment. The increased 60-percent deduction for long-term capital gains and the elimination of the "poisoning" or earned income subject to the 50-percent maximum tax by the deductible portion of long-term capital gains became effective on November 1, 1978.

Only 40 percent of an individual's excess of net long-term gains over net short-term capital losses is now taxed at ordinary income rates, and the balance is generally free of tax. In addition, the untaxed portion of an individual's long-term capital gains is no longer an "item of tax preference" and thus is not subject to the 15-percent "add-on" minimum tax. Further, long-term capital gains no longer have an adverse effect on the application of the 50-percent maximum tax on an individual's personal service income.

However, an investor may be subject to a new "alternative" minimum tax. The alternative minimum tax, if greater than the regular income tax, effectively replaces that tax. It applies at rates of up to 25 percent on taxable income increased by (1) certain "excess" itemized deductions and by (2) the deductible 60 percent of the excess of net long-term capital gains over net short-term capital losses.

## THE BASIC CONSIDERATION: DISPOSAL

An investor becomes the holder of a capital asset when a put or call is purchased. The cost of the put or call is its basis, and its holding period is measured from the date of purchase.

Since December 31, 1977, in order to qualify for long-term capital gain treatment, an asset must have been held for twelve months. Consequently, unless listed options with terms longer than the current standard term of nine months are issued, options will never qualify as long-term capital gains or losses.

Although the *acquisition* of a put is usually treated as a short sale, the disposal of either a put or a call is the action on which federal income-tax responsibility is based. A put or call may be disposed of by the holder in one of three ways:

1. Exercise
2. Sale
3. Expiration unexercised

Taxation of gains and losses realized by option holders depends on whether the option is exercised, sold, or permitted to lapse.

### Call Exercise

Exercise of a call is a way to take a long position in the stock. If a call is exercised, the call holder becomes the owner of the underlying stock.

The holding period of the stock is measured from the exercise date. It does not include the holding period of the call.

The cost basis for the stock includes the cost of exercising the option and the original cost of purchasing the option. Both the brokerage commission when the call is exercised and the commission on purchase of the call are considered to be part of the cost basis for tax purposes.

### Put Exercise

Exercise of a put by its holder involves delivery of the underlying stock against receipt of the strike price.

A capital gain or loss is realized on the sale of underlying stock. The cost of the put is

# tax strategy for holders

# 30

treated as a reduction in the proceeds of the sale, as is the commission on the sale.

The *acquisition* of a put is treated as a short sale unless both of the following conditions are met:

1. The acquisitions of the put and of the stock identified on the holder's records as intended to be used in connection with the exercise of the put take place on the same day (called a "married" put)
2. The put is not exercised or, if exercised, the put is exercised by the delivery of the identified stock

When a put is married with particular shares of stock, holding-period rules apply in determining whether gain or loss on exercise is long term or short term.

### Call Sale

If a call is sold, the holder realizes a capital gain or loss determined by comparing the sale proceeds to the cost of the call.

If the call is worth less when sold than its cost basis, sale results in a currently deductible capital loss. A gain results if the call is worth more when sold than its cost basis. Remember, that gain or loss is short term now that a twelve-month holding period is required for long-term capital gain or loss.

### Put Sale

If a put is sold, the holder realizes a short-term capital gain or loss determined by comparison of the sale proceeds with the cost basis of the put.

The IRS has ruled that sale of a put by a holder is the closing of a short sale if substantially identical property is held short-term at the time of the acquisition of the put or is acquired subsequent to the acquisition of the put.

### Call Expiration

If a call is allowed to expire unexercised, the loss to the holder is a capital loss measured by the cost basis of the call.

### Put Expiration

If a put is allowed to expire unexercised, the loss to the holder is a capital loss, as with a call. But, if the put was married to stock, the cost of the put is added to the basis of the stock. Expiration of a put is considered to close any short sale made by its acquisition.

# TAX STRATEGY FOR CALL HOLDERS

When a call is first traded, its price reflects both the time-limited value of the right to purchase the underlying stock at the strike price and the difference between the market value of the stock and the strike price. The time value declines as the call approaches its expiration date.

At any time, the underlying stock may be selling for less than the strike price, in which case the call is out of the money; or the underlying stock may be selling above the strike price, in which case the call is in the money and has value even when it is about to expire. The following discussion will consider tax strategies available to holders of profitable and unprofitable calls, call purchase in combination with short sale, and the limitations imposed by the so-called wash sale rule.

### Profitable Calls

The holder of a call may have a potential profit whether the call is in or out of the money.

The holder of a profitable in-the-money call only has to decide when to realize his profit and whether to realize it through exercise and sale of the underlying stock or through a closing sale transaction. In making this decision, the holder should consider, among other things, margin requirements and transaction costs. Such costs are generally greater on an exercise and sale of the stock.

In some cases, however, profit can be captured *only* by sale of the option. For example, if time remains before expiration, an out-of-the-money call purchased when the underlying stock was selling considerably below the strike price will increase in value as the price of the underlying stock rises toward the strike price. This profit can be captured only by sale of the call.

If a call is in the money, exercise may be a

satisfactory alternative to sale of the call. However, because of the added commissions, a higher net profit usually results from selling the call rather than exercising the call and selling the stock.

If the call holder wishes to acquire the stock for investment, it may be less costly to sell the call and acquire the stock on the market rather than to acquire the stock through exercise of the call.

In either case, the holding period of the stock begins with its acquisition and does not include the holding period of the call.

Of course, if sound investment policy so dictates, the holder can exercise the call and hold the stock thus acquired for the minimum period required for long-term treatment, deferring the tax on his option gain and possibly converting it from a short-term to a long-term capital gain. The investor retains the full risk of his long position in the underlying stock. However, he can eliminate the risks of his long position following the exercise of his profitable call option by making a simultaneous short sale of the underlying stock or by purchasing a put. These procedures would defer the tax on his option gain into a subsequent tax year.

### Unprofitable Calls

The holder of a call that has declined in value has two ways of establishing a loss for tax purposes:

1. Sell the call
2. Permit the call to expire unexercised

In either case, the transaction is considered to be a short-term capital loss. As with profitable calls and gains, year-end planning may require deferring losses. Among the techniques that may be used for this purpose are buying puts, writing calls, and combining exercise with short sales.

### Call Purchase Combined with Short Sale

A call option, being similar in many respects to a long position in the underlying stock, can be used as a hedge against, or be hedged by, a short position in the underlying stock.

An investor with a profitable call can hedge his profit by a short sale of the underlying stock. Through this strategy, the tax on the profit can be deferred until a later tax year.

On the other hand, an investor with a profitable short position in an underlying stock, by acquiring a call, can lock in the profit (less the call premium and transaction costs) on that position and maintain the potential for additional profit should the price of the underlying stock continue to decline.

An investor may also be able to use the call/short sale combination to his tax benefit when he has an unrealized long-term gain in the underlying stock. By simultaneously purchasing a call and selling the underlying stock short, he can lock in and defer the profit (less the call premium and transaction costs) on his long position in the stock. At the same time, he maintains the potential for additional profit should the price of the underlying stock continue to increase.

### Wash-Sale Rule

The wash-sale rule denies a deduction for losses sustained on the sale of securities if the seller, within a sixty-one-day period beginning thirty days before and ending thirty days after the sale, purchases substantially identical securities or acquires a call option in the same underlying stock. The purchase of a call to defer loss on a sale of underlying stock clearly brings the wash-sale rule into operation if the sale and the purchase of the call fall within the wash-sale period.

# TAX STRATEGY FOR PUT HOLDERS

Put prices reflect both the time-limited value of the right to sell stock at the strike price and the difference between the market value of the stock and the strike price. The time value declines as the put approaches its expiration date. Note that this relationship of put value to stock price is the exact opposite of a call.

The underlying stock may be selling for less than the strike price of the put, in which case the put is in the money. An in-the-money put has value even when it is about to expire because any holder of that put can capture the difference between the cost of buying the stock and the strike price.

If the underlying stock is selling for more than the strike price, the put is out of the money, and its value progressively declines as the expiration date approaches.

## Profitable Puts

The holder of a profitable in-the-money put has the same alternatives as the holder of a profitable in-the-money call: to sell the option or to exercise it. Similarly, the holder of a put, like the holder of a call, will want to consider such factors as transaction costs and margin requirements, among other things, in order to make the better decision.

The simplest way for a put holder to realize gain on a put if the market value of the underlying stock declines is to sell the put. The gain is short term.

If the put holder exercises the option, the exercise is a sale. Exercise requires delivery of the underlying stock by the put holder for the strike price. The gain is long term or short term depending on when the stock was acquired. If the delivered stock was purchased more than the requisite period of twelve months prior to the acquisition of the put and no other sustantially identical stock was purchased in the interim, any gain or loss on exercise is long term. Conversely, if any stock was purchased less than the requisite period before the put was purchased or was acquired after the put was purchased, any gain on the exercise is short term.

The holder of a profitable put may be able to defer the tax on his option gain by exercising the put and delivering borrowed stock, thus effecting a short sale. The gain on the put is then taken into account in computing the gain or loss when closing the short sale. Of course, any gain on the short sale is considered to be short term.

The holder of a profitable put may lock in his gain and defer it to a subsequent taxable year through acquisition of the underlying stock or through the writing of another put on the same underlying stock, much the same as in the call/short-sale combination.

## Unprofitable Puts

The holder of a put that has declined in value has two ways of establishing loss for tax purposes:

1. Sell the put
2. Permit the put to expire unexercised

In either case, the holder will have a short-term capital loss.

In the case of a put married to stock, sale of the put is necessary to establish the loss. Upon exercise, the cost of a married put is added to the basis of the stock.

The put holder's principal tax strategies are, for the most part, defensive: protecting gains on stock or calls and avoiding various tax traps in the short-sale rules that can convert long-term gain into short-term gain, convert short-term loss into long-term loss, and reduce holding periods.

## Short-Sale Rules

Puts purchased by an investor who already has a long position in the underlying stock present a more complicated problem, however, because of the operation of the short-sale rules.

Under the Internal Revenue Code, the acquisition of an option to sell property at a fixed price (a put) is treated as a short sale. A short sale may create either of the following tax scenarios:

1. Elimination of the holding period of the underlying stock with the result that any gain realized on the exercise or sale of the put to be treated as a short-term capital gain
2. Treatment of any loss on the closing of the short sale as a long-term capital loss

The first prong of the short-sale rules, which eliminates the holding period of the underlying stock and makes any gain on the closing of the short sale a short-term gain, applies whenever an investor, on the date of the short sale (the acquisition of the put), has held the underlying stock for not more than twelve months. It also applies if such stock is acquired between the date of the short sale (the purchase of the put) and the closing of the short sale (the exercise, lapse, or disposition of the put).

An important exception to the first prong of the short-sale rules occurs if a put is acquired on the same day as the underlying stock. (To qualify, the stock must be identified in the investor's records as intended for use in exercising that put and must actually be used for that purpose if exercise occurs.) If such a put lapses, however, the cost of the put is added to the tax basis of the identified stock; it is not allowed immediately as a deductible loss. If such a put is exercised with other than the identified stock, the short-sale rules are applicable.

The second prong of the short-sale rules treats any loss sustained on the termination of a short sale as a long-term capital loss, regardless of the actual holding period of the property used to close the short sale, whenever on the date of entering into the short sale, substantially identical property has been held for more than twelve months.

Option contracts have a maximum duration of approximately nine months; therefore, it is not possible to hold an option long-term. Since under the new law the option writer can have only a short-term capital gain or loss at the termination of the transaction, opportunities for effective tax planning are somewhat reduced but by no means entirely eliminated.

In tax planning, option writers must remember that as long as they maintain a writing position, they are subject to being assigned an exercise notice at any time. While there is less likelihood that an out-of-the-money option will be exercised, an exercise becomes more probable as the option moves into the money. This probability increases dramatically as the expiration date approaches or the option is selling at less than its intrinsic value.

### Termination

Taxation of premium income received by options writers is deferred until termination of the transaction. A writing position may be terminated through either exercise, expiration (the lapse of the option), or sale (a closing purchase transaction).

If an option is sold, capital gain or loss results, measured by the difference between the premium originally paid and the premium received in the closing sale transaction.

If an option lapses, the income will be equal to the premium received in the opening writing transaction.

If the option is exercised, the entire transaction is treated as a purchase or sale of the underlying stock. The premium is considered to be part of the purchase or sale price. For a call writer, the premium income increases the amount realized on the sale of the stock. A put writer, on the other hand, must subtract the premium from the price paid for the stock (the exercise price) in determining his tax basis (cost) for the stock.

### How to Determine the Holding Period

If a call is exercised, the holding period of the underlying stock, not the option, determines whether the gain or loss is long term or short term. The holding period of the option cannot be added to the holding period of the underlying stock.

tax strategy
for writers

31

Similarly, the holding period for stock acquired through the exercise of a put begins when the stock is acquired pursuant to exercise of the option, not when the option is written.

# TAX STRATEGY FOR CALL WRITERS

Out-of-the-money calls present a relatively simple starting point, since we may ordinarily exclude the risk of exercise, although that risk is real if the option moves into the money.

The writer's alternatives are either to allow the option to lapse or to engage in a closing purchase transaction. The gain if the option lapses is treated as a short-term capital gain. Likewise, the gain or loss on a closing transaction receives short-term treatment.

On the other hand, the writer of an in-the-money call must consider the tax consequences of the possible assignment to him of an exercise notice.

Following is a brief survey of tax treatment of the premium received by the call writer depending on whether his obligation is terminated by

1. Expiration
2. Closing purchase transaction
3. Exercise

### Termination by Expiration

If the holder allows a call option to expire unexercised, the writer treats the premium as a short-term capital gain realized at the expiration date.

### Termination by Closing Purchase Transaction

At any time before exercise, the writer can enter into a closing purchase transaction; that is, a purchase can be made of an equivalent call designated as a closing transaction. Any gain or loss is short term and measured by the difference between the net amount previously received and the amount paid for the closing purchase.

Option writers considering a closing purchase transaction in an option that expires in a subsequent taxable year may defer the taxation of any gains into the later year to take any losses in the present year.

The investor who chooses immediately to establish his loss may couple his closing purchase with the writing of a similar call in order to maintain a comparable investment position. There is no risk that with such a rollover his loss would be disallowed under the wash-sale rules.

The investor choosing to deter gains must remember that he remains liable on the option and continues to bear the market risk.

### Termination by Exercise

Exercise is initiated by the holder, not the writer. When the writer delivers stock against payment of the strike price specified in the call, a capital gain or loss is realized.

The transaction is treated as a sale of the stock delivered. The premium is considered as part of the proceeds of sale. Total proceeds (the premium plus the payment of the exercise price) are used to determine the amount of the gain or loss.

The holding period of the stock delivered determines whether the gain or loss is long term or short term.

### Tax Postures for In-The-Money Covered Writers

For the writer of an in-the-money call, the tax consequences of a possible exercise depend, among other things, on whether the writer's position is uncovered or covered.

The writer of a covered, in-the-money call may have to take into account a variety of tax considerations. Principally, he must decide between the realization of gain or loss (which may be long term or short term) on his stock and option positions upon exercise through a closing purchase transaction, either alone or in combination with a sale of the underlying stock.

If an exercise notice is received while the unrealized gain on the stock is still short term, it may be advantageous to purchase and deliver new stock for a short-term loss and hold the old stock for long-term capital gains treatment. This technique is useful primarily to the investor who has other short-term gains against which to deduct this short-term loss.

If delivery of the underlying stock held by a call option writer upon exercise would produce a short-term gain, it might be beneficial to engage in a closing purchase transaction and hold the underlying stock for long-term treatment. However, an investor may wish to engage in a closing purchase transaction for other reasons, such as a desire to terminate the option position while maintaining a long stock position in anticipation of appreciation in value.

Writers who hold underlying stock that would produce a long-term capital loss if delivered at exercise are usually better off terminating their writing position either through a closing purchase transaction or the delivery of newly acquired underlying stock, both of which produce a short-term capital loss.

The covered call writer has another alternative at exercise. The long position can be sold at the market and a new purchase of stock can be made for delivery against the call. These transactions create a greater long-term gain and a short-term loss resulting in a tax saving if the investor has other short-term gains and the short-sale rules do not apply.

While the tax advantages in a rising market are considerable, the pendulum returns when prices decline. In this situation, premiums on expired calls are considered a short-term capital gain, but capital losses incurred on the long positions may be long term. The covered writer who owns stock that is not yet long term may wish to realize any loss while it is still short term.

### Tax Postures for In-the-Money Uncovered Writers

The writer of an uncovered call that is in the money has several choices. First, he may effect a closing purchase transaction for short-term gain or loss. Second, he may choose to maintain his position, hoping for a decline in the price of the underlying stock so that the option will lapse. Third, he may purchase the underlying stock and assume the position of a covered writer any time prior to delivering stock pursuant to an exercise notice.

For the most part, these are trading decisions with significance for tax planning only in the timing of the gain or loss from the transaction.

# TAX STRATEGY FOR PUT WRITERS

### In- versus out-of-the-Money Put Writers

Puts are said to be in the money when the exercise price is above the market price of the underlying stock. Writers of in-the-money puts have the choice of entering into a closing purchase transaction or awaiting exercise. A closing purchase transaction may be desirable for the purpose of timing gains or losses between different years.

Of course, if sound investment policy so dictates, the writer of a put may assume a long position in the underlying stock by awaiting exercise. To do so also defers the recognition of any gain or loss on the option transaction, and the investor may be able to convert the position to a long-term capital gain by holding the acquired stock for twelve months.

The stock's holding period begins on the day acquired pursuant to exercise, *not* when the option was written.

Puts are said to be out of the money when the exercise price is below the market price of the underlying stock. The writer of an out-of-the-money put, in basically the same tax position as the writer of a call trading out of the money, can either allow the option to lapse or enter into a closing purchase transaction. In either case, the gain or loss is treated as short-term capital gain or loss. Thus, the only tax consequences of this choice relate to the timing of the gain or loss that is realized.

### Termination by Expiration

If the market rises and stays above the exercise price, the put writer realizes a short-term capital gain when the put expires unexercised. If the holder of a put allows it to expire unexercised, the writer will, under the new law, realize a short-term capital gain.

### Termination by Exercise

As with a call, exercise of a put is initiated by the holder. After exercise, the put writer is left with an investment position in the underlying stock. The transaction is treated by the writer as a purchase of stock.

The cost basis of that stock is the strike price plus commission less the net premium on writing the put. The holding period begins with exercise.

Writing a put generally is not considered as the acquisition of an option to acquire stock, even though it results in acquisition by the writer on exercise. Therefore, put writing is not subject to the wash-sale rules, and the stock acquired by means of an exercised put is subject only to the usual tax rules for investments in stock.

The acquisition date for the stock would appear to be the settlement date, but it is prudent to use the earlier date of exercise or assignment if the stock is to be sold to realize a loss before it becomes long term. If the stock has appreciated and long-term gain is sought, the later date should be used in measuring the requisite period.

### Termination by Sale

Instead of exercise or expiration. The writer of a put has an option to make a closing purchase transaction. As with calls, the writer of a put can enter into a closing purchase transaction at any time before exercise, and any gain or loss realized is treated as a short-term capital gain or loss.

Since the costs of a closing purchase transaction are substantially less than those of the acquisition and disposition of stock on exercise, the writer of a put faced with the likelihood of unwelcome exercise is generally well advised to enter into a closing purchase transaction.

Furthermore, a closing purchase transaction is a possibility when a potential gain exists because the price of the stock has advanced but the put will not expire for some time. Gain or loss on such a closing purchase transaction is now a short-term capital gain or loss.

### Short Selling as a Means of Defense

To protect against the risk of a falling market, a put writer can sell stock short at the same time a put is written. This, however, leaves the writer exposed to the usual short-seller's risk in a rising market. Buying a call covers this risk.

However, the combined cost of all these various transactions might exceed any possible economic benefit. All the gains and losses in this situation are usually short-term capital gains and losses.

# STRATEGY AND PORTFOLIO CONSTRUCTION

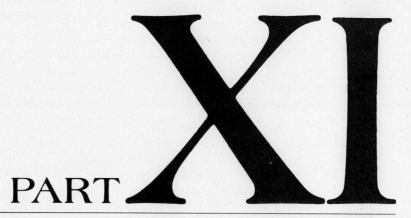

PART XI

## IN TERMS OF INVESTMENT OBJECTIVES

The selection of option strategies is determined primarily by an investor's objectives. Broadly speaking, investment objectives can be classified in the following categories:

1. Increase in income
2. Speculation with limited risk
3. Portfolio diversification
4. Reduction of volatility
5. Protecting of profit or an existing position
6. Taking advantage of an expected substantial move in stock price

The following is a survey of alternate option strategies available for achieving various objectives.

### Increase in income

1. Sell call
2. Sell put
3. Sell straddle
4. Sell combination

### Speculation with limited risk

1. Buy call
2. Buy put
3. Buy straddle
4. Buy combination

### Portfolio diversification

1. Buy call
2. Buy put
3. Buy straddle

option strategy
selection guide

32

### Reduction of volatility

1. Sell call
2. Sell put
3. Sell straddle

### Protection of profit or an existing position: Buy put

1. Buy put

### Taking advantage of an expected substantial move in stock price

1. Buy straddle
2. Buy combination

# IN TERMS OF STRATEGY CATEGORIZATION

The following is a broad categorization of option strategies designed to achieve various investment objectives, along with their advantages and cautions:

### Call Buying

1. Investment objectives
   - a. Speculation
   - b. Protecting a short sale
2. Advantages
   - a. Leverage
   - b. Limited risk
3. Caution
   - a. Depreciating asset
   - b. Risk of total loss

### Call Selling

1. Investment objectives
   - a. Reduction of volatility
   - b. Increase in income
2. Advantages
   - a. Potential income increase
   - b. Hedge potential
   - c. Potential to sell stock above market price

3. Caution
   - a. Option may be exercised at any time
   - b. May prevent large gain due to exercise (opportunity lost).

### Put Buy

1. Investment objectives
   - a. Protection of existing positions
   - b. Portfolio diversification
   - c. Protection of profit
   - d. Speculation
2. Advantages
   - a. Leverage
   - b. Limited risk
   - c. More advantageous than a short sale
3. Caution
   - a. Depreciating asset
   - b. Risk of total loss

### Put Selling

1. Investment objectives
   - a. Increase in income
   - b. Acquisition of stock below market price
2. Advantages
   - a. May increase income
   - b. Can improve market timing
3. Caution
   - a. Below strike option may be put to buyer any time
   - b. Falling stock price may be greater than premium received

### Straddle and Combination Buying

1. Investment objectives: Taking advantage of expected substantial move in stock price
2. Advantages
   - a. No need to guess market direction
   - b. Potential profit in up *or* down markets
3. Caution: Stock must show volatility up or down

### Straddle and Combination Selling

1. Investment objectives
   - a. Acquisition of stock
   - b. Increase in income

2. Advantages
   a. Greater premium income from writing both a put and call option
   b. Improbable that both put and call will be exercised
3. Caution
   a. Possible early exercise
   b. May require substantial margin

## IN TERMS OF BULL- VERSUS BEAR-MARKET INSTRUMENTS

Option strategies may also be classified in terms of their applications as bull- or bear-market instruments.

### *Bull-Market Instruments*

Investors who believe that stock prices are going *up* can utilize several strategies to take advantage of anticipated uptrends. Simpler bull-market strategies range from buying a call to buying its underlying stock.

Buying a call is an alternate course to investing in the underlying security. In many instances, it is less risky and less expensive to control shares of a certain stock with a call than it is to go long on the stock, either outright or with margin. The key to determining these alternate vehicles lies in weighing their risk-reward parameters.

Essentially, a call option purchaser anticipates an increase in the value of the underlying stock by investing a fraction of the cost of the stock as means of obtaining greater leverage on his investment.

***Example:*** During the week ending May 12, 1979, some of energy and gambling calls doubled, tripled, and quadrupled. Standard Oil of California's June 45 soared from 1 to $3\frac{5}{8}$, Joy Manufacturing's August 35 from $\frac{3}{8}$ to $1\frac{1}{4}$, Continental Oil's July 35 from $\frac{13}{16}$ to $2\frac{5}{16}$, Schlumberger's August 70 from $3\frac{1}{8}$ to $5\frac{1}{4}$ and Exxon's July 50 from $1\frac{3}{8}$ to $2\frac{1}{4}$. On a split basis, Bally's August 40 climbed from $2\frac{3}{4}$ to $4\frac{1}{2}$.

In addition, Lockheed's June 20 climbed 271 percent, to $1\frac{3}{8}$, when the equity rose 10.2 percent. Baker International's June 40 was up 246 percent, to $3\frac{1}{4}$, on a 7.8 percent upturn in the stock. Kerr McGee's July 50 rose 233 percent, to $1\frac{7}{8}$, when the shares tacked on 8.6 percent.

***Example:*** During the week of June 25, 1979, big profits were scored on energy calls. Atlantic Richfield's July 70 quadrupled, to $\frac{1}{2}$; Greyhound's July 15 tripled to $\frac{9}{16}$; Fluor's July 45 more than doubled, to $6\frac{3}{8}$; and Burlington Northern's July 50 rose $4\frac{1}{2}$, to $7\frac{1}{4}$. Santa Fe's July 20 doubled to 4, while Mesa Petroleum's July 45 tacked on $4\frac{5}{8}$, to end the week at 19.

***Example:*** Sometimes, calls leaped ahead of the underlying stock. During the week of June 25, 1979, for instance, Continental Oil's July 35 rose $1\frac{1}{16}$ on a $\frac{7}{8}$ hike in the shares, while Louisiana Land's August 30 climbed $3\frac{1}{4}$ when the stock rose $2\frac{5}{8}$.

During the week of August 20, 1979, gold and energy calls led the market. ASA November 25 rose from $1\frac{9}{16}$ to $3\frac{3}{8}$ and Homestake's October 35 from $1\frac{15}{16}$ to $3\frac{3}{4}$. Standard Oil of California's September 50 jumped from $2\frac{7}{16}$ to $6\frac{3}{8}$, Pennzoil's October 45 from $1\frac{3}{8}$ to $3\frac{1}{2}$, and Pittston's November 25 from 1 to $1\frac{3}{4}$.

*Warning:* Call prices can plunge just as sharply as they can rise. For instance, during the week of July 9, 1979 calls were battered both by a 12.63-point downturn in the Dow-Jones Industrial Average and the evaporation of time value in the July series (expiration is on the twenty-first of the month).

***Example:*** IBM July 70 tumbled from 4 to $\frac{3}{4}$, Dupont's July 40 from $3\frac{1}{8}$ to $\frac{7}{8}$, Polaroid's July 30 from $1\frac{9}{16}$ to $\frac{1}{16}$, and Texas Instrument's July 90 from 2 to $\frac{1}{8}$.

***Example:*** In the week of March 26, 1979, call prices on nuclear stocks fell apart after the reactor mishap at Harrisburg, Pennsylvania. Kerr-McGee's April 50 plummeted from 6 to $2\frac{5}{16}$, McDermott's May 20 from $2\frac{3}{8}$ to $1\frac{1}{8}$, and Westinghouse's April 20 from $\frac{11}{16}$ to $\frac{5}{16}$.

### *Bear-Market Instruments*

Investors who believe that stock prices are going down can utilize various strategies in options trading, either with the hope of turning a profit or in order to achieve some measure of protection for their existing stock positions.

Among the simpler options techniques available for use in bearish markets, the choices range upward in risk from buying puts to selling naked calls.

A put option, perhaps least risky of the choices, gives its holder the right to sell 100 shares of the underlying stock at a specified price over a set period of time. A call option, in a sense, is a mirror image of the put. A call gives its owner the right to buy underlying shares.

Conceptually, the purchase of a put is comparable to selling a stock short. But buying the put provides leverage, or the opportunity to invest fairly small amounts of capital with the possibility of a large return if the price of the underlying stock drops far enough.

*Example:* During the second week of July 1979, the price of IBM stock dropped 3½ points, to finish at 70⅛. This decline reflected the company's announcement of a rather disappointing earnings report for its second quarter. Within the same period, some IBM put options doubled.

Among defense strategies in bear markets, selling naked calls is one of the most risky ones. A call is said to be sold (written) naked when the investor neither buys nor owns the underlying stock. His objective is to take in premium income on a stock that he expects either to decline or to remain relatively stable in price during the life of the contract.

The risk in this strategy develops if the stock begins to rise sharply. If a person sells a naked call and the stock begins to climb, his defensive action is usually typically to purchase an identical call option and thereby close out his position. By this process, he limits his loss.

Buying a put, on the other hand, automatically limits the investor's potential loss. In using this bearish technique, he cannot lose more than the price of the purchased option, plus commission charges.

## CALL OPTION PRICE INDEX

### An Index for Consistent Measure

Tracking overall premium levels for price trends in order to better understand stock-market action has been an objective of the investment community for several years. The Chicago Board Option Exchange added a new dimension to the art of option trading when it introduced its call option price index in April 1979.

The index is designed to provide investors with a concise and consistent measure over time of average option price levels on CBOE calls. The index is computed weekly, using Thursday closing prices, and is published each Friday.

Public participants in the options market always have had a tough time determining how much an option is worth. That's because the price, or premium, paid for an option depends on two variables: (1) how close the exercise price of the option is to the price of the underlying stock, and (2) how close the option is to expira-

tion. The CBOE measures premiums on ninety-five six-month, at-the-money calls as a percentage of the underlying stock prices. Since the calls used in the index are at the money, the premiums represent time-value alone.

Because such options seldom exist, the CBOE constructs them by calculating the weighted average of the market prices of the four series most similar to the hypothetical calls. Since the index averages hypothetical options, it does not measure what a trader would pay for a CBOE option. Rather, its chief function is to provide a consistent measure of premium levels over a period of time, and to permit traders to analyze how premiums change before, during, and after a stock-market rally or decline.

### Premium Trends Relative to Market Direction

According to CBOE, it's important to compare the trend of option premiums to the direction of the stock market. Theoretically, premiums should turn up when stocks are climbing or when option traders expect them to rise and decline when stocks are falling, or traders look for a downturn.

# new option trading tools

# 33

Despite its limitations, Wall Streeters regard the new CBOE call price index one more research tool to be added to stock indices, bond yields, P/E ratios, dividend yields and money-supply figures.

# OPTION STRATEGIES RELATIVE TO PREMIUM LEVELS

Option prices (premiums) constantly expand and contract according to market sentiment, interest rates, the price volatility of the underlying securities, and other factors. It is sometimes useful to design option strategies relative to low- or high-premium levels.

# LOW-PREMIUM-LEVEL STRATEGIES

Generally, the purchase of listed puts and calls during periods of low overvalues offers suitable speculating accounts the ability to participate in volatile moves of the underlying security regardless of which direction taken.

Maximum loss would occur if the underlying security is trading at the strike price of the put and call. If the underlying stock advances or declines sufficiently to cover the put and call premiums (plus transaction costs) profits will result (at expiration) in either one or the other option.

Among the main strategies attractive for low-premium levels are (1) stock substitution, (2) hedging a short sale, and (3) put buying.

## Stock Substitution

When premiums are low, it becomes increasingly tempting for an investor who is long an optionable stock to sell that stock and replace it with an in-the-money call on that stock.

This action enables the investor to take out a significant part of his investment in the underlying stock, while retaining the ability to participate in an upward move in the stock.

## Hedging a Short Sale

When premiums are low, an investor who decides to sell an optionable stock short can obtain relatively inexpensive protection against large losses by buying a call.

## Put Buying

Theoretically, the purchase of a low-premium put offers excellent leveraged potential should the underlying security decline by expiration, plus limited upside exposure. However, as in the purchase of all options, the investor is risking the entire premium should the option expire worthless.

# LOW- OR HIGH-PREMIUM-LEVEL STRATEGIES

## Bull Call Spreads

As long as an investor believes a stock will appreciate, he can put on a bull spread in either low- or high-premium-level markets with similar costs and risk/reward parameters. It should be noted that spread transactions involve at least twice the number of commissions as an unhedged long or short position.

A bull spread encompasses buying 1 call on a specific stock and simultaneously selling 1 call on that stock having the same or shorter expiration and a higher strike price.

## Variable Spreads

Generally, variable spreads are "cheaper" when premium levels are high.

A variable spread encompasses buying 1 call on a specific stock and simultaneously selling more than one call, with the same expiration and usually a higher strike price, on that stock.

### Broad Option Strategy

Different market environments call for different option strategies, strategies that are also determined by the overall objectives of the investor, whether individual or institutional.

### Ratio Writing Strategy

If, with the market at a relatively high level, a cautious approach appears to be called for, stress should be on downside protection for the preservation of capital. The hedged option strategy of ratio writing, if well structured, may provide a broad profit zone without compromising downside protection.

### Spreading Strategy

Spreading has rapidly gained in applications as a result of changed margin rules for spreads. The upshot of the margin rules is that spreading has become a small-capital-expenditure investment medium, as the long option is deemed adequate to cover the short option.

### Covered Writing Strategy

Despite the rising importance of spreading and ratio writing, covered writing remains the dominant strategy for the dual purposes of capital preservation and capital enhancement in the world of options.

### Up, Flat, or Down Market

In periods of market uncertainties, the built-in advantages enjoyed by covered option writers versus long common stock holders or call buyers are obvious. In an up market, the covered writer earns the premium and possibly favorable strike-price differentials. In a flat market, the writer earns the option premium. In a down market, the writer may profit if the decline is less than the premium received.

The writer loses only when the decline is more than the premium received.

## PROTOTYPE PORTFOLIO

In the balance of this chapter, a prototype portfolio, based on June 17, 1975, closing prices, illustrates broad option strategies for an option-oriented portfolio of modest amounts, say, between $20,000 and $25,000.

What are the possible approaches for option-bound investors who seek a small, diversi-

# option portfolio strategies

# 34

fied option portfolio for maximum profit potential and minimum risk exposure? The prototype portfolio will help answer that question. For such investors we use the prototype portfolio below for illustrative purposes. It is not, however, intended to reflect the proportional balance of the components, in terms of invested funds, among the three principal categories of option strategies: (1) spreading, (2) ratio writing, and (3) covered writing.

This is becuase the values of particular options chosen for particular option strategies as of, say, June 17, 1975 (being the valuation date of this particular *sample* portfolio), would remain valid only for a limited time.

### Portfolio Segments

The three segments of this prototype portfolio are (1) the spreading segment; (2) the ratio writing segment; and (3) the covered writing segment.

### Spreading Segment

1. "Special situation" spread: bull perpendicular on Eastman Kodak
   Cost: $525 per spread
   Reason: Possible 73.8-percent return in 18 weeks
   Size: 5 spreads, to cost $2,625
2. Bull vertical on Xerox
   Cost: $213 per spread
   Reason: Long call potentially worth 10 points more than the short call
   Size: 5 spreads, to cost $1,065
3. Bull vertical on Deere
   Cost: $200 per spread
   Reason: Narrow spread premium
   Size: 5 spreads, to cost $1,000
4. Bull horizontal on IBM
   Cost: $675 per spread
   Reason: Possible widening of spread premium
   Size: 2 spreads, to cost $1,350

### Ratio Writing Segment

1. 2-to-1 ratio write on Mesa Petroleum
   Cost: $1,875 per write
   Reason: Possible 28-percent return in 18

weeks if MSA remained unchanged at expiration
   Size: 1 ratio write, to cost $1,875
2. 2-to-1 ratio write on Pfizer
   Cost: $2,688 per write
   Reason: Fairly broad profit zone
   Size: 1 write, to cost $2,688
3. 3-to-1 ratio write on Skyline
   Cost: $2,906 per write
   Reason: Broad profit zone
   Size: 1 write, to cost $2,906.
4. 3-to-1 ratio write on Syntex
   Cost: $2,013 per write
   Reason: Broad profit zone
   Size: 1 write, to cost $2,013.

### Covered Writing Segment

1. Leveraged covered write on Merrill Lynch
   Cost: $1,125 per write
   Reason: 28.6-percent downside protection; possible 34-percent return in less than 8 months if MER remained unchanged at expiration
   Size: 1 write, to cost $1,125
2. Leveraged covered write on G. D. Searle
   Cost: $1,263 per write
   Reason: 32.7-percent downside protection; possible 51.6-percent return in less than 9 months if SRL remained unchanged at expiration
   Size: 1 write, to cost $1,263
3. Covered write on Disney
   Cost: $3,963 per write
   Reason: 19.6-percent downside protection; possible 26.3-percent in 18 weeks if DIS were called
   Size: 1 write, to cost $3,963
4. Covered write on Alcoa
   Cost: $3,863 per write
   Reason: 13.9-percent downside protection; 19.1-percent return in less than 9 months if AA were called
   Size: 1 write, to cost $3,863

### Portfolio Cost Composition

The above portfolio would have composition and cost structure as follows:

### *Spreading Segment*

| | Cost |
|---|---|
| 5 EK spreads | $2,625 |
| 5 XRX spreads | 1,065 |
| 5 DE spreads | 1,000 |
| 2 IBM spreads | 1,350 |
| | $6,040 |

### *Ratio Writing Segment*

| | |
|---|---|
| 1 MSA 2-to-1 write | $1,875 |
| 1 PFE 2-to-1 write | 2,688 |
| 1 SKY 3-to-1 write | 2,906 |
| 1 SYN 3-to-1 write | 2,013 |
| | 9,482 |

### *Covered Writing Segment*

| | |
|---|---|
| 1 MER 1-to-1 leveraged write | $1,125 |
| 1 SRL 1-to-1 leveraged write | $1,263 |
| 1 DIS 1-to-1 write | $3,963 |
| 1 AA 1-to-1 write | $3,863 |
| | $10,214 |
| Total portfolio cost | $25,736 |

## ANATOMY OF PROTOTYPE PORTFOLIO

Following is an anatomy of the prototype portfolio.

### *Spreading Segment*

1. Special situation spread: bull perpendicular: This is a low-cost special situation spread where you could possibly end with a 73.8-percent return in 18 weeks even with the underlying stock doing nothing during that intermediate-term option period.

   It is based on perpendicular spread on Eastman Kodak (NYSE–99⅛–EK) structured as follows:

   | | |
   |---|---|
   | Buy EK October 90 at | 13¾ |
   | Sell EK October 100 at | 8½ |
   | Cash layout | 5¼ |

   Also known as a vertical or money spread, a perpendicular spread is an option technique that involves simultaneous long and short positions on the same stock having different strike prices but the same expiration month.

   In bull perpendiculars you buy the low-strike option and sell (short) the high-strike option.

   In our bull horizontal spread on EK, you would need only $525 in cash layout to control a $99-plus stock for 18 weeks.

   If EK remained unchanged at 99⅛ at October expiration, returns would be 73.8 percent over the 18-week time span.

   With EK as a bull perpendicular, the stock's expected upside move would considerably widen the premium spread from the current 5¼ points.

   Every five-point move, or about 5 percent on a $99-value underlying stock, would probably magnify into a move of more than 20 percent, or more than three points in a 13¾-value option.

   Meanwhile, the option premium would widen by about one point, or 20 percent or so, from the present 5¼ to 6¼.
2. Bull perpendicular spread on Xerox: For Xerox (NYSE–67¾–XRX) bulls, a low-cost bull spread on XRX may be construed as follows:

   | | |
   |---|---|
   | Buy XRX October 80 at | 3¾ |
   | Sell XRX October 90 at | 1⅝ |
   | Cash layout | 2⅛ |

   With a 2⅛-point cash layout, a spreader can own a XRX October 80 that potentially could be worth ten points more than XRX 90.
3. Bull perpendicular spread on Deere: The following bull perpendicular spread appears attractive on Deere (NYSE–39½–DE):

   | | |
   |---|---|
   | Buy DE October 40 at | 4 |
   | Sell DE October 45 at | 2 |
   | Cash outlay | 2 |

The maximum profit potential for this bull spread is obtainable with DE moving up to 45.

4. Horizontal spread on IBM: An attractive horizontal spread on IBM (NYSE–203½–IBM) can be structured by the sale of an intermediate-term option to reduce the cost of a more-distant-term option that is believed to be undervalued:

| | |
|---|---|
| Buy IBM January 200 at | 28 |
| Sell IBM October 200 at | 21¼ |
| Cash outlay | 6¾ |

Also known as a calendar or time spread, a horizontal spread is an option technique that involves buying and selling options having the same strike price but different expiration months. In bull horizontals, you long the far-term expiration and sell (short) the near-term expiration.

Historically, the premium differential between an intermediate-term IBM option and a far-term IBM option with three months separating them is wider than the spread premium of 6¾ indicated here.

The spreader's profit is predicated upon a possible widening of the spread premium.

## *Ratio Writing Segment*

1. 2-to-1 ratio write on Mesa Petroleum: Since well-structured partially hedged writing provides a broad profit band without compromising downside protection, the following two-against-one ratio writes appear attractive.

One involves Mesa (NYSE–24–MSA) with the following hedged construction:

Buy MSA at 24
Sell 2 MSA October 25 calls at 2⅜ each
Downside parameter = 18¾
Upside parameter = 28⅛
Profit zone = 9⅜ points (between 28⅛ and 18¾)

A profit zone of 12½ points is thus established, within which the partial hedger will remain profitable.

2. 2-to-1 ratio write on Pfizer: Pfizer (NYSE–30⅞–PFE) is another interesting partially hedged writing situation where you can construct a fairly broad profit zone between the upside and downside breakeven points within which PFE will remain profitable.

A 2-to-1 ratio write on PFE can be structured as follows:

Buy 100 PFE at 30⅞
Sell 2 October 35 calls at 2 each
Downside parameter = 26⅞
Upside parameter = 43⅛
Profit zone = 16¼ points

3. 3-to-1 ratio write on Skyline: More aggressive hedgers may wish to go for a ratio of three to one.

An attractive 3-to-1 write involves selling August 25 calls at 1⅜ per call against 100 shares of Skyline (NYSE–21–SKY), as follows:

Buy 100 SKY at 21
Sell 3 SKY August 25 calls at 1⅜ each
Dowside parameter = 16⅞
Upside parameter = 29¹⁄₁₆
Profit zone = 12³⁄₁₆ points

If SKY stayed unchanged at expiration, the 3-to-1 hedger would realize 24.4 percent in just five weeks.

4. 3-to-1 ratio write on Syntex: Syntex (NYSE–38⅛–SYN) is also promising as a 3-to-1 ratio write involving the sale of three SYN January 40 calls at 6 per call against 100 shares of SYN.

The partially hedged write is indicated by the following construction:

Buy 100 SYN at 38⅛
Sell 3 SYN January 40 calls at 6 each
Downside parameter = 20⅛
Upside parameter = 49⅞
Profit zone = 29⁵⁄₁₆ points

If SYN remained unchanged at expiration, the ratio writer would gain 89.4 percent in less than eight months.

### *Covered Writing Segment*

Two situations particularly attractive for leverage (margined) covered writing.

One would involve G. D. Searle (NYSE–18¾–SRL), a newcomer to the AMEX, whose February 15 option provided a low-cost writing opportunity for very good returns.

The other one would involve Merrill Lynch (NYSE–15¾–MER), which continued to offer one of the most interesting writing possibilities.

1. Leveraged covered write on Merrill Lynch: Due to its predominantly retail business, MER has emerged competitively stronger and is likely to report higher-than-expected June quarter earnings.

   A margined covered write on MER would involve purchasing 100 shares at 15¾ (margined at $787.50) and selling a January 15 call at 3⅜, as follows:

   | | |
   |---|---|
   | Buy 100 MER at | 15¾ |
   | 50% margin at | 7⅞ |
   | Sell MER January 15 at | 3⅜ |
   | Cash outlay | 4½ |

   Thus the option premium reduces cash outlays to $450 and protects the stock down to 12⅜ (27.3 percent).

2. Leveraged covered write on Searle: A leveraged covered writing structure is suggested on G. D. Searle as follows:

   | | |
   |---|---|
   | Buy 100 SRL at | 18¾ |
   | 50% margin at | 9⅜ |
   | Sell SRL February 15 at | 6⅛ |
   | Cash outlay | 3¼ |

   Thus, the option premium from the sale of the deep-in-the-money February 15 call reduces cash requirement to $3.25 and, simultaneously, protects the stock down to 12⅝ (32.7 percent).

   The likely high return is due to the low cash outlay of this leveraged covered writing structure as well as by SRL's deep-in-the-money option.

   Option-oriented investors should be alert to new option opportunities. It would be worth watching first-hour trading for possible aberrations because frequently new options tend to be underpriced or overpriced.

3. Covered write on Disney: The following two covered option writing situations offer the potential for attractive returns if the underlying stock were called away (all on a cash basis).

   One situation involves writing an October 50 option at 7¾ on Disney (NYSE–47⅜–DIS) against 100 shares of DIS, with the option premium reducing the covered writer's cash outlay to 39⅝, as follows:

   | | |
   |---|---|
   | Buy 100 DIS at | 47⅜ |
   | Sell DIS October 50 at | 7¾ |
   | Cash outlay | 39⅝ |

   The reduced investment at 39⅝ also provides the downside protection (16.4 percent).

   If DIS were called away at 50, the gain to the covered writer would total $1,037.50, including $775 from option premium and 2⅝ from appreciation to the called-away price, indicating a return of 26.2 percent in 18 weeks.

4. Covered write on Alcoa: Another covered writing situation involves issuing a January 45 option at 5⅜ on Alcoa (NYSE–44–AA) against 100 shares of stock, as follows:

   | | |
   |---|---|
   | Buy 100 AA at | 44 |
   | Sell AA January 45 at | 5⅜ |
   | Cash outlay | 38⅝ |

   The reduced cash outlay of 38⅝ also provides the downside protection (12.2 percent).

If the underlying security were called away at 45, the gain to the covered writer would total $738, including 5⅜ from the option premium, one point from appreciation to the called-away price, and $100.50 from dividends, indicating a return of 19.1 percent in less than eight months.

## Portfolio Methods

While the prototype portfolio is only valid at the time of construction, what is timeless are the methods of composing an option portfolio through the use of different option media and strategies.

Also timeless are the methods of achieving portfolio leverage through ratio writing and spreading techniques, to maximize investment results, as well as those methods designed to achieve the dual objectives of capital preservation and capital enhancement, particularly during periods of market uncertainties.

# WORKSHOP AND QUESTIONNAIRE

# XII

### Basic Option Worksheet

Since option writing is generally considered the most prudent form of option investing, we will use the basic option writing worksheet for illustrative purposes.

A basic option writing worksheet includes the following elements:

A. Basic data
B. "Buy stock" data
C. "Sell option" data
D. Possible consequences:
    (x) if stock moves above striking price, with option exercised;
    (y) if stock remains unchanged; and
    (z) if stock moves lower.

### Basic Data

a. Date
b. Number of calendar days
c. Name of stock
d. Number of shares
e. Purchase price
f. Option
g. Premium

h. Dividend
   Total dividends

### Buy Stock

1. Cost of stock purchase
2. (Plus) Commission on stock purchase
3. Total stock cost

### Sell Option

4. Gross premium receipt
2. (Minus) Commission on option sale
6. Net premium receipt

### Actual Cash Investment

3. Total stock cost
6. (Minus) net premium receipt
7. Actual cash investment

## POSSIBLE CONSEQUENCES

The following are possible consequences:
    (x) if stock moves above striking price, with option exercised;

option workshop

35

(y) if stock remains unchanged; and

(z) if stock moves lower.

### If Stock Moves Above Striking, with Option Exercised

6. Net premium receipt
8. (Plus) Dividends
9. (Plus or minus) Gain or loss
2. (Minus) Commission on stock purchase
10. (Minus) Commission on exercise
11. Net return
12. Percent gain (line 11 ÷ line 7) for ———— days.
13. Annualized gain* ——————%

### If Stock Remains Unchanged

6. Net premium receipt
14. (Minus) Amount (if any) of option in money
8. (Plus) Dividends
2. (Minus) Commission on stock purchase
15. Net return
16. Percent gain (line 15 ÷ line 7) for ———— days
13. Annualized gain ——————%

### If Stock Moves Lower

3. Total stock cost
6. (Minus) Net premium receipt
8. (Minus) Dividends
17. Investment reduced to
18. Breakeven point (line 17 ÷ no. of shares)

### Illustrative Transaction

Applying the above option worksheet formula to an illustrative transaction on Philip Morris (NYSE–46–MO) on March 19, 1975, that would involve buying 100 shares of MO at 46 and selling one July 50 call at 3⅜, we had the following:

a. Date   3/19/75

b. Number of calendar days   129

c. Name of stock   Philip Morris

—

* Multiply *percent gain* by 360 and divide by number of days.

—

d. Number of shares   100

e. Purchase price   46

f. Option   July 50

g. Premium   3⅜

h. Dividend   $0.225

# APPLYING WORKSHEET FORMULA

### Buy Stock

1. Cost of stock purchase $4,600.00
2. (Plus) Commission on stock purchase $62.00
3. Total stock cost $4,662.00

### Sell Option

4. Gross premium receipt $337.50
5. (Minus) Commission on option sale $15.00
6. Net premium receipt $322.50

### Actual Cash Investment

3. Total stock cost $4,662.00
6. (Minus) Net premium receipt $322.50
7. Actual cash investment $4,339.50

# POSSIBLE CONSEQUENCES

### If Stock Moves Above Striking, with Option Exercised

6. Net premium receipt $322.50
8. (Plus) Dividends $22.50
9. Gain or loss $400.00
2. (Minus) Commission on stock purchase $62.00
10. (Minus) Commission on exercise $65.00
11. Net return $618.00
12. Percent gain (11 ÷ 7) = 14.2 for 129 days
13. Annualized gain 39.6%

### If Stock Remains Unchanged

6. Net premium receipt $322.50
14. (Minus) Amount (if any) of option in money 0

8. (Plus) Dividends $22.50
2. (Minus) Commission on stock purchase $62.00
15. Net return $283.00
16. Percent Gain (15 ÷ 7) = 6.5
13. Annualized gain 18.1%

### If Stock Moves Lower

3. Total stock cost $4,662.00
6. (Minus) Net premium receipt $322.50
8. (Minus) Dividends $22.50

17. Investment reduced to $4,317.00
18. Breakeven point $43.17

### Do-It-Yourself Option Assessment

By application of the above option worksheet formulas, readers should be able to work out their own option sheets as a means of assessing the relative returns of varying option writing possibilities.

### Question-and-Answer Method

The Options Questionnaire is designed to help the reader know on what to focus in the course of studying the subjects covered by this book. The reader can ask himself the following series of salient questions and seeking answers in the book.

This method of reading with a focus is particularly appropriate for a subject matter such as options that requires considerable drill and exercises for a real understanding.

## LISTED OPTIONS AND LISTED OPTIONS MARKETS

1. What is the basic difference between options and short-term warrants?
2. What is the basic difference between the listed options now traded on the national options exchanges and the traditional options traded over the counter?
3. What accounts for the phenomenal growth of listed options in the years since their debut on the Chicago Board Options Exchange?
4. What are the two major innovations of the listed options market?
5. What are the basic exclusive characteristics of listed options?
6. What accounts for the liquidity of the listed options market?
7. What accounts for the potential of listed options to achieve the two normally irreconcilable objectives of maximizing gains and minimizing risks?
8. What accounts for the risk-limiting characteristics of listed options?
9. What makes listed options small-capital-expenditure vehicles for participation in America's top-quality companies?
10. What is the unique guaranteeing function of the Options Clearing Corporation?

call options
questionnaire

36

# OPTION VALUES

11. What is the built-in leverage in option price movements relative to price movements in their underlying securities?
12. What are the general yardsticks to determine the cost or value of options?
13. Is there an intrinsic value for an option?
14. How does one evaluate in-the-money options and out-of-the-money options?
15. How does one determine the best time-period value of options?
16. Why is the largest option premium percentagewise often paid for the shortest period of time? Why is the option premium for the initial three months higher than the next three-month period? How does one take advantage of this time-value aberration?
17. How does one calculate relative overvaluation or undervaluation among options and between options and their underlying securities?
18. Do you need a computer and high-level mathematics to calculate the value of options?
19. What are the principal advantages and disadvantages of computer-based option programs?
20. How does one salvage option values even if anticipated movement in the underlying security should fail to materialize?
21. Why should you be alert to option opportunities especially during the initial trading hours of a newly listed option?

# VARIOUS OPTION STRATEGIES

22. What are the basic option strategies?
23. Which of the following is generally considered to be the most speculative?
    (a) Covered writing
    (b) Uncovered writing
    (c) Straight long stock position
    (d) Straight option buying
    (e) Spreading
    (f) Straddling

24. What should you do if you believe the price of a stock will rise? Buy a call? Is there any other possible approach, especially if you are in a high income bracket and had capital losses?
25. How does one calculate the potential maximum return and exposure for option buyers?
26. What should you do if you believe the price of a stock will decline? Sell a call? Buy an in-the-money call and sell short the underlying security?
27. What are the relative advantages and disadvantages of the above two approaches?
28. How does one calculate the potential maximum return and exposure for option writers (sellers)?
29. What should you do if you believe the stock is going to change very little? Buy the stock and sell a call against the stock? Or buy the stock and sell two calls against the stock? What are the relative advantages and disadvantages of these two approaches?
30. What are the most appropriate market conditions for option writing? For option selling? For option straddling? For option spreading?
31. Which is generally considered more likely to make money, writing (selling) options, or buying options?
32. What is your personal opinion as to the comparative profitability of writing (selling) or buying options?

# OPTION BUYING AND ITS TECHNIQUES

33. What are the principal advantages and disadvantages of option buying?
34. What are the principal call option buying strategies?
35. What are the merits of buying stocks for the purpose of writing call options to obtain additional income?
36. How can you protect against an upward price movement of a stock that you do not own?

37. How does one establish a stock position before receiving the expected funds?
38. How can one buy stocks at below-market prices?
39. How can one control more stock with the same amount of money?
40. How can one acquire an option at no cost?
41. How can you release cash while retaining your market position?
42. How does one hedge against a short sale?

# OPTION WRITING AND ITS TECHNIQUES

43. What are the principal advantages and disadvantages of option writing (selling)?
44. What are the principal option writing strategies?
45. How can you increase your cash return while retaining the security?
46. How can you reduce the cost of the stock that you have acquired?
47. How does one sell stocks at above-market prices?
48. How do you buy-wait-write?
49. When would it be advantageous for you to write options with a view toward their being called away?
50. How does one calculate the potential gain from stocks written for options if and when they are called away?
51. How does one create short-term losses for tax purposes?
52. What are the possible recourses for protecting your uncovered position?

# RATIO WRITING AND ITS TECHNIQUES

53. What are the principal advantages and disadvantages of ratio writing or variable hedging?
54. How does one calculate the potential maximum return and exposure for ratio writers?
55. How does one establish a profit band in ratio writing?

56. How does one calculate the downside parameter for ratio writing?
57. How does one calculate the upside parameter for ratio writing?
58. What are the principal ratio writing strategies?
59. How does one set up a 2-against-1 ratio writing?
60. How does one set up a 3-against-1 ratio writing?
61. How does one buy at discount instead of premium?

# OPTION SPREADING AND ITS TECHNIQUES

62. What are the principal advantages and disadvantages of option spreading?
63. How does one select stocks for spreads?
64. What are the principal option spreading strategies?
65. How does one calculate the potential maximum return and exposure for option spreaders?
66. How does one balance downside protection with upside potential in option spreading?
67. How does one set up a bull horizontal (time or calendar) spread? A bear horizontal spread?
68. How does one set up a bull vertical (money or perpendicular) spread? A bear vertical spread?
69. How does one establish a higher-potential spread position at reduced risk?
70. How does one buy below-intrinsic-value options?

# OPTION STRADDLING AND ITS TECHNIQUES

71. How does one make money without knowing market directions?
72. What is the principal difference between a straddle and a spread?
73. Why is a straddle generally more expensive than a spread, a put, or a call?

74. Why are volatile stocks more desirable for straddling?
75. What are the principal straddle option writing strategies?
76. How can one sell a straddle without a stock position?
77. How does one offset a short position with a straddle?
78. How does one convert two calls into a put and a call?
79. How can one recoup the entire straddle premium with only half the option?
80. How can one achieve profit pyramiding?

# PUT OPTION AND ITS TECHNIQUES

81. What are the principal advantages and disadvantages of put options?
82. What are the principal put option strategies?
83. What is the basic difference between a put option and a short sale?
84. What is the basic difference between a put option and a buy-stop?
85. How can one insulate short-term market breaks?
86. How can one profit from down fluctuations?

# OPTION MARGINS

87. What are the three sets of option margin requirements?
88. What is the difference between the initial margin requirement and the maintenance margin requirement?
89. What is the margin requirement (if any) for covered writing?
90. How does one calculate the margin requirement for uncovered writing?
91. How does one calculate the margin requirement for ratio or variable writing?
92. What are the improved margin advantages for spreading?
93. How does one minimize the cost of spreading?

94. What are the main differences between bull spread margins and bear spread margins?

# TAXES

95. What are the basic tax considerations for option buyers?
96. How does one realize a long-term gain on decline?
97. How does one realize a long-term gain on rise?
98. What are the basic tax considerations for option writers?
99. How does one convert a short-term gain to a long-term gain?
100. How can one create ordinary loss with an offsetting option? With an offsetting stock?
101. If an option writer's obligation is closed by executing a closing purchase transaction, what is the Internal Revenue Service's rule on tax treatment of profits from option writing?
102. If an option is exercised, what is the Internal Revenue Service's rule on tax treatment of an option premium received?
103. If an option expires unexercised, what is the Internal Revenue Service's rule on tax treatment of an option premium received?
104. What are the special tax advantages for straddle writing?
105. What are the most frequently used option techniques for tax-shelter purposes?

# OPTION PORTFOLIOS

106. What are the principal means of increasing the yield for an income-oriented portfolio using options?
107. What would be the most appropriate option programs for conservative accounts whose portfolios are composed primarily of low-cost, quality stocks?
108. What are the alternate income-oriented option strategies for option-oriented portfolios?

109. What are the possible obstacles to reaching maximum yields achievable through income-oriented strategies?

110. What would be the most appropriate portfolio composition for income-oriented accounts in terms of percentage allocation among writing, buying, and spreading segments?

111. What are the principal option strategies for maximizing gains in a growth-oriented portfolio?

112. What is the most appropriate options programs for aggressive accounts primarily seeking capital appreciation?

113. What are the possible obstacles to reaching the maximum gains achievable through aggressive strategies?

114. What is the most appropriate portfolio composition for growth-oriented accounts in terms of percentage allocation among the writing, buying, and spreading segments?

115. What are the principal option strategies for maximizing gains in a balanced (income and growth) portfolio?

116. What is the most appropriate portfolio composition for balanced accounts in terms of percentage allocation among the writing, buying, and spreading segments?

As in the Call Options Questionnaire, the same quiz method is used to help you test your knowledge about put options.

## PUT BASICS

1. What is a listed put option?
2. Why do listed puts result in greater investment flexibility?
3. Why do listed puts enable investors to trade for profit in down markets as well as in up markets?
4. What is the importance of a listed market for puts?
5. Why is a put the mirror image of a call?
6. What are the similarities between a put and a call?
7. What are the major differences between a put and a call?
8. What is an in-the-money put?
9. What is an out-of-the-money put?
10. What is the relationship between put premium and stock price?

11. What are the major factors determining put premiums?
12. What is the volatility of a stock? How do you measure it?
13. Why is volatility important to put buying or selling?

## SIMPLE STRATEGIES

14. What are the basic strategies using puts?
15. What are the two basic strategies from the put buyer's viewpoint?
16. What are the two basic strategies from the put seller's viewpoint?
17. What are the two principal advantages a put buyer has over a short seller in the underlying stock?
18. What is the principal reason for combining a put purchase with buying the underlying stock?
19. Why should one sell a put?
20. What is the principal reason for combining a put sale with selling short the underlying stock?

# put options
# questionnaire
# 37

## PUT BUYING

21. How does an investor profit from an anticipated decline in the price of a certain stock?
22. Why is put buying analogous to buying insurance?
23. Why is put buying a particularly useful protection in connection with purchase of volatile stocks?
24. What is the maximum risk in put buying?
25. What are the similarities between a put buyer and a call buyer?
26. What are the differences between a put buyer and a call buyer?
27. What is the meaning of covered put buying?
28. What is the meaning of uncovered put buying?

## LONG PUT

29. What is a long put?
30. What are the principal uses of buying puts as a trading vehicle?
31. What happens to a put buyer if the stock price at expiration is below the strike price? Above the strike price?
32. How do you dispose of a profitable long put position?
33. How do you exercise a long put position?
34. What is the alternate way to benefit from a profitable long put position other than exercising it?
35. Where is the resale market for puts?
36. What is the third possible approach to exercise or resale?
37. Why is put purchase an alternative to short sale in the underlying stock?
38. What are the two main advantages of put purchase over short sale?
39. Does a stop-loss order have any advantages? Disadvantages?
40. Compare the leverage factor in put buying with that in short sale.
41. What's the meaning of depreciation factor? How does one calculate it?

42. Compare the risk factor in put buying with that in short sale.
43. Compare put buying with short sale regarding margin calls, timing flexibility, taxes, and cash dividend liability.

## LONG PUT, LONG STOCK

44. What is the purpose of simultaneously owning a common stock and a put on the same stock?
45. How can a long put position allow an investor to pursue long-term investment objectives?
46. Why does only put buying provide the complete hedge to a long stock position?
47. What are the two principal applications for a combined long-stock, long-put strategy?
48. How do you protect unrealized profit in a stock position that you do not want to relinquish?
49. How do you freeze a capital gain or loss in stock in a current year and defer the tax consequences to the succeeding year?
50. How do you establish a stock position while establishing a minimum price for its possible liquidation?
51. What is the meaning of "married put"?
52. Compare long puts plus long stock on the one hand with long put plus long call on the other.

## PUT SELLING

53. What kind of underlying stock does one look for when selling a put?
54. What are the two types of put selling?
55. What is an uncovered put?
56. Why does naked put selling place the seller in the same economic position as a conservative covered call writer?
57. Compare the risk/reward factors of a covered call writer with those of an uncovered put writer.

58. What is the meaning of covered put selling?
59. Is covered put selling completely covered?
60. What are the two principal purposes of put selling?
61. How does a put seller choose the exercise price if he is bullish on the underlying stock? If he is bearish?
62. What is the obligation of a put seller?
63. What does the put seller do when he receives an exercise notice?
64. What is the meaning of "closing purchase transaction"?

## SHORT PUT

65. What is a short put?
66. Why does a put seller need ample cash reserve?
67. Why is naked put selling more conservative than its name indicates?
68. What are the two principal ways for a put seller to realize his premium income?
69. How can an investor buy stock at a price below the market price?
70. What is the inherent risk for a put seller with a related stock position?
71. What are the means of defense available to put sellers to minimize their exposure?

## SHORT PUT, SHORT STOCK

72. What is covered put selling?
73. Why is covered put selling only partially covered?
74. Why is short put, short stock a bear put strategy?

## SHORT PUT, LONG STOCK

75. When does an investor sell a put against a long stock position?

76. How does leverage work both ways when an investor sells a put with a position in the related stock?

## PUT SPREADING

77. What is put spreading?
78. Does the basic concept of call spreading apply to put spreading?
79. Explain why a spread is essentially the dollar difference between the buy and sell premiums?
80. What are the meanings of "debit" and "credit"?
81. What is the meaning of "even" spread?
82. Why does spreading enable an investor to trade in more volatile stocks without paying high premiums?
83. Why has the appeal of option spreading been enhanced by margin rules?
84. Why is the cost of spreading high?
85. What is the simple formula for calculating potential spread profit?
86. What is the simple formula for calculating potential spread risk?
87. How do you calculate spread breakeven point?
88. In a bear put price spread, why does the spreader buy a higher strike-price put and sell a lower strike-price put?
89. What is the basic formula for structuring a bear put time spread?
90. How do you roll down a bear put price spread when it becomes profitable?

## PUT TIME SPREADS

91. What is put time spreading?
92. How do you structure a bull put time spread? A bear put time spread?
93. What are the key factors determining the potential profitability in a put time spread?
94. What are the things to watch for in initiating a put time spread?
95. When does a put time spreader use an in-the-money put? An out-of-the-money put? An at-the-money put?

# PUT PRICE SPREADS

96. What is a put price spread?
97. Why is a price spread also called a vertical spread?
98. How do you construct a put price spread?
99. In a bullish put price spread, why does the spreader sell a higher strike-price put and buy a lower strike-price put?
100. Why is a spread essentially a risk-reducing device?

# STRADDLES

101. How do listed puts facilitate trading in straddles?
102. What is the option strategy enabling investors to make money without knowing market direction?
103. When does one buy a straddle? Sell a straddle?
104. Why do straddles provide a means of making money both for the buyer and for the seller?
105. What is a long straddle?
106. Why does a straddle buyer need a substantial move (in either direction) in the underlying stock?
107. How do you calculate the upper and lower profit levels for a straddle buyer?
108. Why is volatility in the underlying stock the key to successful straddle buying?
109. How do you choose the expiration month in straddle buying?
111. What kind of market action does a straddle seller anticipate in the underlying stock?
112. What are the two principal motivations for selling a straddle?
113. How do you calculate the profit parameters for a straddle seller?
114. When does the maximum profit for a straddle seller occur?
115. How do you reduce risk in selling a straddle through use of varied strike prices for the call and the put?
116. Why does "whipshaw" pose a major risk for a straddle seller?

117. Why does one use an out-of-the-money option in structuring a bullish straddle?
118. Why does one use an in-the-money option in structuring a bearish straddle?

# COMBINATIONS

119. What is a combination?
120. Should combination buyers and sellers look for the same characteristics in selecting a stock?
121. What is the purpose of combination buying?
122. What is the purpose of combination selling?
123. What is the importance of volatility to combination buying or selling?
124. How do you structure a combination on the same expiration month?
125. How do you calculate the profit parameters for a combination buyer or seller?
126. Compare a combination with a straddle.
127. How do you incorporate a bullish or bearish bias into combination buying?
128. Why does one use a call closer to being in the money when structuring a bullish combination buying position?
129. Why does one use a put closer to being in-the-money when structuring a bearish combination buying position?
130. What are the different expectations for a combination buyer with or without holding a position in the underlying stock?
131. What is the step-by-step procedure for combination buying?
132. What is the meaning of "lifting a leg" for a combination buyer?
133. What is the maximum risk for a combination buyer?
134. Why does a bullish combination seller use a stable stock?
135. What is covered combination selling?
136. What is uncovered combination selling?
137. What is the motivation for a covered combination seller?
138. What is the motivation for an uncovered combination seller?
139. Why does a bullish combination seller use a put closer to being in the money?

140. Why does a bearish combination seller use a call closer to being in the money?

# PUT MARGINS

141. What is the margin requirement for a long put?
142. What is the margin requirement for a long put, long stock?
143. What is the margin requirement for a short put?
144. What is the margin requirement for a short put, short stock?
145. What is the margin requirement for a put spread?
146. What is the margin requirement for a straddle?
147. What is the margin requirement for a combination?

*Accumulation:*   The process by which an excess supply of stock is absorbed by an expanding demand that, over time, has a favorable effect on the price of the stock.

*Annualized return:*   The calculated hypothetical earnings, extended to a twelve-month period, for an option purchaser or writer (seller) based on the conditions that exist at the expiration of an option contract. Annualized return is the aggregate sum of proceeds from option premium, possible appreciation to expiration, and dividends. This hypothetical return, however, rarely occurs.

*Annualized yield:*   Same as *Annualized return.*

*Arbitrage:*   An offsetting transaction involving almost simultaneous purchases and sales of the same security, or substantially identical securities, in different markets in order to profit from a price differential. In option trading, arbitrage takes advantage of a temporary price discrepancy between options or between the option and the underlying stock.

*At the money:*   An option for which the strike price (or exercise price) is the same as the price of the underlying security.

*Bank guarantee letter:*   Letter issued by an exchange-approved bank certifying either of the following: (1) The writer of a put has cash on deposit at that bank to cover the purchase of the underlying stock should the option be exercised; or (2) in the case of a call, that a writer has deposited the underlying stock with the bank. The bank will deliver the stock upon exercise.

*Bear horizontal spread:*   An option spread involving the purchase of a near-month expiration and the sale of a more-distant-month expiration.

*Bearish:*   The investment attitude of an investor who believes a stock or stocks will decline.

*Bear market:*   A market in which the general trend of securities prices is down.

*Bear spread:*   A strategy involving the simultaneous purchase of one type of option (put or call) and the sale of another of the same type, both on the same stock. The purchased option must have a higher strike price than the sold option. Both should have identical expiration dates. This strategy is based on an investor's expectation of a decline in the stock price.

# glossary

*Bear straddle writing:* Selling (writing) one call option against cash and one put option against a long position.

*Bear vertical spread:* Buying a higher-strike option and selling (shorting) a lower-strike option (the reverse of a bull vertical spread).

*Beta:* A measure of a stock's sensitivity to the movement of the general market in recent years.

*Bull horizontal spread:* An option spread involving the purchase of a more-distant-month expiration and the sale of a near-month expiration.

*Bullish:* The investment attitude of an investor who believes a stock or stocks will advance.

*Bull market:* A market in which the general trend of securities prices is up.

*Bull spread:* A strategy involving the simultaneous purchase of one type of option (put or call) and the sale of another of the same type, both on the same stock. The purchased option must have a lower strike price than the sold option; both should have identical expiration dates.

*Bull straddle writing:* Selling one call option against a long position and one put option against cash.

*Bull vertical spread:* Buying a low-strike option and selling a high-strike option. A bull vertical spread is sometimes called a bull perpendicular or a bull money spread. It is the reverse of a bear vertical spread.

*Butterfly:* An option spread consisting of the sale of two intermediate options and the purchase of two options with strike prices of equal distance from the short options, in the ratio of 1:2:1. A butterfly is sometimes called a sandwich spread.

*Buying a spread:* Putting on a spread at a debit; to pay out more for an option spread than is received. It occurs when an investor buys the more expensive of two options and sells the less expensive.

*Buying a straddle:* Purchasing a put and a call covering the same underlying security with the same exercise price and expiration date.

*Buying in:* Eliminating the option writer's obligation that arises from having sold a call option by means of purchasing a similar call option and designating it a closing transaction.

*Buy stop:* An option strategy whereby an uncovered option writer executes an order normally on the basis of the strike price plus option premium. The purpose of a buy stop order is to limit an unknown loss.

*Calendar spread:* Also known as a time spread or horizontal spread, a transaction involving the simultaneous purchase and sale of options with the same strike price but different expiration dates on the same underlying stock.

*Call:* A contract to buy 100 shares of a specified stock at a specific price (the exercise or strike price) at any time within a given period of time.

*Called:* Another term for "exercised," an indication by the buyer of a call to the writer of a call that the indicated underlying security must be delivered.

*CBOE:* The Chicago Board Options Exchange.

*Class of options:* All listed option contracts of the same type covering the same underlying security, e.g., all listed Exxon Corporation call options.

*Close to the money:* An option strike price close to the current price of the underlying stock. In close-to-the-money options, time value, as a factor in determining the premium, is at its maximum.

*Closing call:* The purchase by an option writer, normally uncovered, of a call option with the same expiration date and striking price as the previously sold one.

*Closing purchase transaction:* A transaction in which an investor who has previously written an option intends to liquidate his preexisting position as a writer. This liquidation is accomplished by buying in a closing purchase transaction an option having the same terms as the option previously written. Such a transaction has the effect of cancelling an investor's preexisting position as a writer, instead of resulting in the issuance of an option to the investor.

*Closing sale transaction:* A transaction in which an investor who has previously purchased an option intends to liquidate his preexisting position as a holder. This liquidation is accomplished by selling in a closing sale transaction an option having the same terms as the option previously bought. Such a transaction has the effect of liquidating the investor's preexisting position as a holder of the option, instead of resulting in the investor's assuming the obligation of a writer.

*Closing transaction:* The purchase or sale of an option for the purpose of offsetting and cancelling an existing open position resulting from a prior sale or purchase.

*Combination:* Any strategy involving the purchase or sale of both puts and calls.

*Consolidation:* A pause in a market trend, with the expectation that the trend will be resumed in the same direction.

*Continuous auction market:* A marketplace which provides a continuous process for holders and writers of options to liquidate their positions.

*Conversion:* The process of converting one side of a straddle option contract into the other side; the strike price remains the same.

*Conversion charge:* The cost of converting the put portion of a straddle option contract into a call. See also *Reverse charge*.

*Correction:* A price decline or pull-back, or a price reaction.

*Cover:* The purchase of stock, or an option on it, in order to fulfill a naked commitment.

*Covered call writer:* The writer of a call option who owns the underlying stock upon which the option is written.

*Covered put writer:* The writer of a put option who owns another put with the same or higher exercise price on the same underlying stock.

*Covered writer:* The writer of an option who, as long as he remains a writer, owns the shares or other units of an underlying security covered by the option.

*Covered writing:* Selling (writing) an option contract involving a number of shares covered by an equal number of shares owned, and preparing to deliver these shares in the event that the option buyer calls for delivery through exercise in his option right.

*Cycle:* The months in which options expire.

*Deep in the money:* An option whose price has risen substantially above the intrinsic value.

*Diagonal spread:* A combination of time and price spread involving the simultaneous purchase and sale of options of the same class that have different exercise prices and different expiration dates.

*Discount option:* An option on which the premium plus the exercise price is less than the current market price of the underlying security.

*Downside parameter:* The downside price level of the underlying security below which a ratio writer will incur a loss.

*Even spread:* A spread on which the cost of the long option equals the cost of the short option.

*Exercise:* To request the writer to deliver the stock at the stated price (call) or to pay the stated price for stock delivered to him (put).

*Exercise notice:* Written statement of an option holder's intention to exercise the option.

*Exercise price:* The price per share at which the option buyer may buy (in the case of a call) or sell (in the case of a put) 100 shares of the underlying stock. The exercise price is also known as the strike price.

*Expiration date:* The date on which the option contract expires. Expiration dates for listed options are standardized and are always three months apart. No more than three expiration dates are traded on a particular option at a particular time.

*Expiration month:* The months in which options expire.

*Far option:* That portion of a spread option whose expiration date arrives last.

*Half hedge:* Writing (selling) two option contracts each for 100 shares of the underlying security owned.

*Hedge:* A means of protecting against financial loss, usually by offsetting a long (buy) position in one stock or option with a short (sell) position in a related stock or option.

*Horizontal spread:* A spread involving simultaneous buying and selling of options having the same strike price but different expiration months. A horizontal spread is also known as time or calendar spread.

*Initial margin:* The minimum margin required when an option transaction is initiated. Long calls and long puts must be paid in full. CBOE regulations require a $2,000 initial equity in a margin account when a new transaction is effected. Thereafter, maintenance requirements come into consideration.

*In the money:* An option contract on which the exercise (strike) price is below the current market price of the underlying stock.

*Intrinsic value:* The difference between the current stock price and the exercise price of the option. A call option is said to have intrinsic value when the stock price is greater than the exercise price. A put option is said to have intrinsic value when the stock price falls below the exercise price.

*Leverage:* The profit potential per investment dollar; highly leveraged investment situations are those in which the profit or loss potential per dollar is great. The universal companion of high leverage is high risk.

*Limited risk:* In respect to options, the fact that option buyers can never lose more than the initial cost of the option.

*Limit order:* An order to buy or sell at a specified price or better.

*Liquidity:* Conversion of a noncash asset to cash and back again. In listed options, liquidity is due to the existence of a continuous secondary market.

*Listed call option:* A contract given under the auspices of options exchanges (such as CBOE and AMEX) entitling the buyer or holder, at his option to buy on or before a fixed date 100 shares of a specific widely held, actively traded security at a predetermined price.

*Long option:* An option that has been purchased.

*Maintenance margin:* Provisions set up by the New York Stock Exchange concerning the minimum equity level required of an account after the initial margin requirements have been met.

*Margin:* The amount of borrowing or credit that a broker is permitted to extend to his customers in option transactions.

*Mark to the market:* The recomputation each day by a broker of an investor's margin requirement; if the account requires more money, the investor must supply it immediately.

*Married put:* A put option and stock acquired on the same day. The stock must be identified as intended to be used in connection with the exercise of the put to qualify for certain tax benefits. The holding period of the stock is figured in the normal manner, unaffected by the existence of the put.

*Maximum return:* The calculated greatest possible yield for an option purchaser or writer (sell) based on the conditions that might exist at the expiration of an option contract. Such return is the aggregate sum of proceeds from option premium, possible appreciation to expiration, and dividends.

*Money spread:* A spread involving the simultaneous purchase and sale of options with the same expiration month but different strike prices. A money spread is also known as a vertical or perpendicular spread.

*Naked writer:* An option writer who does not own the shares or other units of the underlying security covered by the option. A naked writer is also known as an uncovered writer.

*Near option:* That portion of a spread option whose expiration date arrives first.

*Neutral strategy:* The strategy an investor uses when it is thought the stock's value will not move appreciably over the near term.

*On the money:* An option for which the exercise price is equal to the market price of the underlying stock; also known as at the money.

*Opening purchase:* A transaction in which an investor becomes the holder of an option.

*Opening sale:* A transaction in which an investor becomes the writer of an option.

*Open position:* A position following (1) an option sale wherein the option has not expired or been exercised; or (2) an option purchase wherein the option has not been exercised or nullified by becoming worthless at expiration.

*Option:* A business contract that allows an investor to buy or sell stock in 100-share units at a certain price (known as the exercise price or strike price) over a certain period, regardless of how high or low the price of the stock moves during that time.

*Option period:* The time period during which the option buyer must exercise or lose his right to buy according to the terms of the option contract.

*Options Clearing Corporation:* The central options clearing agency that assumes the obligation and becomes the purchaser to the option seller and seller to the option buyer immediately after sale and purchase orders are matched between the option seller and the option buyer. This agency is just for listed options, but not for over-the-counter option transactions.

*Out of the money:* The situations in which the exercise price of a call is higher than the market price of the underlying stock or the exercise price of a put is lower than the current stock price.

*Over the counter (OTC) options:* Options that are not sold under the auspices of listed options markets and thus expiration dates and exercise prices are not standardized.

*Parity option:* An option for which the premium plus the exercise price equal the market price of the underlying security.

*Partial covered writing:* Selling (writing) an option contract involving a number of shares that exceeds the number of shares owned.

*Perpendicular spread:* A spread involving simultaneous buying and selling of options having the same expiration month but different strike prices. A perpendicular spread is also known as money or vertical spread.

*Position One, Sell Two:* An option strategy whereby a ratio writer sells two options against 100 shares of the underlying security held.

*Premium:* The price that the buyer pays the seller (writer) for the right (option) to sell stock to him at a later date and at a specific price (puts), or buy stock from him (calls).

*Price spread:* A spread involving the purchase and sale of options of the same class having common expiration dates, but different exercise prices; also known as a money or vertical spread.

*Profit band:* A profit protection zone formed by the upside and downside breakeven points within which a ratio writer will remain profitable as long as the price of the underlying security stays between these two parameters.

*Put:* A contract giving the right to sell to the writer the stated number of shares (typically 100) of the underlying security within a stated period of time at the stated exercise price. Puts are usually acquired when the buyer expects a stock to decline during the life of the contract.

*Ratio spreading:* An option strategy whereby a spreader may choose to construct his spreading position by varying the ratio of his long and short options; also known as a variable spread.

*Ratio writing:* An option strategy whereby an option writer (seller) may choose to partially hedge his position by combining the writing of one or more covered options with that of one or more uncovered options on the same underlying security. Ratio writing is also called variable hedging.

*Regulation T:* The Federal Reserve Board rule governing, among other things, the amount of credit (if any) that initially may be extended by a broker to his customer.

*Return on cash flow:* The yield on an actual dollar commitment, indicating leverage based on cash flow.

*Reverse charge:* The cost of covering the call portion of a straddle option into a put. This charge is normally smaller than the conversion charge. See also *Conversion charge.*

*Reverse horizontal hedge:* A variation of ratio spreading whereby the spreader buys two near-term options and sells one far-term option having the same strike price.

*Risk/reward ratio:* A potential loss relative to a potential gain in a proposed strategy, expressed as a ratio.

*Sandwich spread:* An option spread consisting of the sale of two intermediate options and the purchase of two options with strike prices of equal distance from the short options in the ratio of 1:2:1. A sandiwch spread is also called a butterfly spread.

*Secondary market:* A marketplace for the disposal (selling or buying) of previously bought or sold options through closing transactions.

*Series of options:* Options of the same class having the same exercise price and expiration month.

*Short position:* The writing of an option or the selling of underlying stock without actually owning the stock at the time of the transaction.

*Spread:* The simultaneous purchase and sale of options on the same underlying stock. These may have the same strike price with different expiration months or different prices with the same or different expirations. The spread itself is the difference between the amount spent for the buy premiums and that gained on the sell premiums.

*Spread (bear):* An option strategy whereby an investor (1) sells (shorts) the far-term option and buys the near-term option; or (2) sells (shorts) the low-strike option and buys the high-strike option.

*Spread (bull):* An option strategy whereby an investor (1) sells (shorts) the near-term option and buys the long-term option; or (2) sells (shorts) the high-strike option and buys the low-strike option.

*Spread in credit:* A spread for which the cost of the long option is less than that of the short option.

*Spread in debit:* A spread for which the cost of the long option is more than that of the short option.

*Spread premium:* The differential between buying and selling option premiums.

*Standardized expiration dates:* A feature of listed option contracts, the contracts terminate on fixed dates, in sharp contrast to over-the-counter options, which can expire on any one of the business days of the year.

*Stop point:* The stock price that triggers investor action should the shares of the stock reach that price.

*Straddle:* Purchase or sale of an equal number of puts and calls on the same underlying stock with identical exercise prices and expiration dates.

*Strike price:* The price per unit at which the holder of a listed call option may purchase the underlying security upon exercise. The strike price is also called the exercise price.

*Taking cover:* A transaction whereby an uncovered (naked) option writer may, during the life of the option, buy the underlying security, thereby becoming a covered writer.

*Tangible value:* For a listed call option, the difference between the market value of the underlying security and the exercise price of the option. Tangible value is also called intrinsic value.

*Three-against-one writing:* An option strategy whereby a ratio writer sells three options against 100 shares of the underlying security held.

*Time spread:* A spread involving simultaneous buying and selling of options having the same striking price but different expiration months. A time spread is also called a calendar or horizontal spread.

*Time value:* That part of an option premium reflecting the remaining life of the option. The more time that remains before the expiration date, the higher the premium, because more time is available for the value of the underlying security to change.

*Total return:* A concept of investment return based on aggregate yields from invested capital from dividends, option premiums, and capital gains earned from option writing activities.

*Two-against-one writing:* An option strategy whereby a ratio writer writes two calls against 100 shares of the underlying security held.

*Uncovered call writer:* A call writer who does not own either the underlying security upon which the option is written or a long call of the same class with an equal or lesser exercise price than the call he has written.

*Uncovered put writer:* A put writer who does not hold a long put of the same class with an equal or higher exercise price than the put he has written.

*Uncovered writer:* An option writer who does not own the shares or other units of the underlying security covered by the option. An uncovered writer is also called a naked writer.

*Underlying security:* A security underlying an option contract against which a call or put option is traded.

*Upside parameter:* The upside price level of the underlying security above which a ratio writer will incur a loss.

*Variable hedging:* An option strategy whereby an option writer (seller) may choose to partially hedge his position by combining the writing of covered option(s) with that of uncovered option(s) on the same underlying security. Variable hedging is also called ratio writing.

*Variable spread:* A spread in which the number of contracts purchased is different from the number of contracts sold.

*Vertical spread:* A spread involving simultaneous buying and selling of options having the same expiration month but different strike prices. A vertical spread is also called a money or perpendicular spread.

*A*

Arbitrage, 10–11
  mathematical approach, 10
  nature, 10
  price determination, 10
  and time spreads, 57
At-the-market options, 14–15
At-the-money short put, long
    stock, 120
Averaging down, with long puts,
    96

*B*

Balance in portfolios, 39
Bearish combinations, 156
Bear horizontal:
  in spread margins, 70
  in time spreads, 54
Bearish approach:
  to put time spreads, 134
  to straddles, 147–148
Bear market, in listed options,
    189–190
Bear spread margin:
  for calls, 51–52
  versus bull spread margin, 58
  and vertical call price, 60–63
Breakevens:
  in portfolios, 36
  in put price spreads, 137
Bullish approach:
  to straddles, 147
  to put time spreads, 133
Bull call spread strategy, 192
Bull horizontal:
  in spread margins, 70
  in time spreads, 54
Bullish combinations, 156
Bull market option market,
    189–190
Bull spread margin:
  for calls, 51
  versus bear spread margin, 58
  vertical call price, 58–60

Buying call options, 205–206
Buying in, 43
Buy high/see strikes:
  calls, 60
  call price spreads, 60
Buy-stop, 44
Buy-wait-write, 40–41

*C*

Calls, 5–7
  and puts, 79
  reasons for buying, 6–7
  reasons for selling, 7
Call backed, 50–51
Call exercise, tax strategy, 175
Call expiration, tax strategy, 176
Call margin, 67–71
  and credit relations, 68
  initial requirements, 68
  maintenance, 69
  margin-account-only transac-
    tions, 68
  nature, 67
  put options, sale of, 69
  Regulation T, 68
  requirements, 68
Call option price index, 191–192
  and consistent measure, 191
  and premium trends, 191
Call options questionnaire,
    204–208
  buying, 205–206
  margins, 207
  markets, 204
  portfolios, 207–208
  spreading, 206
  straddling, 206–207
  strategies, 205
  values, 205
  writing, 206
  versus puts, 207
  ratio writing, 206
  taxes, 207
Call price spreads, 58–65
  bear vertical spreads, 60–63

  buy high/sell low strikes, 60
  examples, 61–62
  key measurements, 62
  margin, 60–61
  strike prices and premiums, 61
  workout against, 62–63
  bull vertical spreads, 58–60
  buy low/sell high strikes, 60
  discount, 69
  examples, 59–60
  low-cost, 59
  as trading vehicle, 59
  diagonal spreads, 65–66
  nature, 58
  sandwich spreads, 63–66
  key consideration, 64
  leverage, 63
  structure, 63
  workout against, 64–65
  verticals, bull versus bear, 58
Call purchase and short sale, tax
    strategies, 177
Call sale, tax strategies, 176
Call spreading, 48–52
  call backed versus stock backed,
    50–51
  defined:
    in credit, 50
    in debit, 50
  margin:
    bear, 51–52
    bull, 51
    spreads, 50
  nature, 49
  risk, 52
  as two options in one, 49
Call strike, in relation to premi-
    ums, 61
Cash dividends on long puts, 93
Cash flow in portfolios, 35
Certificateless securities, 9
Combinations, 152–161
  aiming at high, 156
  bullish versus bearish, 156
  buying:
    with short stock position, 157

# index

with stock position, 157
without stock position, 157
defined, broad versus narrow, 153
leglifting, 155
long call, long put, 153–154
nature, 152
procedure, 154–155
same expiration month, 153
selling:
   bearish approach, 159–160
   bullish approach, 159
   components, 160
   covered, 160
   and related stock position, 158
   with short stock position, 160
   short call, short put, 158
   static stock, 158
   uncovered, 158–159
   varied ratio approach, 160
versus straddle, 161
   buyings compared, 161
   relative dollar risks, 161
   sales compared, 161
variable ratio buying, 157–158
and volatility, 152–153
Commissions in put spreading, 128
Covered put buying, 88
Covered put writing versus covered, 106–108
Covered call writing, 12–13
strategies, 193
Covered combinations, 160
Covered writing segment of portfolio, 194, 197
Credit in call margins, 68

D

Diagnonal spreads:
   with call price, 65–66
   time spreads, 54
Discounts:
   in bull vertical spreads, 69
   time spreads, 54
Discounts:
   in bull vertical spreads, 69
   in call price spreads, 69
Diversifying with long puts, 96
Downside, short put, long stock, 122

E

Exercise notice, 106

H

Hedging:
   long put, long stock, 99
   in put writing, 118–119

I

If-called-away portfolio, 39–41

Initial margin:
   calls, 68
   puts, 163
In-the-money options, 15
   covered call, 181–182
   puts, 78
   short put, long stock, 120
   uncovered, 181–182
   versus out-of-the-money puts, 182

L

Leglifting, in combination, 155
Leverage:
   in call price spreads, 63
   double with short put, long stock, 121–122
   with puts, 78
Listed options market, 8–11, 204
Long call, long put, 153–154, 166
Long options versus short, 14
Long puts, 90–97
   as alternative to short sale, 91–93
   diversifying, 96
   nature, 90
   protection for, 93–94
   selling versus exercising, 95–96
   and speculation, 90–91
   short sale profits, 96
   as trading vehicle, 96
      averaging down, 96
   when to buy, 94–95
      absolute versus relative risks, 94–95
Long put, long stock, 89, 98–101
   buying, 98
   complete hedging, 99
   hedging, 99
   versus long put, long call, 101
   nature, 98
   protection of profit, 99–100
Low P/E, high yield, 36–38

M

Maintenance margin:
   for calls, 69
   for puts, 163
   for short puts, 111
Margin:
   for call spreads, 50
      calculation, 60–61
   options, 207
   for inputs, 162–167
      in combinations, 166–167, 212–213
      put selling, 109
   for spreads, 70–71
   for straddles, 150–151
Margin calls on long puts, 93
Margin-account-only transactions for calls, 68

Maximum investment yield on portfolio, 36
Maximum return on portfolio, 35–36
Multiple options:
   in time spreads, 55
   in variable hedging, 44

N

Naked call writing, 116
Neutral approach, to put time spreads, 133

O

Options:
   at-market, 14–15
   basics, 5–7
   covered, strategies for, 12–13
   in-the-money, 15
   market for, 8–11
   out-of-the-money, 15
   premiums, 13–15
   short versus long, 14
   strategy, 187–190
   workshop, 201–203
Options Clearing Corporations, 9
Option writing for portfolios, 35–39
Out-of-the-money, 15
   puts, 78, 95
   short puts, long stock, 120

P

Portfolios:
   balance, 39
   breakevens, 36
   cash flow, 35
   formulas, 35
   low P/E, high yield, 36
   maximum investment yield, 36
   maximum return, 36
   option-oriented, 39
   prototype, 193–198
   premiums, 35–36
   return, 35–36
Premiums:
   low, strategies for, 192
   measure of, 35–36
   options in general, 13–15
   in put buying, 192
   in short sale, 192
   in straddles, 144
   in stock substitutions, 192
Price index for calls, 191–192
Profit:
   with long puts, 93
   with long put, long stock, 99–100
   two-ways in put time spreads, 131
   in straddles, 144

Profitable calls, tax strategies, 176–177
Profitable puts, tax strategies, 178
Prototype portfolio, 193–198
Puts, 77–80
  buying side, 79
  and calls, 79
  versus calls, 77–78
  in-the-money, 78
  leverage, 78
  nature, 77
  out-of-the-money, 78
  premiums, 79–80
    and stock *beta*, 80
    and underlying stock price, 80
Put buying, 87–89
  versus call buying, 88
  covered versus uncovered, 88
  long, 88–89
  nature, 87
  risk, 87–88
Put exercise, tax strategies, 175–176
Put expiration, tax strategies, 176
Put margin, 162–167
  in combination, 166–167
  for long put, 163
  for long put, long stock, 163
  minimum requirements, 163
  for put spread, 165–166
  for short put, 163–164
  for short put, short stock, 164–165
  for straddle, 166
    long call, long put, 166
    short call, short put, 166
Put option questionnaire, 209–213
  basics, 209
  buying, 210
  combinations, 212–213
  long, 210
  long put, long stock, 210
  margin, 213
  price spreads, 212
  selling, 210–211
  sale, 69
  short, 211
  short put, long stock, 211
  short put, short stock, 211
  spreading, 211
  straddles, 212
  strategy, 209
  time spreads, 211
Put price spreads, 127, 135–140
  bear, rolling of, 139–140
  bearish approach, 138–139
  bullish approach, 136
  nature, 135
  potential profit/risk, 137–138
Put selling:
  basics, 105–109
  covered versus uncovered writing, 106–108
  exercise notice, 106
  exercise price, 108–109

  method, 105
  nature, 105
  tax strategy, 176
  writing margin, 109
Put spread, 125–129
  concepts, 125
  construction, 127–128
  debit and credit, 126
  dollar difference, 125–126
    relative versus absolute, 126
  margin, 128–129
  simultaneous long and short, 126
  tax strategies, 128
  time spread, 127
Put strategies, 81–84
  buying, 81–82
  buying put and stock, 82–83
  nature, 81
  selling, 83
  selling stock short and put, 83–84
  summary, 84
Put time spreads, 130–134
  bearish approach, 134
  bullish approach, 133
  different expiration months, 130
  nature, 130
  neutral approach, 133
  put versus call time spread, bearish, 134
  stock price movement, 131
  time passage, 131
  two ways to profit, 131
  widening, 131
Put writing versus out-of-the-money, 114–115

R

Ratio:
  determination in variable hedging, 44
  spreading, 57
    different strike prices, 57
    reverse horizontal hedge, 57
    two-to-one, 57
  writing:
    for calls, 206
    strategy, 193
Ratio writing segment for portfolios, 194, 196
Regulation T, and calls, 68
Relative dollar risks;
  in combinations, 161
Revenue Act of 1978, 173–174
Reverse horizontal hedge, 57
Risk:
  known versus unknown in short put, 110–111
  limiting:
    on long puts, 93
    in put buying, 87–88
  reducing:
    in put spreads, 136

  in short straddle with long stock, 148–150
  in time spreads, 56
  relative versus absolute:
    in long puts, 94–95
    in put spread, 126
    in variable hedging, 43
Rolling a bear spread, 139–140

S

Salvage value on long put, 93
Sandwich:
  as call price spread, 63–65
  in time spreads, 54
Secondary market, 9
Section 1234, 74
Sell-stop versus put purchase, 67
Short call, short put, 166
Short-life warrant on covered call, 13
Short options versus long, 14
Short puts, 110–117
  closing out, 112
  defense of, 116–117
  differing puts, 113–114
  effective cost, 113
  financial preparation, 111
flexibility, 114
  margin requirements, 111
  nature, 110
  profitable repurchase, 112–113
  profit levels, 111–112
  risk, 110–111
  writing:
    in- versus out-of-the-money, 114–115
    procedure, 111–112
Short put, long stock, 118–120, 121, 211
  double leverage, 121–122
    downside, 122
    upside, 122
  hedged, 118–119
  nature, 118
  selection of strike price, 120
Short put margin, 163–164
Short put versus short put, long stock, 106
Short put, short stock, 164–165, 211
Short sale:
  as alternative to long put, 91–93
  in combinations, 157
  premium levels, 192
  profits and long puts, 96
  tax rules, 178–179
  in variable hedging, 43
Short-term portfolios, 39–40
Speculation with long puts, 90–91
Spread:
  bearish approach, 136
  with calls, 49–52, 206
    price, 58–66

with puts, 211
strategy, 193
in time spread, 56
Spreading segment of portfolio, 194, 195–196
Spread margin, 70–71
on bear horizontal, 70
on bull horizontal, 70
on vertical spreads, 70–71
Static stock in combinations, 158
Stock backed, 50–51
Stock substitution, 192
Stop-loss orders, 96–97
flexibility, 97
sell-stop versus put purchase, 97
timing error, 97
trading halts, 97
Straddles, 143–151
bearish approach, 147–148
bullish approach, 147
with calls, 206–207
versus combinations, 161
long, 144
margin, 150–151
long, 150
puts, 166
short, 150–151
and market direction, 143–144
nature, 143
premium, 144
profit levels, 144
puts, 212
short, 146, 148–149
with long stock, 148–150
whipsaw, 146
Strategies:
broad, 9–10, 193
for bull call spreads, 192
for calls, 205
covered writing, 193
and market, 193
ratio writing, 193
for spreading, 193
for variable spreads, 192
Strike price:
covered call, 13
long put, 95
in ratio spreading, 57
short put, long stock, 120

T

Tax Reform Act of 1976, 173
Tax strategies, 175–79
call exercise, 175
call expiration, 176
call holders, 176
call purchase and short sale, 177
call sale, 176
general discussion, 175
profitable calls, 176–177
profitable puts, 178
put exercise, 175–176

put expiration, 176
put holders, 177–178
put sale, 176
unprofitable calls, 177
unprofitable puts, 178
short sale rules, 178–179
wash sale rule, 177
Tax planning:
general, 173
present rates, 174
Time spreads, 53–57
and arbitrage, 57
bear horizontal, 54
bull horizontal, 54
diagonal, 54
early exercise, 57
expiration, 56
horizontal, 53
long call, 55
low-cost spreads, 55
multiple options, 55
nature, 53
and near-term expiration, 55
premiums, 55
risks, 54
sandwich, 54
small capital expenditure, 54
spreads, 54–56
strike price, 54
vertical, 53
volatility, 54
Time value of covered call, 12–13

U

Uncovered:
combination selling, 158–159
partially, 44–46
in variable hedging, 42–44
Underlying stock price, puts, 80
Unprofitable calls, 177
Unprofitable puts, 178
Upside, short put, long stock, 122

V

Value of call, 205
Variable hedging, 42–46
buying in, 43
buy-stop, 44
off setting call option, 43–44
with multiple options, 44
parameters, 45
partially uncovered, 44–46
position one, sell two, 44
profit band, 45
ratio determination, 44
risk, 43
selection criteria, 44
short sales, 43
taking cover, 43
three against one, 46
uncovered, 42–44
writing against cash, 115–116

Variable ratio buying in combinations, 157–158
Variable spread strategy, 192
Varied ratio approach, 160
Vertical spread margin, 70–71
Volatility:
in combinations, 152–153
in options, 14
in long puts, 94
in puts, 80
in time spread, 54

W

Wash sale, tax rules, 177
Whipsaw in short straddles, 146
With stock position in combinations, 157
Workout:
against calls, 62–63
against sandwich spreads, 64–65
Workship on options, 201–203
Writing:
calls, 181–182
in-the-money covered, 181–182
in-the-money uncovered, 181–182
termination by closing purchase, 181
termination by exercise, 181
termination by expiration, 181
holding period, 180–181
puts, 182–183
in- versus out-of-the-money, 182
termination by exercise, 183
termination by expiration, 182
termination by sale, 183
and short selling, 183